BORDEAUX

A Legendary Wine

BORDEAUX

A Legendary Wine

By Michel Dovaz

Photography by Michel Guillard

Translated by John Lee

Abbeville Press Publishers

NEW YORK LONDON PARIS

In memory of Héléna
— M. D.

Front cover: Bordeaux wine bottle
Back cover: Château d'Yquem
Endpapers: Bordeaux limestone

English-language edition
Editor: Jeffrey Golick
Designer: Celia Fuller
Production Manager: Lou Bilka

Originally published as *Bordeaux: terre de légende*
Copyright © 1997 Éditions Assouline
English translation copyright © 1998 Abbeville Press

First English-language edition
2 4 6 8 10 9 7 5 3 1

Library of Congress Cataloging-in-Publication Data
Dovaz, Michel
[Bordeaux terre de legende. English]
Bordeaux, a legendary wine / by Michael Dovaz; photography by Michel Guillard; translated by John Lee.
p. cm.
ISBN 0-7892-0449-5
1. Wine and wine making—France—Bordeaux. I. Title.
TP553.D64613 1998
641.2'2'0944714—dc21
98—15672

CONTENTS

PREFACE

In the modern world everything happens quickly; the only constant is that things will change. Despite this endless state of flux some things remain dependable; the more time passes, the more compelling these fixed landmarks become. They become models, archetypes, symbols, and end up as legends. The Rolls Royce has become the symbol of the luxury automobile, Champagne has become synonymous with celebration, and sometimes fame can become so powerful that a brand is turned into a concept. The French call a car horn a Klaxon, the British call a vacuum cleaner a Hoover, and Americans call a white wine Chablis. Do we use Bordeaux to mean any red wine? No, because the word has been stoutly defended. Nevertheless, Bordeaux wine is now so celebrated the world over that it has become the archetype of red wine.

The entire world conforms to the standards of Bordeaux, envies it, and copies it. Thus Bordeaux grape varieties—particularly cabernet sauvignon—are planted in vineyards everywhere. Thus, in every country, wine is matured in wood, even to excess. Thus the wines of the four corners of the globe are stored in Bordeaux-shaped bottles.

What is behind this exemplary success story? The entirely random creation, over thousands of years, of a unique soil; weather conditions that particularly favor the development of subtle aromas in the grapes; and lastly, the tireless efforts of people who in three centuries have built up a legend.

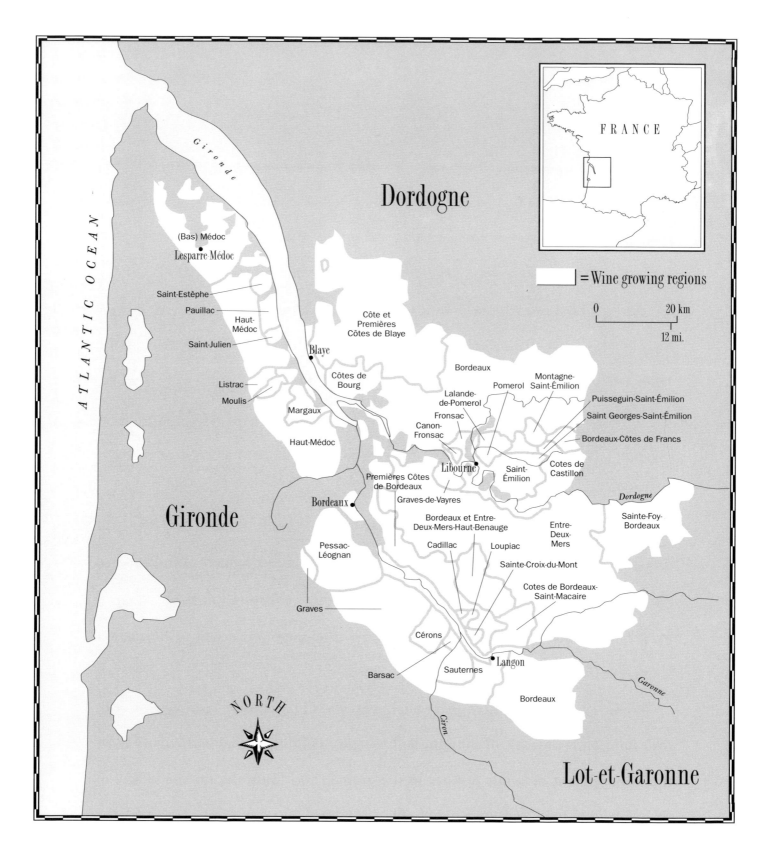

FRANCE

= Wine growing regions

0   20 km
12 mi.

Dordogne

ATLANTIC OCEAN

Gironde

Gironde

(Bas) Médoc
Lesparre-Médoc

Saint-Estèphe
Pauillac
Haut-Médoc
Saint-Julien

Listrac
Moulis

Margaux

Haut-Médoc

Blaye

Côte et Premières Côtes de Blaye

Côtes de Bourg

Bordeaux

Montagne-Saint-Émilion

Pomerol

Lalande-de-Pomerol
Fronsac
Canon-Fronsac

Puisseguin-Saint-Émilion
Saint Georges-Saint-Émilion
Bordeaux-Côtes de Francs

Libourne

Saint-Émilion

Cotes de Castillon

Dordogne

Premières Côtes de Bordeaux

Bordeaux

Graves-de-Vayres

Bordeaux et Entre-Deux-Mers-Haut-Benauge

Entre-Deux-Mers

Sainte-Foy-Bordeaux

Pessac-Léognan

Cadillac

Loupiac

Sainte-Croix-du-Mont

Cotes de Bordeaux-Saint-Macaire

Graves

Cérons

Barsac

Sauternes

Langon

Ciron

Bordeaux

Garonne

NORTH

Lot-et-Garonne

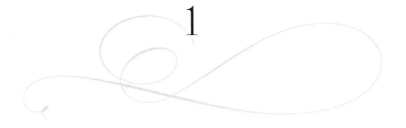

The Birth of the *Terroirs*

Understanding the formation of the *terroirs* of Bordeaux —the distinctive soils grapevines are grown in, and their subsoils—would be a very simple affair if only the layers of sediment were stacked neatly on top of each other. Unfortunately, it does not work that way. Even the different marine deposits of the Primary, Secondary, and Tertiary periods do not lie horizontally; the mechanics of plate tectonics have resulted in a collapse toward the west-southwest. On this uneven base rivers or the wind have deposited piles of gravel and sand, which have since been subjected to considerable erosion. The earliest gravel deposits came from the Pyrenees, the second layer from the Massif Central. These deposits and removals of material extended over more than two million years, resulting in a highly varied outline that, although similar in make-up to the Marmande sector, has nothing of that area's tidy flatness.

One might think that the viticultural geologist would be content to study the ground down to depths of around thirty feet, on the principle that vine roots rarely get beyond and often get nowhere near such depths. But that would underestimate the importance of drainage and the water table; it would ignore slopes and hillocks; it would fail altogether to explain the nature of favorable *terroirs,** why they are just where they are, and why there are so few of them.

In the Bordeaux region, we have no need to go all the way back to the Primary and Secondary (Paleozoic and Mesozoic) periods, as we might if we were studying, say, the vineyards of the Jura or Provence. We shall merely mention the end of the Tertiary (late Miocene), when marine sediments—Bordeaux limestone, also known as starfish limestone, and Fronsac sandstone—appeared. Both of these are

---

* *Terroir* (pronounced terWAHR), from *terre*, meaning earth or soil. The word *terroir* refers not only to the soil but also the whole natural environment of a place, including geology, climate, microclimate, etc., all of which makes a given plot suitable for, in this case, winegrowing. As Jancis Robinson explains it in her *Wine Course* (Abbeville):

"While the macroclimate of a wine region may govern whether it is capable of producing rich wine grapes at all, the subtle characteristics of a much smaller area—a particular vineyard, or even part of a vineyard—may determine the sort of wine that can be produced from that area. These characteristics include the climate of that smaller area, its mesoclimate (for long called its '*microclimate*'); its soil; the lie of the land, or its topography; and the effects each of these three elements have on each other. Any gardener, or even garden observer such as myself, can see at a glance (on a frosty morning, for example) how each part of the garden is heavily influenced by all these characteristics. The French, typically, have one elegant word for this long list of natural characteristics: *terroir*."

widespread on the Right Bank of the river Garonne around Saint-Emilion, Pomerol, and Fronsac. Also in this period the formation of the Pyrenees was almost complete, and the entire Left Bank, from Langon (and beyond) to the lower Médoc, was submerged in Pyrenees gravel. These *graves*—areas of stony soil—butted up against the Eocene limestone of the Blayais, the region on the Right Bank around Blaye.

We today find this Pyrenean material in various vineyards of the Sauternes, Léognan, Martillac, and Listrac. It was also during the Pliocene epoch that the valleys came to look the way we see them today. Tectonic motion was still not complete, which explains the aymmetrical deposits, along with the effects of large-scale erosion, either combined with or leveled by deposits of sand blown across from the coastal Landes region.

A little over a million years ago (1,300,000 B.P. [before the present] to 1,100,000 B.P.), a second wave of gravel arrived: Günz gravel (i.e., dating from the Günz glacial stage), originating in the Massif Central and the Limousin and carried down by the rivers Garonne and Dordogne. To these gravel deposits we owe the finest *terroirs* of the Bordeaux region, particularly those of the four first growths in the 1855 classification—Haut-Brion, Margaux, Lafite, Latour—as well as Mouton, promoted to first-growth status in 1973.

For a million years, then, the most important elements have been in place, although a further three ice caps both abraded older deposits and added new ones. Between 700,000 and 600,000 years ago, the Mendel ice cap planed smooth the Barsac plateau, cutting up and eroding the soil just about everywhere, but depositing gravel around Lalande de Pomerol, creating the *terroir* of the Lagune, spreading into the Médoc to Labarde. Around this time, the Gironde estuary was settling into its present-day position.

During the Riss (200,000 to 120,000 B.P.) and Würm Glaciations (30,000 to 13,000 B.P.) the motions more or less canceled each other out: sand was deposited, then carried away again. Sea levels were as much as 164 feet (50 meters) lower during the Würm glaciation, and the deposits were all submerged shortly afterward during the Flandrian age (11,000 B.P.) when the sea rose back up to today's level. Nevertheless, during the course of those 200,000 years, the

terroirs lived dangerously; the layers of gravel responsible for the great wine-growing soils might easily have disappeared under 3 to 10 feet (1 to 3 meters) of sand and sometimes more. This sand was deposited by some extremely violent westerly winds (not until the nineteenth century was the pine forest in the Landes planted to hold down the sand). Everyone in France is familiar with a huge mountain of sand called the Pilat dune; and it is easy to see how the Médoc vineyards occupy the land facing the Gironde, and how the Bordeaux-Lesparre road marks a kind of boundary between the vineyards to the northwest and the Landes pine forest planted in the sand to the southwest. Such an invasion is not restricted to the Médoc region alone; it happens throughout the vineyards of the Gironde, including the Sauternes and the Right Bank, taking in the Blaye and Bourges regions as well.

During the Riss glacial stage, the winds were so violent that no sooner was the sand deposited than it was carried away again. The *croupes* or hillocks were protected in this way as the sand fell into the estuary and farther north, on the Right Bank. Following the Riss glaciation, some exceptional floods dredged out the estuary once more and remodeled the landscape, though the sand deposited during the Riss glaciation is visible throughout the vineyard. After ninety thousand years of calm weather, the *terroirs* faced one last ice age, the Würm glaciation. Unlike previous ice ages, this one was short, lasting just over 30,000 years (the Günz lasted 200,000 years, the Mindel and Riss each almost 100,000). The sand from the Landes—which has the peculiarity of being black, having been colored by untransformed humus—then launched another assault, eventually extending beyond the line of the future Bordeaux-Lesparre road and spoiling the soil for growing vines right up to the classified growths of today. It is very visible south of the Bordeaux-Lesparre road. The great *terroirs* survived and resisted this invasion; others, such as the Bas-Médoc, the Haut-Médoc, and locally Lalande de Pomerol, saw their winegrowing potential diminished. In the Sauternes, acres of good soil disappeared under the sand.

The final danger facing the quality *terroirs* was not the wind, but the sea. During the Flandrian age, 10,000 to 12,000 years ago, the level of the river Gironde rose again, half of the coastal gravels disappeared, and the lowlands were submerged

Nevertheless, during the course of those 200,000 years, the *terroirs* lived dangerously; the layers of gravel responsible for the great wine-growing soils might easily have disappeared.

in mud, sand, and peat. In the Bas-Médoc, in the marshland farther upstream, and again on the banks of the Gironde, the phenomenon of submergence contributed to the creation of the rich, heavy soils known as the *palus.* Unsuitable for producing quality wines, these soils nevertheless did give rise to the *vins de palus,* which played an active role in the history of Bordeaux wine.

Thus, for ten thousand years, the scene had been set; the great soils were in place and ready. Now man only needed to discover their potential—but that would be a long time coming.

Glaciation	Years ago	Period
Donau	3–5,000,000	Tertiary
Günz	1,000,000	
Mindel	650,000	
Riss	150,000	Quaternary
Würm	20,000	

The formation of the Bordeaux *terroirs* began at the end of the Tertiary period and was most significantly shaped during the Quaternary period.

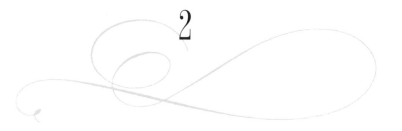

Bordeaux History

From Ausonius to the Pontacs

It was the Romans who introduced winegrowing to the Bordeaux region, as to the rest of the country, about two thousand years ago. They had already done so several centuries earlier in the Narbonne, and although the grape varieties of Italy thrived in those sunny climes, the same cannot be said for the Bordeaux region. There is something of a mystery about this not so very southern location, as with the northern Rhône vineyard: in both cases, there is no room for the southern varieties. Where does the Allobrogian grape, in which some see the ancestor of the Mondeuse, and the Biturican—supposed to be the ancestor of the cabernets—come from? Let us leave the Allobrogian to the mists of Lyons to take a closer look at the Biturica vine, which takes its name from the Bituriges, the people of Bordeaux at that time. Roger Dion holds that it originated in Spain. E. Etienne finds a family likeness with the vine known as Basilica, which came from

Albania. Whatever its origin, it was planted in the outskirts of Burdigala (the ancient name of Bordeaux) two thousand years ago, which was about when the Bordeaux vineyard came into being. It owed its prosperity to a whole range of factors, for Burdigala had become a town of merchants, importing wines from Italy, later from Narbonne, and soon afterward from Gaillac, before redispatching them to the other provinces. The "Chartrons" of the period—essentially brokers—dated back before the local producers, but they very soon grasped the advantage of being both producers and merchants.

Within a few centuries, local production had achieved a reputation. A golden age began, as can be seen from the remains of a number of villas of the time. Ausonius, writing in the late fourth century, waxes lyrical about the fame of the wines of Burdigala. An extremely wealthy local dignitary, Ausonius knew what he was talking about, for he was a producer himself, no doubt in several different places, being the owner of eight villas in various parts of the region, at

OPPOSITE
Arnaud II de Pontac, proprietor of Haut-Brion, c. 1600. Half a century later, his descendants would invent the notion of the growth and the "new French claret."

14

ARNAUD II
DE PONTAC
ÉVÊQUE DE BAZAS
1672 - 1603

Pauillac, Naujac (Saint-Seurin), Lucaniacus (Saint-Emilion), and elsewhere.

What do we know about the wines of the fourth century (and earlier)? Only that they survived countless invasions, although trade did suffer as a result. There were two reasons for their survival: the invaders were thirsty, and the priests were saying more and more masses.

The night of the Dark Ages then spread over the Bordeaux area, which was annexed to the duchy of Aquitaine soon after the year 1000. In the wake of the marriage of the beautiful Eleanor of Aquitaine to Henry Plantagenet, king of England, in 1152, the wine trade with England began to pick up again, but La Rochelle was more active than Bordeaux, exporting large quantities of white wine, produced in the hinter regions of the port. Bordeaux's first big chance was when Eleanor's son Richard came to the throne in England; now a king drank Bordeaux wine. The town's second chance came in 1224, when Louis VIII occupied the Poitou, including of course La Rochelle. The port of Bordeaux then grew in proportion as La Rochelle fell into decline. Meanwhile the Bordeaux region was becoming the exclusive supplier to England. On the strength of its successes, the town built up a monopoly in production, sales, shipping, and retailing of wines. To this end any means were allowed, including the setting up of what amounted to privileges to sell the local wines first, with the wines from upcountry being saleable only after no Bordeaux wine was left. All shipments were under tight control, as the only port empowered to export was Bordeaux itself. The Bordeaux wines of this time are famous for having been involved in the first comparative tasting session on record, reported by Henri d'Andeli in 1224. Eighty wines from all over Europe were involved, including one from Saint-Emilion and one from the town of Bordeaux. Neither of the two Bordeaux was particularly outstanding, which is hardly surprising, as until the thirteenth century the wines from the southwest of France with the best reputation were those from the Poitou-Charentes area. The winner of this tasting competition, which had been arranged by the king of France, was a sweet wine from Cyprus. Such a tasting can only be of historical interest, in any case, for how can dry wines be compared with sweet, or red with rosé or white?

Although we have no descriptions of the drinking qualities of the wines of the Middle Ages, we do know how they were made: the grapes were trampled underfoot, and the must was placed in vats and fermented for several days. The newly developing wine was racked, and when fermentation was completed it was sold and drunk immediately. It was a light rosé (hence the name claret), and probably cloudy. Its alcoholic content was low (maybe 8 percent); it was low on tannin, and volatile acidity gave it a vinegary taste. Understandably, it did not keep well, even in barrels subjected to regular topping up (filling to replace evaporated wine). As the months went by, it got less and less palatable, which is why prices were high for young wines, gradually falling off as the year wore on. When the new wine came on the market, whatever remained of the wine of the previous year was sold off cheap. If such wines were available today, they would be of interest to no one.

The early white wines—luxury wines, more complex to make because the grapes were pressed—must have been a more interesting proposition. They were fermented in casks, as are the best wines of today, but were produced in very limited quantities, as only the large estates had their own winepress. There was proper red wine too, but it did not have much of a following, being astringent, tannic, concentrated, and very probably more or less off, because once the claret had been drawn off, the remaining juice was left on the marc, or solid residue, unprotected (no sulfuring was done). To be refined, it would have needed to age, whereas it could only be drunk young, as indeed it was. It was not until the fifteenth century that it became general practice to press the (red) marc, and hence that *vin de press* wine came into being, and the notion of blending gained currency.

Two events of note were to mark life in Bordeaux: the planting of the *palus*—the rich, fat, alluvial soils—and the conquest of Aquitaine by France in 1453. The planting of vines on the *palus* was the work of the burghers of Bordeaux, who, as we have seen, enjoyed certain privileges. Although they did not know it, these burgher producers were paving the way for the coming of the great wines. We have come a long way since then, and the *palus* soils were rather unsuitable for grapevines, but they offered a number of advantages.

One was the possibility of opening a *bourdieu,* which would very quickly take on the meaning of a winery—a production plant with purpose: built premises, comprising not only a press but also a vineyard, with a planting of selected grape varieties (doubtless the cabernets—and also petit verdot and malbec). Those wines that were actually made into reds, no longer just *rosés de saignée* with press wine added, had color, and were almost powerful. They had one huge advantage over the fragile *graves* wines (those from grapes grown on rocky soil): they traveled well. Furthermore, the rich soils of the *palus* produced high yields.

Dutch Influence

Despite various political and military events, England held on to her dominant position in the commercial activity of Bordeaux; but the powerful Dutch navy and the ingenuity of the Dutchmen were to play havoc with three centuries of habit. The English enjoyed claret, while the Dutch preferred the solid *palus* wines. They, or their customers in northern Europe, had something of a taste for white wines, particularly the sweet whites (to this day, we can still see marked on some Monbazillac labels the phrase *marque hollandaise,* or "Dutch brand," which dates back to that period). The Sauternes area was covered in white vines to keep up with demand. The Dutch also introduced a new technique that was to revolutionize enology (if we may use that word in this context) in the late fifteenth century: the "Dutch match," or the practice of sulfuring, the combustion of sulfur as an antiseptic agent (and also a yeast selector, but that was not known at the time). The Dutch fumigated the casks, which meant, first, that the wines were no longer oxidized, and second, that they could be kept sweet (this is known in modern parlance as *mutage*—artificial interruption of fermentation—with sulfur dioxide).

From then on, wine began to speak, as the soil and the grape were no longer muffled by oxidation. The dynamism of the Dutch merchants was to have numerous repercussions: they invented the wine merchant's business—the art of creating a wine to suit one's needs by mixing and blending,

fortifying and aromatizing. The notion of stabilizing (sulfur, alcohol, clearing by racking) gained currency. The Dutch merchants even reasoned that it was pointless shipping the water contained in the wine; it could be eliminated prior to boarding by distillation, to be reintroduced upon delivery. To this strangely logical reasoning we owe the invention of cognac—but that is another story.

A Turning Point:
The Seventeenth Century

Up to this point, Bordeaux had merely been tuning its instrument. All that was needed to create great wines was now in place. Commercial competition would also play a role, as the English market—always a buoyant one, with its refined, demanding consumers, who had considerable spending power —was invaded with wines from all over, including Portugal and Spain. What could be done to stand out against the crowd, to give the region its brand name, its characteristic style, its inimitable quality? Arnaud de Pontac, the first president of the Bordeaux Parliament and more importantly, owner of Haut-Brion, was the first to sell his wine under a château name. This initiative met with instant success, all the more amazingly since he sold his wine at prices well above anybody else's. We have proof of this in reading the diary of Samuel Pepys (1633–1703) for April 10, 1663: "Here drank a sort of French wine, called Ho Bryan, that hath a good and most particular taste that I never met with." Pepys drank that wine in a tavern. He is the first to have commented on a Bordeaux growth, and although he later mentions other wines, he would never write another word on French wines, which goes to show how surprised he was on tasting this "new French claret." The Pontacs continued to win over the English market by deliberately targeting the very wealthiest; in 1666 they opened the Pontack's Head in London, the most elegant restaurant-cum-grocery in town, and the most expensive.

So what was so very particular about the "Ho Bryan" that so struck Samuel Pepys? Not having any tasting descriptions to work on, we must make do with deductions drawn

*Sulfuring the vines with bellows in the nineteenth century;
the vines here are few and far between.*

from the available techniques of the day. The wine must have been fine, for *tirage au fin* seems to have been an innovation introduced at Haut-Brion. It was woody, having been in new casks, although only briefly. Lastly, it must have been selected, for it is unthinkable that wine sold carrying the estate's name at a very high price (four times the going rate) could have been anything but the very best.

From the Pontacs to Napoleon

In no time, other productions had gained influence. By the turn of the eighteenth century the English were using the word *cru* (growth) for the wines of Lafite, Latour, and Margaux. It should be noted that all these châteaus belonged to the upper crust of Bordeaux society, the *noblesse de robe* who owed their patents of nobility to administrative or legal posts bought by them or their ancestors. Hence the inescapable conclusion—and things are no different today—you cannot make great wines without investing a great deal of money. This justifies the rather strange categories of wines invented by the Bordeaux vintners: *cru ouvrier* (worker growth), *cru paysan* or *artisan* (peasant or artisan growth), *cru bourgeois*, and *cru classé* (classified, or aristocratic, growth). Each growth

was measured on several scales: a quality scale; a socio-professional scale; and a price scale.

The people of Bordeaux were practical people and soon observed

1. that the best wines were being sold at higher prices;
2. that the wealthiest owners had monopolized the best soils;
3. that to make a great wine required money and professionalism; and
4. that there was a close link between a proprietor's economic and social status and the quality of the wine from his estate.

The eighteenth century was the century of "furious planting," an expression coined by the steward Boucher, who in 1724 drew up a report requested by the authorities, who were worried that over the previous thirty or forty years wheat had been replaced by vines. Baron Montesquieu (1689–1755), that apostle of liberalism, was opposed to the ban placed in 1731 on planting except with the king's permission. This ban was in fact no more heeded than the one decreed by Domitian in the year 92, and it provides us with some information as to what was known about the soils at the time, as Boucher states in his report that nothing should be done against the vines planted "in the *graves* of the Médoc, the *graves* of Bordeaux, and the slopes."

For the historian of the eighteenth century there is ample documentary evidence. While organoleptic descriptions are few and far between, there is a wealth of detail concerning how wine was made. We know exactly what went on at Château Margaux, then the property of the marquis d'Aulède, a relation of the Pontacs. The white wine grapes were harvested in the morning, the red grapes in the afternoon, only after the dew had evaporated. Total or partial destemming was practiced, and a selection process led to the making of a "second wine." The timing of running off the wine was decided after tasting. The wine was housed in new oak casks, for which the wood came from northern Europe. In its broad outlines, winemaking today has changed very little from the method perfected three centuries ago, with one important difference: to the *grand vin* was added about 10 percent of white wine (from the sauvignon blanc grape, apparently), a practice dropped during the nineteenth century.

While the parliamentary classes deserve tribute for creating the great Bordeaux wines, it should also be noted that they defended by hook or by crook a protectionist privilege that would nowadays be considered unacceptable. No doubt it was based on a very ancient usage; certainly the kings of England had been granting such a privilege as early as 1342, back in the time of Edward III, a custom upheld by all the subsequent English and French kings, up to Louis XVI. The French economist and statesman Anne-Robert-Jacques Turgot (1721–1781), a liberal, tried unsuccessfully to have it abolished by a decree of 1776. In 1785, Louis XVI, the hesitant king, renewed that privilege for a further nine years. It took the French Revolution finally to see it off, on August 4, 1789. The Revolution had far-reaching repercussions for Church possessions, which were turned over to the nation but had no great effect on the great estates. They changed hands—sometimes just on paper, at that—but neither their structure nor their output were affected.

The early nineteenth century was marked by the publication in 1801 of *Treatise on the Vine* by Antoine Chaptal, a chemist who was also a government minister, and who was responsible, if not for inventing the process of chaptalization, at least for giving it widespread currency.

More and more books came out as wine became a subject for study. The Bordeaux vineyard emerged from the upheaval of the Revolution and the race for quality continued, unlike many other regions where it was a race for quantity only. This situation was worsened by the "new winegrowers," the purchasers of national possessions. It is not so much that refinement was equated with the ancien régime; the newcomers were there not to get involved in politics or moral issues but to make money—a great deal of money—and quality was not what they were about. Very fortunately, the large *domaines* were beyond the means of such buyers, and this is how the future classified growths escaped their downfall.

In 1811, a legendary year, new heights were reached with the "wines of the comet," but the consequences of the Napoleonic wars were to affect even the biggest producers, with several estates gradually changing hands. Despite numerous political upheavals in the mid-1800s, the vineyards were back on track toward prosperity, and preparations were under way for the Great International Exhibition of 1855. Until 1851 the vine had been generous enough, reproducing almost spontaneously by layering, and enjoying robust health; but in that year a cryptogamic disease—powdery mildew—made its appearance. Within three years it had reduced production by 70 percent. This had unforeseen and long-lasting consequences, as certain *domaines,* still marked by the scars of powdery mildew, failed to reach their acknowledged rankings in the 1855 classification.

The 1855 Classification

It is often said that "in Bordeaux they are mad about classifications." This is not quite true; they have merely applied great ingenuity to making the most of a document that was in no way intended for the general public. These classifications were originally proposed to streamline trade relations, and also to allow the tax authorities to work out a basis for assessing contributions. The first classification dates back to 1647;

it does not concern growths that did not already exist, but rather categories of wine: *palus* wines; white wines of Sauternes, Médoc, and Graves; Côtes de Bordeaux, Saint-Emilion, Blaye, and Bourg (in decreasing order of worth). The ranking was based on the prices applied in transactions with the Dutch buyers who monopolized the market during the seventeenth century, a curious admixture of the market price list and the administrated price. In 1698 the steward of Guyenne, Bazin de Bezons, specified that the most valuable wines were those of the Médoc, Graves, and Sauternes. In 1716 the chamber of commerce mentioned four or five wines, among them the Pontacs, as being the most sought after by the English. Finally, in 1776, for tax reasons, the steward Dupré de Saint-Maur drew up the first classification, himself using the phrase "classification of wines in the Guienne." In this extensive and exciting classification, we note that the priciest of all is Margaux at 1500 louis, followed in equal second place by Lafite, Latour, and Haut-Brion (1200 louis). The steward, who had a modern outlook, describes these wines as being "the four great growths" and Margaux as "the first growth of the top four." There follow in joint next place Léoville and Rauzan at 1000 louis. Then come Montbrison (Durfort-Vivens), Gorse (Palmer), Mouton, Kirwan, Mission, Carbonnieux, Pichon, Lascombe, and so on (750–800 louis).

Saint-Maur did not draw this classification out of his hat; he consulted the brokers, whose language he spoke. The brokers become the key figures in Bordeaux trading; it is they who drew up the 1855 classification. When the steward comments on the *palus* wines, which, it should be remembered, reached their top price in 1647, he expresses himself like a merchant: "This sort of wine that is essential in order to arrange the lowlier Médocs." This says it all; before the Revolution, each wine had its place, from the greatest to the humblest. On his way through Bordeaux in 1787–88, future president of the United States Thomas Jefferson confirms Saint-Maur's classification in his notebooks, but adds some interesting information on the Sauternes district. His classification is (1) Yquem; (2) Filhot; (3) Suduiraut (Président du Roy); (4) Lafaurie-Peyraguey (Président Pichard). All these wines were sold more cheaply than the wines of Médoc or Graves of similar reputation (about 300 louis). But Jefferson's notebooks present a further interest. Through the merchants, we know the price of the wines, but we do not know what they tasted like. Only the wine drinkers can tell us this, but they write either very little or nothing at all. The first interesting comment comes from Samuel Pepys, then several from John Locke in 1677, Arthur Young in 1787, and finally Jefferson. We learn from Jefferson what nowadays we might term the peak of a wine. He recognizes the notion of maturing and improvement with age, observing how the (Sauternes-style) whites keep for much longer, and are at their best for anything up to fifteen or twenty years. He is also attentive to vintage, which was also reflected in selling prices (Margaux 1772 had doubled in price). He goes on to say that the best wines to be bought in his day were those of the year 1784, the only good year since 1779.

Before the Revolution, wines were enjoyed and talked about exactly as they are today, with a ranking of growths by quality, good vintages and the not-so-good ones, peak, and selling price. To make life easier for themselves, the brokers drew up purchase price lists. The broker chose the wines for the merchant, the *négociant*; a professional winetaster, he had an eye what we now call the price-quality ratio, so he knew the price of the wines, being the person actually responsible for fixing it, in conjunction with the producer. This being the case, it will come as no surprise that the brokers' union was approached by the president of the chamber of commerce of Bordeaux, Duffour-Dubergier, with a view to drawing up "a full list of the classified red wines of the Gironde, and another for the great white wines." The drawing up of such a list was in fact nothing new; in his 1816 topography of all known vineyards, A. Julien had already

THE CLASSIFIED BORDEAUX GROWTHS

The 1855 Classification

REDS		WHITES

REDS

First growths

Château Haut-Brion .... Pessac
Château Lafite-Rothschild .... Pauillac
Château Latour .... Pauillac
Château Margaux .... Margaux
Château Mouton-Rothschild ...... Pauillac
(promoted in 1973)

Second growths

Château Brane-Cantenac .... Cantenac
Château Cos d'Estournel .... Saint-Estèphe
Château Ducru-Beaucaillou .... Saint-Julien-Beychevelle
Château Dufort-Vivens .... Margaux
Château Gruaud-Larose .... Saint-Julien-Beychevelle
Château Lascombes .... Margaux
Château Léoville-Barton .... Saint-Julien-Beychevelle
Château Léoville Las Cases .... Saint-Julien-Beychevelle
Château Léoville-Poyferré .... Saint-Julien-Beychevelle
Château Montrose .... Saint-Estèphe
Château Pichon-Longueville .... Pauillac
Château Pichon-Longueville
Comtesse de Lalande .... Pauillac
Château Rausan-Ségla .... Margaux
Château Rauzan-Gassies .... Margaux

Third growths

Château Boyd-Cantenac .... Cantenac
Château Calon-Ségur .... Saint-Estèphe
Château Cantenac-Brown .... Cantenac
Château Desmirail .... Margaux
Château Ferrière .... Margaux
Château Giscours .... Labarde
Château d'Issan .... Cantenac
Château Kirwan .... Cantenac
Château Lagrange .... Saint-Julien-Beychevelle
Château la Lagune .... Ludon
Château Langoa-Barton .... Saint-Julien-Beychevelle

Château Malescot-Saint-Exupéry .. Margaux
Château Marquis d'Alesme-Becker . Margaux
Château Palmer .... Cantenac

Fourth growths

Château Beychevelle .... Saint-Julien-Beychevelle
Château Branaire-Ducru .... Saint-Julien-Beychevelle
Château Duhart-Milon .... Pauillac
Château Lafon-Rochet .... Saint-Estèphe
Château Marquis de Terme .... Margaux
Château Pouget .... Cantenac
Château Prieuré-Lichine .... Cantenac
Château Saint-Pierre .... Saint-Julien-Beychevelle
Château Talbot .... Saint-Julien-Beychevelle
Château La Tour Carnet .... Saint-Laurent-de-Médoc

Fifth growths

Château d'Armailhac .... Pauillac
Château Batailley .... Pauillac
Château Belgrave .... Saint-Laurent-de-Médoc
Château Camensac .... Saint-Laurent-de-Médoc
Château Cantemerle .... Macau
Château Clerc-Milon .... Pauillac
Château Cos-Labory .... Saint-Estèphe
Château Croizet-Bages .... Pauillac
Château Dauzac .... Labarde
Château Grand-Puy-Ducasse ..... Pauillac
Château Grand-Puy-Lacoste ..... Pauillac
Château Haut-Bages-Libéral ...... Pauillac
Château Haut-Batailley .... Pauillac
Château Lynch-Bages .... Pauillac
Château Lynch-Moussas .... Pauillac
Château Pédesclaux .... Pauillac
Château Pontet-Canet .... Pauillac
Château le Tertre-Rotebœuf ...... Barsac

WHITES

First superior growth

Château d'Yquem .... Sauternes

First growths

Château Climens .... Barsac
Château Clos Haut-Peyraguey ..... Bommes
Château Coutet .... Barsac
Château Guiraud .... Sauternes
Château Lafaurie-Peyraguey .... Bommes
Château Rabaud-Promis .... Bommes
Château Rayne-Vigneau .... Bommes
Château Rieussec .... Fargues-de-Langon
Château Sigalas-Rabaud .... Bommes
Château de Suduiraut .... Preignac
Château La Tour Blanche .... Bommes

Second growths

Château d'Arche .... Sauternes
Château Brousset .... Barsac
Château Caillou .... Barsac
Château Doisy-Daëne .... Barsac
Château Doisy-Dubroca .... Barsac
Château Doisy-Védrines .... Barsac
Château Filhot .... Sauternes
Château Lamothe (Despujols) ..... Sauternes
Château Lamothe (Guignard) ..... Sauternes
Château de Malle .... Preignac
Château de Myrat .... Barsac
Château Nairac .... Barsac
Château Romer-du-Hayot .... Fargues de Langon
Château Suau .... Barsac

Saint-Emilion Classification
(revised in 1996)

First classified great growths

CLASS A
Château Ausone
Château Cheval Blanc

CLASS B
Château l'Angélus
Château Beau-Séjour Bécot
Château Beauséjour (Duffaut-Lagarosse)
Château Belair
Château Canon
Château Figeac
Château La Gaffelière
Château Magdelaine
Château Pavie

Château Trottevieille
Clos Fourtet

Classified great growths
Château L'Arrosée
Château Balestard La Tonnelle
Château Bellevue
Château Bergat
Château Berliquet
Château Cadet-Bon
Château Cadet-Piola
Château Canon-La Gaffelière
Château Cap de Mourlin
Château Chauvin
Château Corbin
Château Corbin-Michotte
Château Curé Bon

Château Dassault
Château Faurie-De-Souchard
Château Fonplégade
Château Fonroque
Château Franc Mayne
Château Grand Mayne
Château Grand Pontet
Château Grandes Murailles
Château Guadet Saint-Julien
Château Haut Corbin
Château Haut Sarpe
Château La Clotte
Château La Clusière
Château La Couspaude
Château La Dominique
Château Lamarzelle

Château Laniote
Château Larcis Ducasse
Château Larmande
Château Laroque
Château Laroze
Château Matras
Château Moulin du Cadet
Château Pavie Decesse
Château Pavie Macquin
Château Petit Faurie de Soutard
Château Le Prieuré
Château Ripeau
Château Saint-Georges Côte Pavie
Château La Serre

Château Soutard
Château La Tour du Pin-Figeac (Giraud-Bélivier)
Château La Tour du Pin-Figeac (J.-M. Moueix)
Château La Tour Figeac
Château Tertre Daugay
Château Troplong-Mondot
Château Villemaurine
Château Yon-Figeac
Clos des Jacobins
Clos de l'Oratoire
Clos Saint-Martin
Couvent des Jacobins

Graves Classification (1959)

Château Bouscaut .... Cadaujac (red/white)
Château Carbonnieux .... Léognan (red/white)
Domaine de Chevalier .... Léognan (red/white)
Château Couhins .... Villenave d'Ornon (white)
Château Couhins-Lurton .... Villenave d'Ornon (white)
Château Fieuzal .... Léognan (red)
Château Haut-Bailly .... Léognan (red)
Château Haut-Brion .... Pessac (red)

Château Laville Haut-Brion .... Talence (white)
Château Malartic-Lagravéire ...... Léognan (red/white)
Château La Mission Haut-Brion ... Talence (red)
Château d'Olivier .... Léognan (red/white)
Château Pape-Clément .... Pessac (red)
Château Smith-Haut-Lafitte ...... Martillac (red)
Château La Tour-Haut-Brion ..... Talence (red)
Château La Tour Martillac .... Martillac (red/white)

published a classification including four first growths—the same four—and seven second growths (Rauzan, Palmer, Léoville, Larose, Mouton, Pichon-Longueville, and Calon). Eight years later W. Franck published his own classification, comprising four classes, and that was followed by another by the broker Paguierre in 1829.

In 1846 an English professor, Charles Cocks, brought out *Bordeaux, Its Wines and Claret Country,* a French edition of which appeared in 1850, issued by the Bordeaux publisher Michel-Edouard Féret with the title *Bordeaux et ses vins classés par ordre de mérite.* This work is frequently revised and updated and has run to fifteen editions, the latest as recently as 1995!

Charles Cocks's 1850 classification is almost identical to the one drawn up by the brokers' union of the wines of the Gironde to determine the order in which the wines should be presented at the Great Universal Exhibition of 1855 in Paris, an exhibition called for by Napoleon III. This classification had no more influence than previous ones. It did, however, take on an official character, becoming the sacred document that it has remained ever since, untouchable with one exception, in 1973, when Mouton-Rothschild was promoted from second to first class.

One notable eccentricity of the 1855 classification is that it has no place for the wines of the Right Bank (which include Saint-Emilion), and no Graves apart from Haut-Brion. As far as Graves wines are concerned—the Pessac-Léognan *appellation d'origine contrôlée* (AOC) wines of today—three historical domains sold off as national possessions (Mission, Pape Clément, and Carbonnieux) had still not recovered from their change of ownership. The other, smaller ones simply do not seem to have impressed the Bordeaux brokers. Saint-Emilion is a rather different case. Trade in these wines

passed through Libourne, where the brokers of Bordeaux did no business. The bills of the very old and famous firm of brokers, Tastet-Lawton, are quite clear; the name of Saint-Emilion figures only very rarely, and the prices indicated are low. The English market was the one that set high prices, whereas the wines of Saint-Emilion were sent not to England but to France and northern Europe, where the market was not inclined to make expensive purchases. It was not until the second half of the nineteenth century that Saint-Emilion wines began to command prices comparable to those of the Médocs. As for Pomerol, this was to take even longer, and did not happen until the second half of the twentieth century.

Classification of Saint-Emilion and Graves Wines

The syndicate for the defense of Saint-Emilion AOC wines successfully submitted an application for classification of the wines of Saint-Emilion, and decrees published in 1955 and 1958 divided these wines into four categories, five if we take into account the subdivision into A and B of the *premier grands crus classés:*

A grape harvest scene. For the great growths, the grapes are handpicked.
Nothing has changed except a tractor has replaced the oxen.

* two class-A *premier grands crus;*
* ten class-B *premier grands crus;*
* seventy classified *grands crus;* and
* *grands crus,* nonclassified wines.

The wines' classifications, on the basis of the precedent set by the 1855 classification, imply that the soil, vinestocks, winemaking process, and other such considerations are taken into account. In addition, to avoid the rigidity of the 1855 classification, this one comes up for review every ten years.

Such flexibility seems logical enough; it does raise some serious practical problems, however. First of all, it rules out the classification of particular *terroirs;* short of some climatic or geological catastrophe, they can never change. Second, declassification or promotion are only decided upon after tasting the wine production of previous years, which have already been sold on the basis of their current ranking. To change their classification is therefore to recognize that they were sold as belonging to a class that in fact did not correspond to the claimed quality, thereby defeating the whole object of the exercise. The classification of the wines of Saint-Emilion was revised in 1985 and 1996.

Similarly, 1953 and 1959 decrees made official the classification of the white and red AOC wines of Graves, wines

that since 1987 have been labeled AOC Pessac-Léognan. This classification, for which no statutory revision is provided, has no internal hierarchy.

From Napoleon III to the Present Day

The second half of the nineteenth century marks the dawn of a golden age. You only need to take a stroll round the Médoc to see why; during that period, châteaus were springing up like mushrooms. Everyone wanted to follow the example set a few dozen years earlier by the marquis de la Colonilla, who on becoming a marquis changed his name and had Château Margaux built. The entire banking profession seemed to be purchasing each his own vineyard and the building to go with it. Nothing was too fine for them, including the wine, as witness the unbelievable oriental winery built for Gaspard d'Estournel that so astonished Stendhal. This construction continues to serve its original purpose, and its novelty has still not worn off: it is the most photographed monument of the Médoc. Within a few decades, the vineyard's output (Cos d'Estournel, *deuxième cru classé* of Saint-Estèphe) had doubled and exports tripled. Powdery mildew was by now just an unpleasant memory, banished by the method of spraying sulfur championed by a winegrower at Ludon, the comte de la Vergne. It was also at Ludon that they invented the idea of training the vines on wire; not far from there, at Giscours, Théophile Skawinski ingeniously designed a rational fermenting room and perfected various carts for the vineyard at a time when scientist Jules Guyot was working out a new method of pruning. Work on the vines became easier, yields went up, and wine began selling well; nothing, it appeared, could contain this euphoria. But in 1867, ominously, a few *palus* vines at Floirac began to wilt. Nothing much was done about it, although increasing numbers of similar occurrences had been observed in the vineyards of Provence since the years 1863–64. Phylloxera was identified by Planchon of Montpellier in 1868. In the Bordeaux region, it was only in the years around 1870–72 that people who had been so far unconcerned finally started to worry.

Following as many useless conferences as candles had been lit in churches, it was concluded that phylloxera did not survive when the vine was waterlogged during the winter; that the larvae of this plant louse failed to hatch in sand; that phylloxera could be fought off by injecting carbon sulfate gas into the ground, using a stake for a syringe; that plants imported directly from America were resistant to phylloxera; and that it was possible to graft French vines onto American rootstock. In the Bordeaux area, these obsevations led to increased planting in areas liable to flooding, i.e., *palus* and lowlands, and mandatory treatment with carbon sulfate for all other vineyards. In 1880 work commenced to replant the entire vineyard with grafted stock.

Dwindling wine production sent prices up, so overall, given the increased yields due to fertilizer and in view of the large quantity of *palus* wine, the situation turned out to be less of a catastrophe than might at first be thought. Although the quality of the great wines was not affected, since the old vinestocks were treated with carbon sulfate and so continued to thrive, the same cannot be said for the less ambitious wines made from the young vines, and "improved" with a certain amount of *palus* wine.

While phylloxera was eating into the vineyard, as if a high price were going to have to be paid for those years of

plenty, the grapevine was struck by another new blight. The branches went brown, the leaves turned white, the flowers black, and the rare grape bunch yellow, gradually withering into grayishness. Again, it was Planchon who identified the cause of this disease: a fungus called downy mildew. Like phylloxera, like oidium, or powdery mildew, it had been imported from America without anybody noticing, concealed about the vines bought in the United States. It has been said that the first American grapevines were planted by way of experiment. The result was powdery mildew. To study the resistance to powdery mildew of the American vines, more of these were imported, introducing phylloxera in the process. And finally, when huge quantities of American stock was brought in to replant the vineyard destroyed by phylloxera, stowaway downy mildew came over with them. The mildew spread like wildfire. Output dropped by half, and wine prices doubled. At Château Dauzac—a classified fifth-growth Margaux—they had got into the habit of daubing a bluish mixture of copper sulfate and lime on the vines along the roadside, so as to prevent "finger blight"—theft of the grapes by passersby. When the steward realized that those vines were not affected by mildew, Bordeaux mixture had just been invented.

After these three calamities from America, the vine—which until then had been a rugged plant—became constant prey to all sorts of pests, and has remained so to this day. It may be supposed (for something has to be supposed) that first, the numerous treatments inflicted on the vine have been and still are modifying the ecological balance; and second, that the genetic heritage of the different varieties has been damaged, either naturally or following selection for the purpose of improving plant's yield at the price of its sturdiness.

In 1900, the wine producers' peace of mind was restored. They had successfully overcome the American diseases, although replanting work with grafted stock would not be complete until 1914, and chemists were developing products offering preventive and curative treatment. Operating costs soared, however, and the golden age was followed by an age of financial imbalances, with the threat of an age of poverty. The paradox was that while the vineyard acreage had gone down (by roughly 74,000 acres, or 30,000 hectares, in the Bordeaux

Château de Beaumont (a bourgeois growth, built during the golden age of the nineteenth century). To this day it commands a huge vineyard.

vineyard), output had increased substantially (1850 = 26 million gallons, 1865 = 66 million, 1875 = 80 million, 1900 = 130 million gallons). This increase was due to the young vines, fertilizers, and the *palus*. It was by no means a local phenomenon; throughout France, vineyard acreage had dropped, and replanting in the plains had been going ahead. Vines with yields of 1.143 tons per acre had been ripped out and replaced with sturdy varieties that could comfortably handle outputs of 5.72 to 11.43 tons per acre in Languedoc. Such overproduction of small wines, with the great wines remaining expensive, was something new. The scene was set for a highly volatile situation, with the market collapsing and even the top-class growths affected. Sales at knockdown prices led people to make wines that were not wine at all, but made with sugar—poor-quality stuff laced with a drop of the genuine article. While the Bordeaux region did not experience a winegrowers' revolt such as occurred in Languedoc and Champagne, it did not entirely escape unemployment and labor claims. In this depressed climate the *négociants*, who, it will be recalled, buy wine in cask, raise it, and bottle it, tended to

water down the best wines with less costly vintages. We should not be too scandalized at this practice, which was common enough, as is borne out by the word *hermitager*, which appears in the old dictionaries, meaning to dilute with Hermitage wine. This, however, was to "arrange" a wine to get the best out of it, whereas the new practice was purely intended to increase profit, if not merely to sell at all, by bringing the price down. The faked and doubtful wines did nothing to produce a healthy market; hence the development of the notion of a wine's origin and defense thereof. As of 1911, the Bordeaux label was restricted to the wines of the Gironde. Senator Capus, a Bordeaux man by adoption, would found the Institut National des Appellations d'Origine (INAO), but that was not until 1935.

In spite of everything, production increased to generally around 160 million gallons.

In 1924 Baron Philippe de Rothschild, in open hostility to the wine merchants, took the radical step of guaranteeing the authenticity of his wine (Mouton) by bottling it himself. He tried unsuccessfully to prevail upon the first growths to

OPPOSITE
Above, the vinegrower's tools. Below, the vines. Note how they are trained on wood. In the mid-nineteenth century, wood was being replaced by wire.

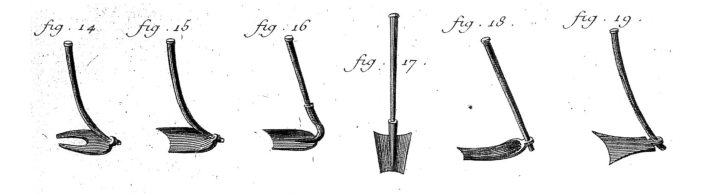

fig. 14   fig. 15   fig. 16   fig. 17   fig. 18   fig. 19

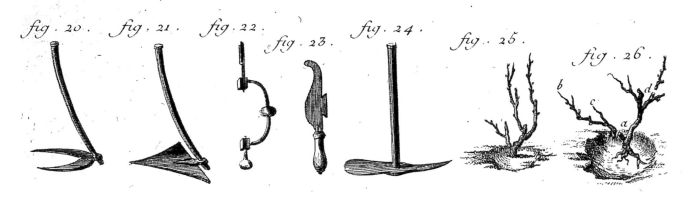

fig. 20.   fig. 21.   fig. 22.   fig. 23.   fig. 24.   fig. 25.   fig. 26.

fig. 29.

fig. 28.

fig. 27.

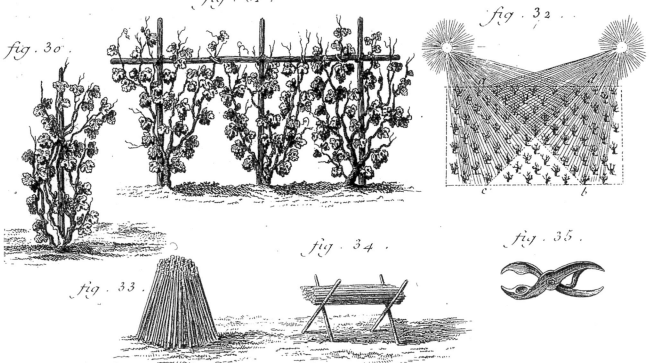

fig. 31.

fig. 32.

fig. 30.

fig. 34.

fig. 35.

fig. 33.

The
mildew
spread
like wildfire.
Output dropped
by half, and
wine prices
doubled.

Plan of "Margaud" during the eighteenth century—now Margaux.
The château had not yet been built, but the garden and lawn were
already in their present-day positions.

Plan
du chateau de
MARGAUD

Margaud est une tresbelle maison qui
a De Beaux jardins. Son seigneur amasse
quantitée de vin, et L'on tient quil en
fait quelque fois pour plus de cinquante
mille livres par an

Les Vignes de ces quartiers sont Echalassées
avec des Echalats comme au tour de
paris, et non celles de Saintonge qui
n'en ont point.

follow suit, but it was only after the war that mandatory château bottling of first growths became acceptable.

The great vintages of 1928 and 1929 were a delight for the producers; however, the terrible month of October 1929 saw the Wall Street crash, which had dire consequences in Europe as of 1931, with falling sales and exports. To make matters worse, 1930, 1931, 1932, and 1933 were poor vintages. This was no longer just a slump: the wine trade was positively poverty-stricken. All the properties went up for sale, but there were no buyers. Bordeaux became a disaster area, and 10 percent of the vineyards were dug up.

With the end of the war came an end to the quota system and fixed selling prices. The 1945, 1947, and 1949 vintages were enough to cheer up even the gloomiest of souls. Gradually tractors began to replace horses, with fast spraying techniques proving an effective weapon against powdery and downy mildew, thereby ensuring higher yields and guaranteed quality. These new features were mostly the prerogative of the Left Bank.

1956

The frost of February 1956 hit the vines hard. Nothing like it had been seen since 1870. The Médoc was snowbound; thus protected, it was less hard hit, as its coastal position took the edge off the cold. Sauternes, Saint-Emilion, and Pomerol, on the other hand, with hardly any snow, experienced Siberian cold, the thermometer plunging well below the grapevine's lower limit of 10°F (–12°C). A quarter of the vineyard was destroyed, including 30 to 50 percent at Saint-Emilion and 50 to 75 percent around Pomerol. This catastrophe was an opportunity to reorganize grape production, with more merlot, more bouchet, and less malbec. While in this region the

wines that came after 1956 are definitely no longer quite the same as those made before—if only because of the age of the vines—1956, due to the frost, and 1959 and 1961, due to the heat, mark a watershed in Bordeaux wines. Of course, to pick on any one particular date is somewhat arbitrary, as producers do not all change their equipment in the same year. And although there were concrete vats back in the time of Chaptal, and shiny stainless steel tanks at the Haut-Brion Mission in 1926, it is nevertheless true that 1956 to 1961 saw both a change of equipment and a change in mentalities.

In Summary

The rich grape harvests in the great heat of the 1959 and 1961 vintages brought it home to producers that, unless you could control fermentation temperatures, winemaking was a hit-or-miss affair, and it was time to hang up the old Alfa-Laval coil in a museum. Stainless steel vats became more common (Haut-Brion began to use them in 1961, Latour in 1964), cooled by sprinkling, then fitted with ring circulation enabling wine to be either cooled or heated. From then on, huge control panels measured and controlled the temperature of each vat to within a tenth of a degree. From that control desk, pumping over and punching down, among other operations, were controlled.

The more sophisticated the equipment, the more skilled the operator had to be. Enologists—a profession unheard of in 1945—took charge of this complex machinery, and the consultant enologist became an important person. The best-known of these, Professor Emile Peynaud, displayed his specialist knowledge to masterly effect when he was called to Château Margaux in 1977, and in 1978 confounded all expectations by producing one of the outstanding wines of

In front, the pleasure garden. At the back, the vineyard.

that vintage. It was later claimed that there was such a thing as a "Peynaud wine." You cannot be adviser to over a hundred and fifty Bordeaux châteaus without leaving some kind of a mark, but this most famous of enologists has always fought shy of giving wines his own personal stamp, claiming rather that the enologist's role is to bring the best out of the soils. Granted there is no such thing as a Peynaud wine, there is maybe such a thing as a Peynaud method, which epitomizes modern enology as practiced around Bordeaux. It might be summarized as follows:

1.

pick ripe grapes;

2.

sort them;

3.

destem them completely;

4.

adjust pumping over according to extraction.
Here the enologist becomes an artist, as the quality of extraction is assessed by tasting;

5.

run off the juice according to the wine desired.
Here a further tasting is required;

6.

mature the wine in new casks, provided it has the necessary stature (further assessment); and

7.

decide on the end of maturation and bottling.
Final tasting by our enology artist.

So we can see that the job of the enologist involves two lines of activity: one purely technical, justifying the Italian job description for such professionals, "enotechnician"; the other involving the wine taster's subjective appreciation.

The work of the enologists has been decisive in shaping the modern post-1961 Bordeaux red, which may be characterized having undetectable volatile acidity, lower acidity level, and riper, rounder tannins. This has led wine drinkers to say that the "new Bordeaux" is mellower, which from an organoleptic standpoint is exactly right. On the other hand, the same wine drinkers are mistaken when they cast doubt on these wines' aging qualities. They do not have less tannins, just better tannins.

What About the White Wines?

The typology of Sauternes wine has been settled for so long now (over a century and a half) that a vertical tasting of Château d'Yquem reveals that the wine is always its same old self. As regards sweet wines, modern enology has only made a few minor technical enhancements: more sparing use of sulfur dioxide (a necessary move indeed!) and improved maturing. The progress of barrel fermentation can only promote the quality of these wines.

We have placed the birth of a new generation of red wines after 1961. The dry white wines went through a veritable revolution in the 1980s. Led by Denis Dubourdieu, owner of Clos Floridène (AOC Graves), but primarily an enologist with a reputation for his work on white wines, a number of estates in Pessac-Léognan have completely reviewed their vinification methods. To achieve greater complexity, they have abandoned fermentation in vats in favor of fermentation in casks; they use (and maybe sometimes overuse?) lees stirring or *bâtonnage* (more flavors, more fat) and are currently producing some remarkable white wines. Until this transformation took place, the only whites international wine lovers got excited about were Haut-Brion and Chevalier domaine whites; now all the classified growths among the AOC Pessac-Léognan whites are doing well, as well as a few nonclassified ones. Such acclaim is fully deserved.

PAGES 36–37

The vineyard of Haut Cos d'Estournel, classified AOC Saint-Estèphe second growth. This semi-oriental building is not a residence but a winery, built by Gaspard d'Estournel in the nineteenth century in tribute to the wines "back from India," of which he was more or less the inventor, and the Arab horses that were his passion.

PAGES 38–39

In the Château Margaux vinothèque. Note the old, deeply mold-spotted Bordeaux bottles, and the capsules missing from the bottles in the back row; these corks have been renewed.

3

The Soil

Since the eighteenth century people have been studying the factors that give rise to the birth of a growth, of a wine. Some places are blessed by the gods, and attempts have been made to find out why and how they have been so blessed. When talking of a particular place, one immediately thinks of the *terroir*, in the broadest sense of the word—a soil and subsoil that enjoy a certain climate or microclimate.

In the Bordeaux area as elsewhere, everything has come about through empiricism and memorized empiricism; some call it tradition, and others history. The division of the *département* of the Gironde—to which the Bordeaux regional appellation and fifty-six local appellations are restricted—is not the work of geologists taking samples from all over, listing them, and classifying them according to their geological affini-

ties: it is the result of usage. Certainly usage incorporates parameters that may be relatively temporary, such as the distance between the place of production and the place of consumption—so crucial in former times and now irrelevant—or social and economic and administrative influences, feudalism, big landowners, politics, influences that survive in some shape or form to this day. Hence the danger of setting situations or status once and for all, even though they are the result of a long history. Has not the classification of 1855, excellent though it was, left us in perpetuity with a photograph taken nearly a hundred and fifty years ago (see chapter 2) and only very slightly modified in 1973?

In a general way, the pragmatism of the Bordeaux wine maker works well and leaves some room for adjustment—not

PAGES 40–41
Luxury wines can only be produced in refined surroundings: here, at Château de Malle, a classified second growth (AOC Barsac) is made. The château is also listed as a historic monument.

OPPOSITE
A true rarity: a horse working the fields of Saint-Emilion.

enough for some people, or in a way that is too cumbersome and slow-moving, but which nevertheless enables the domaines, techniques, and the wines themselves to evolve.

Thus the *terroirs*, or to be more precise, their boundaries, are set; yet they are not as hard and fast as one might think. There is a certain amount of leakage between the neighboring communes of Pauillac and Saint-Julien, although they have different appellations, just as we detect a hint of Saint-Estèphe in the Pauillac of the renowned Château Lafite; but this should offend nobody, for it is true that, despite ever more sophisticated geological research, this notion of the *terroir* has by no means unlocked all its secrets. And a good thing too, for if we had all the answers, we might have the hubris to attempt man-made *terroirs* to order, instead of contenting ourselves with adding a very superficial dose of fertilizer. The only human intervention possible in this area is draining (of which more later).

To put the question more plainly, what do we know about the affinity, or lack of affinity, between the vine and certain soil types; and on a subsidiary basis, can each appellation or group of appellations be distinguished or justified in terms of a given soil? We may start looking for an answer to this question by a process of elimination. Wet areas are unsuitable for growing the grapevine, for the simple reason that the roots of the vine cannot survive in permanently wet conditions: they rot. This explains why, when you move up the Médoc region starting out from Bordeaux (on the Margaux-Pauillac road and beyond), you find large areas with no vines. It will be noted that these areas always coincide with a dip in the road, which only has to rise a few meters for you to come to a few more vines spread out to the left. These high points are the famous *croupes* we read about in descriptions of Bordeaux vineyards. Granted that the vine does not like wet soils, are all dry soils equally suitable? That would be an oversimplification, but it may be inferred from the above that soils known as hydromorphic soils, which retain water, are not compatible with wine. This is why the notion of filtering soils was invented, and why this filtering capacity is measured; it is also why, conversely, the soil's water retention capacity is also measured. These studies either tie in with or confirm work carried out by grain size distribution specialists on soil compactness.

It should be noted that although it is a crucially important factor, soil permeability needs to be complemented by the location of the water table, whose level will of course vary, depending on the time of year. The water question appears to be fairly straightforward—although the vine, or more precisely its roots, will devise solutions enabling it to make the best of a variety of soil types, as we shall see when we come to listing the *terroirs* of the main appellations—but the question of the chemical makeup of the soil is so complex that we have to make do with certain approximations. Chemical analyses carried out on the soil include the organic matter (carbon, nitrogen, etc.), calcareous rock type (active or not), capacity for producing chlorosis, potassium content, magnesium and lime content, phosphoric acid, and lastly, oligo-elements. Specialists locate imbalances and make up for them with fertilizer, but those same specialists are in total ignorance as to the organoleptic consequences for the wines of the chemical compounds in the soil. If it were merely a matter of adding iron slag to the soil to give extra depth and a flavor of black truffles to one's red wine, everyone would be doing it, and we could produce *terroirs* on demand. The complexity of the processes, their interactions, and the transformations produced by the plant material all pose great problems, although science may be able to come up with some solutions. But how long will it take, and what is it all going to cost?

FETE DES VENDANGES
BORDEAUX les Samedi 11, Dimanche 12, Lundi 13 SEPTEMBRE
REPRÉSENTATIONS SUR LES QUINCONCES DE 3HS. A 6HS.
BACCHUS TRIOMPHANT

Left Bank

Médoc

We begin with the Médoc, as it is the most straightforward, the most homogenous, the most obvious of the soil types, although this homogeneity is more marked to the east of the Haut-Médoc. In this part of the Haut-Médoc, we find all the growths listed in the 1855 classification even though this classification was made solely in terms of wine prices, without regard to the nature of the soil. However, when we draw the geological map of the Haut-Médoc, we see that all the classified growths are planted on gravelly soils. We also note that as soon as the proportion of clay begins to rise, the brokers who drew up this classification began to lose interest in the wines. If we needed to demonstrate the influence of the *terroir* on wine styles, it would be sufficient to quote this example. What is the makeup of this soil? A low percentage of clay and silt, and hence a low particle-size distribution (less than 50 microns), but 90 to 95 percent of mixed gravel and sand with maximum filtering capacity, having a particle-size distribution of 0.5 mm, and mostly 1 mm to 2.5 mm! This ideally poor soil forces the vine roots to delve as far down as possible, thereby more or less making rainfall variations a nonfactor. This, in fact, is the very *terroir* that would immediately spring to mind if we had to design one.

AOC Margaux

A great soil dating from the Günz glacial stage of Garonne gravel on a clay limestone/marl base, all the more unusual for having been further carved out by the Gironde, which changed its course during the Mindel and Riss glaciations.

AOC Saint-Julien

A whole commune given over to working the Günz gravels (more than 20 inches) on a thin iron pan base. On the western flank, the sands of the Landes moors have been trying their best to flood one of the Médoc's finest *terroirs*, fortunately with no great success.

AOC Pauillac

High-quality Günz gravels, the coarsest known in the Gironde vineyard, at Latour and part of Lafite. To the east of the commune is a mixture of Günz and Pyrenees gravels. A number of small rivers and streams have given these incomparable gravels their relief.

AOC Saint-Estèphe

The famed rock of Saint-Estèphe, a clayey marine limestone, forms the bedrock under the major part of the commune. It is overlaid with anything between 6½ and 33 feet (2 and 10 meters) of gravelly alluvium deposited during the Ice Age. Added to this are various more or less clayey marls, and a little wind-deposited sand. In a word, clayey, chalky gravel with filtering qualities suitable for the grapevine.

AOC Moulis

The commune of Moulis has one major defect—it does not overlook the river Gironde, from which it is separated either by the commune of Arcène or by Lamarque (both AOC Haut-Médocs). Is it because it has this off-centered position to the west that Moulis has no classified growths? We may think that this commune is being eaten away by the moor sands of the Landes from the west. Certainly there is no lack of sand, but it is mixed in with heavy, clayey-calcareous Pyrenees gravel. Farther east, the strange limestone hollow of Peyrelebade is backed by gravelly hillocks dating from the Günz glacial stage. The superiority of this type of gravel is once again evident with Château Chasse-Spleen and Château Poujeaux.

AOC Listrac

This soil is characterized, particularly in the western and southwestern sector, by its clayey gravels of Pyrenean origin.

If it were merely a matter of adding iron slag to the soil to give extra depth and a flavor of black truffles to one's red wine, everyone would be doing it.

This soil type is suited to the merlot grape, which is indeed very highly regarded at Listrac. After the Peyrelebade kettle, on the western side, we admire a fine gravel hillock at Médrac (Château Peyredon-Lagravette).

AOC Pessac-Léognan

The Left Bank keeps singing the same old song—the supremacy of the graves, whether they be Garonne, Pyrenees, Günz, Mindel or Riss gravels. To simplify: on Tertiary calcareous rock, and more occasionally on Tertiary molasse (Smith-Haut-Lafite, Carbonnieux), alluvial deposits reach 167 to 233 feet (50 to 70 meters). The gravel layers are Pyrenean in origin toward Haut-Bailly, Pape Clément, Martillac, and Chevalier, and Garonnese dating from the Günz glacial stage toward Smith-Haut-Lafite, Carbonnieux, Olivier (in part), and Haut-Brion; Mission Haut-Brion has the benefit of both. There are also Riss and Mindel gravels at Bouscaut and Couhins. In most instances, we can tell from their relative position in the soil strata where the gravels came from.

AOC Graves

The Graves *appellation d'origine contrôlée* area extends to Langon and beyond, making way for Sauternes in its central section. On the whole, despite its quality, this *terroir* is not as remarkable as that farther north. The gravels are much finer, to the point of becoming like sand, and even sometimes like silt. Clay or chalky clay is also present and accounts for the space taken up by white wine varieties. As a general rule, the calcareous bottom soil dating from the Tertiary is never far away.

The Sauternes Inclusion

This inclusion is preceded by the three communes of Cérons, Illats, and Podensac, which are entitled to produce very sweet white AOC Cérons wines, when they do not produce dry white Graves. This clayey-calcareous soil on starfish limestone contains little gravel.

AOC Barsac

The low-lying Barsac plain lost its Günz gravel and was powdered with Mindel red sand (Climens, Coutet, and other Barsacs).

AOC Sauternes

The communes entitled to the Sauternes appellation (Bommes, Fargues, Preignac, and Sauternes) have a distinctively tormented relief. Higher ground to the south, with fine, heavy Pyrenees gravel (Rieussec, Lamothe, Guiraud, upper Yquem). To the north and west, lower down, is course Günz gravel similar to that found at Pauillac (Tour Blanche, Rayne-Vigneau, Suduiraud, Rabaud, lower Yquem). A noteworthy feature is that Château d'Yquem lies at the top of a hill of sandy clay, mostly clay, so much so in fact that in the mid-nineteenth century, 62 miles (100 kilometers) of drains were laid to remove the moisture from the soil.

Right Bank

If we leave the south and head for Bordeaux, the Right Bank is dotted with numerous appellations, in the same spirit as the Left Bank, doubtless on a less grand scale, although the Left and Right Banks are very close in geological terms, with a starfish limestone base and fine clayey calcareous or siliceous gravel.

Saint-Emilion

This appellation presents no single geological type. The Saint-Martin plain stands apart, a unique feature in the Bordeaux region, a huge block of fissured limestone covered with 8 to 27 inches (20 to 70 cm) of clayey calcareous earth. This calcareous rock is everywhere to be seen, and the wines of Clos Fourtet, Ausone, and Pavie lie in old quarries that have been

PAGES 54–55
Changing posts, replacing wires—such are the off-season jobs.
Note the gravelly soil and the rounded pebbles.

turned into vast cellars. The presence of this limestone can also be observed by visiting the monolithic church in the center of the town of Saint-Emilion.

The second notable soil type at Saint-Emilion is the hillside variety. Here the arable soil is very shallow, no more than eighteen inches deep. The soil is sandy or calcareous clay on a molasse base.

The third soil type at Saint-Emilion is that found at the foot of the slopes, where the arable soil is obviously deeper, up to six feet deep. The molasse base is covered with very sandy or sandy clay soils, which cannot claim to have the high agricultural qualities of the other *terroirs* of the Saint-Emilion area. This description would not be complete without mentioning the sector to be discovered by going from Saint-Emilion to Pomerol.

Two first growths are to be found here: Cheval Blanc and Figeac. They differ from other Saint-Emilion wines in the grape varieties used, which take into account the particular soil type here—Günz gravel on a sandstone base, with a surface relief somewhat reminiscent of the Haut-Médoc—a quality *terroir*.

Pomerol

The Günz gravel mentioned with reference to the northwest of Saint-Emilion (Figeac, Cheval Blanc), continues along the plain of Pomerol, again on a sandstone base. In this overall configuration, Pétrus occupies a sill all on its own. It is unique in that it has practically no gravel and because the sandstone acts as a foundation to a sandy clay weald, drained by the domed shape of the molasse base. Here again the very unusual varietal mix at Pétrus (95 percent Merlot) is justified by the unusual soil type.

Fronsac

Here there is no gravel, but a calcareous plateau covered, as at Saint-Emilion, with slopes of red sandy clay and molasse.

If we continue up the Gironde estuary, we come to Côtes de Bourg and Blaye, with their more compact red clay and white siliceous soils.

THE FIFTY-SEVEN AOC WINES IN BORDEAUX
(✳ = *classified growths*)

REDS

Bordeaux/Bordeaux supérieur

✳ PREMIÈRES CÔTES DE BLAYE/BOURG or CÔTES-DE-BOURG/ BORDEAUX-CÔTES-DE-FRANCS/CÔTES DE CASTILLON/ GRAVES DE VAYRES/PREMIÈRES CÔTES-DE-BORDEAUX/ SAINTE-FOY-BORDEAUX

✳ MÉDOC/HAUT-MÉDOC/MARGAUX/MOULIS/LISTRAC-MÉDOC/ SAINT-JULIEN-PAUILLAC/SAINT-ESTÈPHE

✳ GRAVES/PESSAC-LÉOGNAN

✳ SAINT-EMILION/SAINT-EMILION grand cru/LUSSAC-SAINT-EMILION/ MONTAGNE-SAINT-EMILION/PUISSEGUIN-SAINT-EMILION/ SAINT GEORGES/SAINT-EMILION

POMEROL/LALANDE-DE-POMEROL

FRONSAC/CANON-FRONSAC

ROSÉS

✳ BORDEAUX ROSÉ/BORDEAUX CLARET/ CRÉMANT DE BORDEAUX (SPARKLING)

DRY WHITES

✳ BORDEAUX/BORDEAUX SEC/CRÉMANT DE BORDEAUX/ ENTRE-DEUX-MERS/ENTRE-DEUX-MERS HAUT-BENAUGE/ BORDEAUX HAUT-BENAUGE

✳ BLAYAIS/CÔTES-DE-BLAYE/PREMIÈRES CÔTES-DE-BLAYE/ CÔTES-DE-BOURG/BORDEAUX-CÔTES-DE-FRANCS/GRAVES DE VAYRES

✳ GRAVES/PESSAC-LÉOGNAN

SWEET WINES

Bordeaux supérieur

✳ PREMIÈRES CÔTES-DE-BORDEAUX/CÔTES-DE-BORDEAUX-SAINT-MACAIRE/SAINTE-FOY-BORDEAUX/GRAVES SUPÉRIEURS

✳ SAUTERNES/BARSAC/CÉRONS/CADILLAC/LOUPIAC/ SAINTE-CROIX-DU-MONT.

4

The Climate

You cannot make good wines without ripe, healthy grapes. Having said that, it is only a small step to deducing that sunshine and low rainfall are the keys to success. If we pursued this line of reasoning further, we would come to the conclusion that the best region in France is the Roussillon. So where does this reasoning fail? While health and ripeness are vital prerequisites, the conditions in which ripening takes place are also extremely important. Like the wine itself, the grape needs to be handled gently. Any extreme conditions are damaging to it. It is not enough that grapes be perfectly ripe; they must be good grapes that are perfectly ripe. Excessively sweltering conditions will increase sugar levels but burn the subtle aromas in the grapes.

From the viewpoint of the vacationer, the climate in the Bordeaux is less than ideal. It is a temperate climate with a maritime influence combining average sunshine and relatively high rainfall, especially in summer, which is a particularly difficult time of year for the grape. This means two

things. First, the slow ripening of the grapes protects and stimulates their aromatic richness. Second, such strict and arduous conditions afford no security, hence the great importance attached to the Bordeaux vintage, this being a much less sensitive issue in the vineyards of the south.

Sauternes, a Special Case

Weather conditions required to make a good sweet wine are substantially different from those necessary or sufficient for other types of wine. More precisely, the health and ripeness of the grape is a general requirement, but when the adventure of the red grapes is over, the adventure of white grapes destined to produce sweet wines is only just beginning. Once the grapes are ripe, the weather can in fact be too fine! The years 1978, 1982, and to a lesser extent 1985 are proof of

OPPOSITE
*Young vine. It will take another four years to start producing AOC-quality grapes,
and at least ten years before the grapes can be used for a great wine.*

58

In order to avoid the rot becoming gray rot—for it to become "noble"—the mists and fogs need to lift and the grapes need to dry out in the sun.

this. Unquestionably excellent years for reds, they were only a partial success for the sweet whites: the hot, dry Indian summer favorable to overripening worked against the growth of *Botrytis cinerea,* the "noble rot." For botrytis to develop, it is crucial that mist or fog envelop the vineyard. This is why the vines are always close to a lake or river: in the Sauternes area, it is the river Cérons; elsewhere it is the Loire, the Rhine, the Bodrog (Tokay), and so on. Also, in order to avoid the rot becoming gray rot—for it to become noble—the mists and fogs need to lift, to allow the grapes to dry out in the sun. In short, fog is needed in the morning, sunshine in the afternoon. As long as the rain holds off, such conditions are ideally met in the Sauternes, as they were in 1988, 1989, and 1990.

OPPOSITE
White grapes and yellow leaves . . . drought or chlorosis, or both!

PAGES 62–63
Enlarged view of the laboratory in which light is converted into sugar.
Special channels will take the sugar off to the grape berries.

5

The Grapes

The grape varieties that go into producing the wines of the various Bordeaux appellations are set by appellation decrees, as is the case everywhere in France. In some cases (the great Bordeaux vintages not included), the minimum or maximum proportion of any given grape is even set out.

No doubt the distinctive quality of the different appellations gains by this rule, although outlawed blends may be viewed as a hindrance to the imagination—and to the development of new wines. It is a sobering thought that had such measures been introduced in the late eighteenth century, something that could easily have happened, the merlot grape would have no place in Bordeaux wines—so there could be no such wine as a Pétrus—whereas merlot currently covers twice the surface area planted with cabernet sauvignon; and

the major Bordeaux variety would doubtless be malbec, which was abundant at the time, and has since been pulled up almost everywhere!

Red Wine Varieties

Cabernet Sauvignon

The cabernet sauvignon grape is the king of the Médoc. It has extended its kingdom across the globe for two reasons: first because, as the king of the Médoc, it caught everybody's attention, and second, because it is a "plastic" variety—it can produce outstanding wines anywhere at all, provided the grapes ripen. This is a quality it shares with the king of the

PAGES 64–65
Vines loaded with white grapes.

OPPOSITE
The bloom on the skin of the grape. Here are the yeasts that will find their way through the must and trigger alcoholic fermentation.

white wine varieties, Chardonnay. Cabernet sauvignon has always been grown in the Médoc (and in the Gironde as a whole), say those who claim that "Biturica," the "new" grape variety mentioned by Pliny, was none other than cabernet sauvignon. It was definitely present in the eighteenth century, when it was known as *vidure* (or perhaps *biture**). This fine variety has every reason to please: small, thick-skinned grapes, late budding that eliminates risk from frost, incomparably powerful tannins, and an aromatic subtlety that is only brought out after lengthy aging, thereby giving the wines of the Médoc and Graves their infinite complexity. On the downside, it does not do well in cold or clay soils, which is why it prefers the Left to the Right Bank.

Cabernet Franc

The presence of cabernet franc is duly recorded as early as 1784 in the Saint-Emilion area, where it was—and still is—known as Bouchet, which became Bouchy farther south. It represents approximately 20 percent of the Médoc vineyard. Its greatest claim to fame is of course being the major ingredient in the *premier grand cru* Château Cheval Blanc. The question here is this: why plant cabernet franc when you can plant cabernet sauvignon? Cabernet franc is less tannic and often less acid, and is often taken for a scaled-down version of cabernet sauvignon. However, this is being less than fair and disregards its finesse, its black currant aromas, which are so marked in the Bourgueil AOC Loire wines, and its ability to ripen in climates that are too cool for cabernet sauvignon —hence its presence at Saint-Emilion.

Merlot

It is often said that the merlot grape plays second fiddle to cabernet sauvignon. This, however, in no way corresponds to the actual surface areas occupied by the two varieties; there

is twice as much merlot in the Gironde as cabernet sauvignon. Of course the yield per acre is much higher than that of cabernet sauvignon, it produces more sugar, it has lower acidity and lower tannic potential, and the skin on the grapes is thinner, and therefore more fragile. It buds early, ripens early, and is subject to a shriveling of the newly formed grapes due to cold, wet weather, a phenomenon known as *coulure*. But, to put it another way, if we state that it is solely responsible for making Château Pétrus what it is, there is no answer to that argument. In the Médoc and the Graves, with only 20 to 25 percent, it plays a relatively backstage role, but it makes up for this on the Right Bank, at Saint-Emilion and Pomerol, where it has taken over two thirds of the vineyard. Unlike the cabernets, this variety is never quite so happy as in clay (Pétrus) or clayey gravel. Its introduction into the Gironde is fairly recent: mid-eighteenth century on the Right Bank, nineteenth century on the Left. Its origin is a complete mystery. The merlot grape produces a richly colored, lush, full-bodied wine with velvety tannins. It is criticized for its easy charm, in contrast with the strict severity and introverted character of wines produced from cabernet sauvignon grapes.

Petit Verdot

This is a variety of the Médoc that is said to have been used here for a very long time; it was mentioned as early as 1400. Is petit verdot the same thing as "petite vidure"? We have some reason to think so, as it does belong to the cabernet family (Cabernet = vidure, which suggests that the grape variety mentioned by Pliny was in fact verdot. This would make sense as it is the oldest known variety in the region.). Petit verdot plays the same role as salt in pastries; only a small amount is grown in Médoc, but the classified vintages, including the greatest of these, make a point of cultivating it. Wine from the petit verdot grape is deeply colored, tannic, spicy and rich in aromas. Unfortunately, this variety is the latest maturing of the cabernet vines, so it only ripens in good years.

Malbec

We mention this grape in passing, as there is not much of it left, on the Right Bank, in the areas around Bourges and Blaye, but owing to its place in the history of the great Bordeaux

wines, it cannot be passed over. It was probably the main red grape variety prior to the invasion of the cabernet sauvignon and merlot vines at around the time of the French Revolution. Malbec wines are deep colored, mellow, round, fruity wines, with low acidity and plenty of tannin, but not too much. Currently malbec is best expressed in the Cahors AOC wine, where it is known as Auxerrois.

Carmenère

This grape belongs to the cabernet family but was not replanted after the phylloxera epidemic, having already been severely hit by powdery mildew. This fall-off in enthusiasm is explained by its low yield and susceptibility to disease. This is a pity because the carmenère grape makes excellent wine, as witness the one remaining château—a bourgeois growth, Château Dilon—that continues to grow a decent patch of it out of respect and curiosity. It yields a deep-colored, fruity, full-bodied, fairly soft wine, almost voluptuous, especially when compared with the astringency of the Médoc. It still figures in the appellation decree for Médoc wines, and maybe it is time the nurseries began to take an interest in making a serious selection of carmenère vinestocks.

White Wine Varieties

Semillon

Whatever people may say, semillon remains the number-one white wine variety of the Bordeaux vineyard: it is easy to grow, and it produces a bumper crop. Against that it has to

PAGE 69
Perfectly ripe white grapes, bearing small marks indicating that the noble rot is setting in.

PAGES 70–71
The vital mist that helps produce botrytis (the "noble rot") here envelops the small houses in front of Château d'Yquem.

PAGES 72–73
Here is a healthy, ripe harvest. These grapes will be separated from their woody stalks (destemmed), crushed, and then placed in fermenting vats. Once matured, the wine from these grapes will bear the label "Pichon Longueville, comtesse de Lalande."

face the trends of fashion: it is criticized for its discreet aromas and the time needed for it to come fully into its own. This is something of a paradox, for wine lovers, particularly those in the English-speaking countries, assess the quality of a wine in terms of its staying power, and yet they appear to forget that semillon is the white grape with potentially the longest-lasting quality of all. Its wines are fat, alcoholic, with low acidity and a slight hint of beeswax. However, due to its sensitivity to oxidation, it is for good winemakers only. With time and cellaring, it takes on a rich complexity. Semillon wines are nearly always blended with sauvignons: a little sauvignon wine blended with a large amount of semillon wine. The sauvignon is the complement but the dominant variety, especially when the wine is young. Later on this relationship is reversed: this second-period variety with its thin-skinned grapes takes the noble rot very well. So we are not surprised to find it in Sauternes wines, in which it can represent anything between 80 and 100 percent. We also have some reason to believe that this old regional vinestock originally came from the Sauternes area. A great grape variety that has nothing but indifference for media coverage.

Sauvignon

Do we need to mention this "ravaging savage" (*sauvignon* may derive from *sauvage,* "savage")? It teams up with the semillon grape, although in complete contrast to it, as it produces sinewy, aromatic wines that are often acidic and, with one or two exceptions, do not improve with age. It finds its best expression on the calcareous soils of Pouilly and Sancerre. In the Bordeaux region, although immediately identifiable, it is not so distinctive. It gives their character to the wines of Entre-Deux-Mers and the white wines of the various Bordeaux Côtes and Côtes de Blaye *appellation contrôlée* wines. Among the prestigious Pessac-Léognan wines, it plays a major role, 100 percent at Couhins-Lurton, 85 percent at Malartic-Lagravière, 70 percent at Domaine de Chevalier, and 30 to 40 percent in the others. It is the only variety used in Château Margaux's Pavillon Blanc, demonstrating that it is perfectly capable of playing a solo part. Barrel aging definitely tones down sauvignon's tendency to overdo things, for it can sometimes give the impression that it is parodying

In the hierarchy of nobility, semillon is a duke of old stock, whereas sauvignon often resembles a count who owes his rank to fashion.

itself. In the sweet wines, it makes up about 20 percent of the blend (as in Yquem), but this figure can be anything between 0 and 50 percent. While the grapes willingly lend themselves to the noble rot, they are often picked before they are too "roasted," so as to preserve at least some of their aromatic potential. Also, the grape matures ten days earlier than the semillon grape. In the hierarchy of nobility, semillon is a duke of old stock, whereas sauvignon often resembles a count who owes his rank to fashion.

Muscadelle

Muscadelle is to the white grape varieties as petit verdot is to the red. Those who grow it praise its late budding, which protects it from frost, its musky scent, and its useful yield; those who do not grow it (such as Yquem) emphasize the lack of complexity of Muscadelle wines and complain of the frailty of this variety, which catches every possible disease. Its adepts retort, "That is precisely what we expect of it, for that way we are forewarned and can treat the entire vineyard!" Both for the dry and the sweet whites, Muscadelle grapes make up about 3 to 4 percent.

In the Bordeaux region—on the Right Bank—one finds a few other white wine varieties of minor interest (merlot blanc, colombard, etc.). They are not allowed in the prestigious appellations.

PAGES 76–77
A well-earned rest. Cold weather is necessary, as it purifies everything. But it can get too cold (as in 1956); the vine can survive at −20°C, but not for long. If the vine gets no rest during the winter, as happens in some climates, it will produce two or even three harvests in a year, and will die two or three times more quickly.

PAGES 78–79
The sap rises, the vine weeps.

PAGES 80–81
If there is no frost, if there is no rain, if the sun shines, if the bees come out . . . the grapes will form. Altogether a very iffy affair.

The Four Seasons of the Vine

The leaves have fallen, the vine is going to sleep. All that remains to be done is to cover its feet for the winter.

Before it reawakens, the vinegrower will be getting it into condition for a new year. The legal nonvegetative period—for in France everything to do with wine is governed by rules and regulations—extends from November 1 to March 31. The vinegrower will make the most of this hibernation of the plants to remove the useless shoots from the vine. The vine has to be pruned because it is a carefree and extremely lively climbing plant, prone to sprout off in overlong shoots, making more wood than grapes. The whole complex art of the vinegrower involves channeling this vigor into producing fruit. Legend has it that Saint Martin noticed that the vines whose branches had been lopped by grazing goats bore more bunches of better-looking grapes. Certainly Saint Martin and his goats could have invented pruning, but we may suppose that these engaging quadrupeds did their cutting in rather haphazard fashion, and worse than that, in the middle of the growing season, which is against all the rules—although crop thinning, which is indeed done in the summer, can prove extremely useful.

Winter Pruning

From the first snip of the secateurs, the vinegrower knows whether it is quality or quantity he is after. Depending on the number of "eyes" he leaves on each vinestock, he modulates

PAGES 82–83

This picture is worth studying closely, as it says it all about the Médoc. The vines look as if they have been planted on level ground; in fact, the ground slopes in all directions, forming a parcel of land known as a croupe. This is Cos d'Estournel.

OPPOSITE

Detail of a harvester's clothing.

PAGES 86–87

Plastic has replaced wood, but the hods are still with us. As in former times, the pickers pick while the carriers carry.

the load. A heavy load obviously brings a higher yield, but high yields result in dilute wine.

So it is important, if quality is what we are looking for, to prevent the vine from overdoing things by pruning to six or eight eyes. Pruning serves other purposes as well. On the Left Bank, more than elsewhere, it tends to keep the height of the vines in check, and low vines can draw greater benefit from the fine soil; it also takes into account the productive capacity of each plant by catering to their individual needs. "Nothing is as good as pruning in March," goes the saying; however, on the great estates, obviously work begins earlier than that in order to be completed in time for the vegetative cycle to start up again, which is when the temperature of the soil reaches 50°F (10°C).

The pruning method depends on both the grape variety and regional customs. It evolved over time until it finally became established during the nineteenth century, although there is no evidence that new methods are not going to come into fashion over the coming years, as witness the "lyre-shaped" vines that are giving very promising results in the white grapevines of the Right Bank. Generally speaking, the red vines are pruned according to the "double Guyot" method, and the white following the "single Guyot" and "Cot" methods.

Summer Pruning

We have all had the opportunity of admiring vineyards that looked like very tidy gardens. Each *rège* or row of vines has the appearance of a hedge that has been sheared on its sides and top. Special machinery has been developed to prevent the plants from growing too far upward and outward, but without cutting it back too hard. The surface area of leafage is vital, being the seat of the process of photosynthesis, which leads to the production of sugar by the vine, sugar that subsequently migrates along with other substances to the grapes.

In the last few years vinegrowers have been forced to take on a new task known as summer pruning, crop thinning, or *vendange verte*. This involves eliminating already formed bunches so as to restrict the yield and improve the quality of the future wine and gain added concentration. It is a difficult decision for those whose job it is to produce grapes to eliminate them, particularly as they cannot be sure how many there are going to be until the grapes are actually picked. It is an unavoidable measure, however, given that grape varieties are increasingly productive and being tended with ever greater skill.

Working the Land

In the fall, everything begins with plowing between the rows of vines and earthing up the foot of the vines to protect them. In the summer, the soil will again need turning over with a hoe. In view of the frequency and repetitive nature of such tasks, vinegrowers have been led to look into other farming—or rather nonfarming—methods. "The soil cannot breathe anymore, the earth is being turned into concrete," argue those against the use of weed killer. The quality vineyards are plowed. Another form of nonfarming, or minimal farming, of the vineyard involves grassing techniques. Controlled selective grassing, whether partial or not, permanent or not, has its enthusiasts, but seldom in the great vineyards.

It is the vinegrower's job to ensure that the soil remains fertile. There is no question of a quality vineyard taking the

PAGES 88–89

The grapes are then transferred from the hods to the pannier, and from there they will be tipped into a large tub called the conquet.

OPPOSITE

The grapes are transported in wicker baskets, following a centuries-old tradition, as this process allows juice squeezed out from any bruised grapes to escape.

easy way out by using artificial NPK (nitrogen-phosphoric acid-potassium) fertilizer, which has been responsible for so much poor wine; the goal is merely to restore what has been lost to the plant. Regular soil analysis makes it possible to achieve this result and offset any possible soil deficiency.

This leaves the question of the diseases that have increasingly hit the vine since 1845, a story that we have already related above. There are two types of treatment: external ones, involving spraying, and internal—"systemic"—treatments. The effectiveness of the chemical substances is not in dispute; however, they can have unforeseen consequences that may affect the wine itself. We have even seen one great Bordeaux château call in all of its bottles, the way automobile manufacturers do with cars, after an undesirable (although nontoxic) taste had got into the wine following chemical treatment applied to the grapes when still on the vine. Researchers are looking into two ways of cutting back such tiresome application of chemicals or doing away with it altogether. The first is organic farming, which involves stimulating predators that destroy the vectors, or carriers, of diseases that damage the vine. The other is genetic engineering: the modification of the genetic makeup of the grape varieties to make them resistant to the various attacks to which *Vitis vinifera* is vulnerable, and to which the other species of *Vitis* are immune.

As the cycle of vegetation begins to slacken off, it is time to prepare for harvesting. Setting the date of the harvest is extremely important, as the quality and style of the wine depend on it. This is why public proclamation of the harvest was introduced, as vinegrowers had always tended to harvest too soon so as to reduce risks arising from a possible worsening of weather conditions.

To produce a good wine, one needs to harvest the grapes when they are ripe, Olivier de Serres wrote in 1600. Such ripeness is fairly straightforward to determine, and there is even a "ripeness index," which is in fact the sugar-to-acid ratio. The grape is fully ripe when its stops gaining extra sugar, which is also when it stops losing acidity, as A. d'Armailhac, who owned and worked a vineyard and wrote a book on wine, stated in 1855. He even went on to say, "This moment of perfect ripeness must not be overstepped."

Ripeness is also important if one is to avoid producing a heavy, inelegant wine. Such arguments have encouraged owners of the great vineyards to look into harvesting machinery. Was not this a way to avoid being tied down by the working hours of squads of grape pickers? But until such time as these harvesting machines find a better way of removing the grapes than beating them off, they will not be involved in the making of ambitious wines. Research into a new generation of machinery capable of "seeing" bunches of grapes and picking them is currently underway, so we shall just have to wait and see.

Harvesting the Noble Grapes

In the Sauternes vineyards, the use of a machine is out of the question. Picking grapes roasted by *Botrytis cinerea* requires a skilled worker, who sorts and chooses only the bunch or part of a bunch that has been subjected to noble rot. Those left on the vine will continue to develop and will go into the picker's basket on a subsequent visit. Still others will be left to ripen even further. And this may happen over and over again, ten times over if necessary! Of course, this is why this method of harvesting is a costly and a difficult business; such pickers need to be specialists ready to go the extra mile. There is also a risk of losing grapes to worsening weather, with some bunches ending up not worth picking at all.

7

Making the Wine

The vintner is the captain of a ship in heavy seas. He does not come up onto the bridge every day—storms are seasonal things—but upon his every decision hangs the future of the ship. It all begins with the arrival of the harvest. Let us take a straightforward example, where it is not raining and so there is no need to set up a system to remove rainwater or dry the grapes. The grapes are tipped out onto a conveyor belt for sorting. Sorters stationed on either side remove leaves, underripe bunches, and rotten or damaged grapes. If the grapes are red, they go into a destemmer-crusher, an appliance that has come in for all kinds of enhancements, and which separates the berries from the stalks (the woody part that holds them together). The wood is eliminated while the grapes are crushed. This corresponds to the familiar barefoot treading in the vat, where the foot exerted exactly the right supple pressure to crush the grape without brutalizing it. Before this, the vintner will have decided whether to destem all the grapes or only part of them; this depends on the ripeness of the stalks and the type of wine he is seeking. When the necessary equipment is available, a physical process may be applied on the must; this is inverse osmosis, which tends to concentrate the must by eliminating a small proportion of the water contained in it. The must is then placed in a large stainless steel vat—which is where the wine is actually made, since what goes in is must, and what comes out is wine. This winemaking machine, this vat, is fitted with a dual mechanism. First, it is wrapped in a set of coils in which a fluid circulates, which may be either hot or cold, to either cool the must or warm it up. Second, in a process

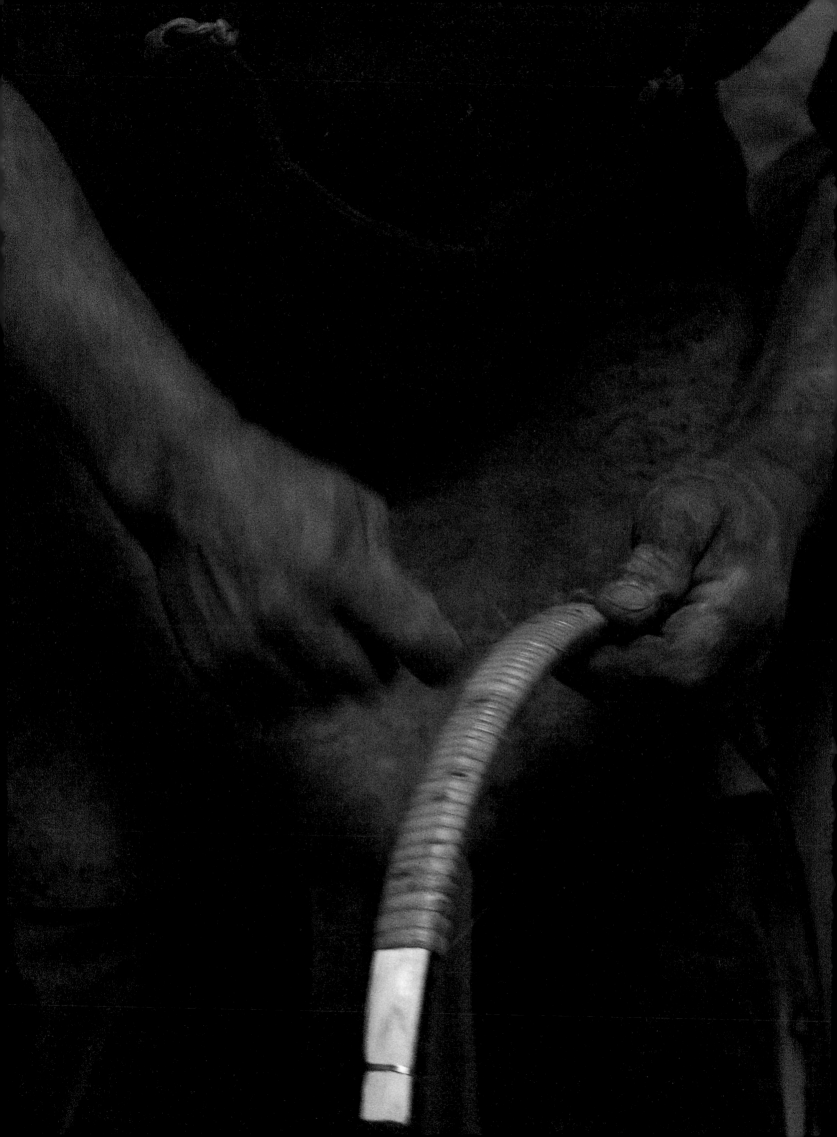

The vintner is the captain of a ship in heavy seas.

PAGES 106–7

It takes five or six egg whites to fine a barrel. The yolks are left in the shells and play no part in the operation.

PAGES 108

Drawing off a glass also offers a chance to taste what is in it.

PAGES 112–13

A wine that is not perfectly limpid is neither an honest nor a commercial wine.

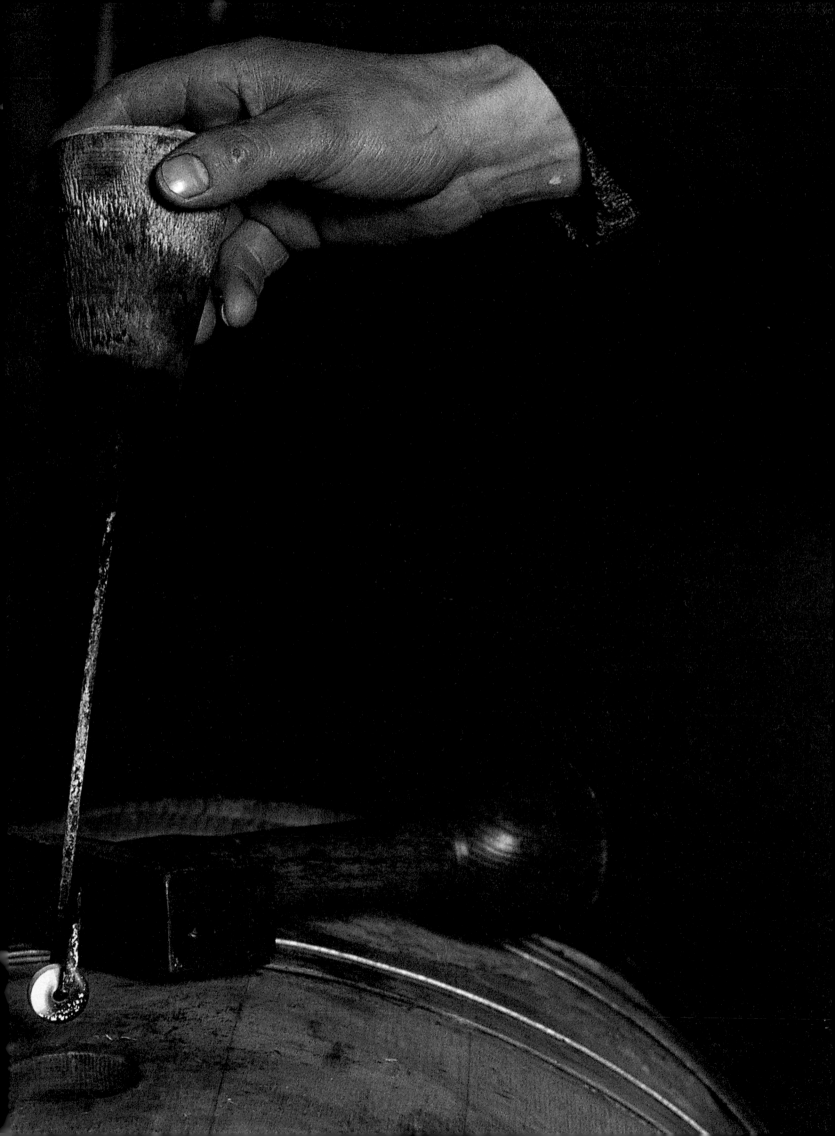

In recent times, the dry whites have risen to the level of the best reds and the incomparable sweet whites.

PAGE 115
Gluing on a label the old-fashioned way at Château Lafite. Labeling is done on the bottling line.

PAGES 116–17 AND OPPOSITE
Bottle storage.

known as "pumping over," a device with a pump and piping enables liquid to be drawn off from the bottom of the vat and discharged at the top, where the solid parts of the must have formed the "cap." This cap deserves all the vintner's care and attention, as is it made up of the coloring and aromatic elements that will give the wine its fine color and "nose." In bringing up liquid in this way, the future ingredients of the wine are leached out of the cap. Since leaching is facilitated by heat and alcohol, the vintner's art is all about controlling temperature at the highest possible levels without endangering the yeasts, which begin to suffer at 93°F (34°C), and controlling the frequency and duration of pumping over. If this is overdone, too much material will be extracted, resulting in undesirable aromas, and the wine will lose its balance and be unable to fulfill all its promise. If pumping over is inadequate, on the other hand, the wine will become light, its voice reduced to a murmur.

Once the fermentation period is over, the vintner is faced with a new problem: should maceration be prolonged in order to gain the benefit of the solvent properties of the alcohol? And should the wine be heated or not? Finally, the wine is removed from the vat and separated from the solid matter, or pomace, which is also removed and pressed. The wine that flows from the press is known as *vin de presse* (press wine). It is very dark and thick, full of tannin, not so fine, but powerful. It will be refined before partly rejoining the *vin de goutte*—the juice that has been drained off from the vat—in the blend.

Before this the vintner, seconded by his consultant enologist, will have tasted each individual vat, as they are all bound to be different and of uneven quality. Only the best ones will be set aside, in separate varieties—for each grape is vinified separately. It is at this stage that the first wine—the *grand vin,* the best vats of each variety—is born. Vats that fail this selection process will produce the second wine, which will not be given the château label. It may happen that a vat does not give satisfaction at all, and its contents will be eliminated and sold off in bulk to a wine merchant. Or a third wine may even be produced! These selections are an institution specific to Bordeaux wines, being applicable only to vineyards on a scale such as are found in that region.

Once the blend has been assembled, when the vintner has incorporated maybe 5, 10, or 15 percent of press wine, the wine, which may or may not have been racked, is taken to the winery, where another question needs to be answered: does the wine have the necessary stature to warrant maturation entirely in new casks, or should a certain amount of it be aged in barrels that have already held wine for a year or two? This question does not arise in the case of first-growth wines, which are always aged in brand-new wood.

The barrel-aging process, including racking operations to refine the wine, extends over a variable period, again at the discretion of the vintner, who knows that the wine gains a woody flavor from the cask but that you can have too much of a good thing, and that "oak tea" has fortunately gone out of fashion. Also, wooden cooperage offers a very slightly oxidizing environment, so a wine that is barreled for too long "dries out," a common fault in wine. There is no hard-and-fast rule in this area; here again, it is entirely a matter for the wine taster to decide.

It now remains to proceed with fining and filtration prior to bottling the wine. These practices are so universal that they hardly call for any comment, except regarding the degree of filtration. Overfiltering can destroy the richness of a wine.

White Bordeaux wines once owed their reputation to the sweet wines. In recent times, however, the dry whites have risen to the level of the best reds and the incomparable sweet whites. Since neither the soil nor the grape varieties have changed, their new status is entirely due to the vintners, who have taken on board state-of-the-art winemaking techniques and learned a great deal from those masters of white wine, the Burgundians. When the harvest of white grapes comes to the fermenting room, it is sorted, just like the red. But already the vintner has to make a choice: to leave the stemmed grapes to macerate with the skins, "skin contact" being highly popular with American enologists; or to send the grapes straight off

to the press. What is the purpose of skin contact? To bring out the flavoring ingredients that, in both white and red wine grapes, are located inside the skin of the grape berry, not in the juice. Skin contact increases flavor extraction from the skins to the juice. Cold and nitrogen are used both to prevent fermentation and to ward off oxidation, the Achilles' heel of white wines and the winemaking process in general. This prefermentation process achieves its purpose, but are the aromas extracted the desired ones?

Over the last few years presses have been greatly improved, and the juice is protected from oxidation; it is also clear, i.e., much less clouded by suspended material—vegetable matter that is liable to pass unwanted flavors into the must. In fact the vintner's first task is to add a small amount of sulfite to the must (to protect it against oxidation) and to clarify it.

This opens up two possible courses: either to make a wine full of aromatic freshness, and so to house the must in big stainless steel vats with strict temperature control, or the altogether more ambitious solution of seeking to obtain a flabby, complex wine for laying down, by draining the must into new casks, leaving it to ferment and to mature in these barrels, with regular lees stirring (a process the French call *bâtonnage,* designed to place the fine deposit back in suspension). Either way, the vintner will have protected the wine against bacterial attack, particularly by the lactobacillus, which is responsible for malolactic fermentation. Therein lies a great enological difference between white Burgundies, which are subjected to malolactic fermentation, and Bordeaux whites, which are not.

After taking responsibility for blending procedures, the vintner consigns the wines to new or old casks, as the case may be. Regular tasting is carried out to monitor maturation and decide when to bottle. From there the wine goes through the standard routine—stabilization by refrigeration, followed by fining and filtration.

The same stages are followed when making sweet wines, except that skin contact is irrelevant to grapes botrytized with noble rot.

For several years now, doubtless taking their inspiration from the way *eiswein* (ice wine) is made, some producers have been practicing cryo-extraction, a very straightforward technique that involves placing the grape harvest in crates inside a huge refrigerator. The grapes begin to freeze, or more precisely, the water content of each berry freezes. All that is now required is to press the moderately frozen grapes. The ice, being incompressible, remains in the press, while the extra-concentrated juice runs off.

The maker of sweet wines has a specific problem to solve: how to achieve a balanced wine. Sweet wine differs from dry wine in that it contains what is known as residual sugar. Sugar is not converted into alcohol because the yeasts that bring about this transformation have died off after fermentation. Ideally, in a natural process that we might regard as suicidal, the yeasts eat the sugars and produce alcohol, although the yeasts cannot survive in alcohol. Once the alcoholic content reaches 16° the yeasts die. This interruption of fermentation is called *mutage*—here by the natural effect of the alcohol. I say natural, because no extra alcohol has been added to reach the fatal 16° mark. If we had added alcohol, which is forbidden, we would have left the realm of winemaking and moved into spirits with a natural fortified wine—the *vin doux naturel* of which Banyuls, Maury, and Rivesaltes are typical French examples. To return to our sweet wine naturally muted at 16°, let us suppose that the must of this wine has a natural potential alcohol content of 18° (i.e., 18° of alcohol if all the sugar were converted), and that its ethanol by volume is only 16°; this leaves a potential 2° of convertible sugar. We will define such a wine with the formula 16 + 2. This wine, which is strong in alcohol, will be moderately sweet. Since to obtain one degree of alcohol takes 17 grams of sugar, 16 + 2 therefore corresponds to 16° of alcohol and 34 g of residual sugar. The wine taster knows that this wine is poorly balanced, that the alcohol-to-sugar ratio is wrong, that this wine, with its potential 18° of alcohol, would be better if its alcohol content were lower and it contained more residual sugar, for

example 14° of alcohol and 4° of residual sugar (14 + 4 or 14° of alcohol and 68 g of residual sugar). How is this result to be achieved? The winemaker will need to mute the wine when it reaches 14°, and to do that the yeasts will have to be inhibited. This can be done by injecting a small amount of sulfur dioxide (SO_2) into the wine. This is a simple and straightforward operation, but one which needs to be performed with great accuracy, for too much sulfur dioxide not only gives the wine an unpleasant taste but is also illegal, as the maximum allowable sulfur dioxide levels are set out in the official texts. Sweet wine is matured in wood, regardless of whether it was made in vats or barrels. Stabilization and clarification follow standard procedures, although sweet wines are not easy to filter.

But are all these vinification techniques, perfectly mastered by the Bordeaux producers, the exclusive prerogative of the wine growers of the Gironde? Not so: today there are no longer any secret winemaking techniques or regional recipes. Certainly, winemaking procedures are not identical wherever you go. For instance in Bordeaux extraction is performed by pumping over; in other areas they prefer a method known as punching down, but pumping over is also employed in California and Australia, as are temperature control and aging in new oak.

No region or appellation can explain its characteristic quality or the quality of its production by some special or more careful winemaking technique, for no one has a monopoly over any given technique, any more than anyone can claim to be more professional than everybody else.

Finally, we must remember that the producer proposes his wine, but the consumer is the only judge as to its quality. The best producer is the one who is on exactly the same wavelength as the consumer—or, perhaps, one who has the power and charisma to mold the consumer's taste.

LABELS

FORMERLY, WHEN BOTTLES WERE HANDBLOWN, THEIR CONTENT COULD ONLY BE APPROXIMATED. THAT IS WHY IT WAS ILLEGAL TO SELL WINE IN BOTTLES; IT HAD TO BE SOLD BY THE CASK OR BARREL.

HAVING PURCHASED THE WINE IN THIS WAY, THE BUYER MIGHT THEN HAVE IT BOTTLED. THE BOTTLES WERE MARKED WITH THE BUYER'S IDENTIFICATION, INITIALS, COAT OF ARMS, AND MONOGRAM. IN 1735, BY REQUEST OF THE CHAMPAGNE PRODUCERS WHO HAD NO CHOICE BUT TO SELL BY THE BOTTLE, THE MARKETING OF BOTTLED WINE WAS MADE LEGAL. COME THE REVOLUTION, SOME ESTATES (LAFITE AND CARBONNIEUX AMONG THEM) WERE BOTTLING PART OF THEIR WINE.

ON THE FIRST LABELS, A SMALL RECTANGLE OF PAPER, ONLY THE ESTATE NAME WAS MENTIONED. GRADUALLY, HOWEVER, THE WINE MERCHANTS DISCOVERED WHAT A USEFUL ADVERTISING MEDIUM A LABEL COULD PROVE TO BE. DURING THE SECOND HALF OF THE NINETEENTH CENTURY, THE LABEL TOOK ON THE FORM THAT IS FAMILIAR TO US TODAY. IT WAS NOT UNTIL THE TWENTIETH CENTURY, HOWEVER, THAT THE LAW TOOK AN INTEREST IN LABELING, IMPOSING A MINIMUM OF MANDATORY INFORMATION WHILE BANNING CERTAIN TERMS THAT WERE JUST TOO FLATTERING TO BE TRUE.

PAGES 126–27

The glass sheds "tears"; the wine has "legs," it is fat and rich.

PAGES 128–29

The age of a wine can be measured visually by its color: a red wine will turn orangey brown with age, then to a dark rosé onionskin color. A white wine will darken from being a light color to gold, golden amber, mahogany, dark mahogany, and black.

PAGES 130–31

Tasting governs blending. Here, the contents of the different vats of Château Margaux await tasting to assess their quality and compatibility.

Drinking Bordeaux Wines

The Bordeaux vineyard extends over 265,870 acres (110,000 hectares) and produces 6 billion bottles each year, bearing fifty-seven different appellations. All types of wines are made here, except *vin jaune* (yellow wine). Red wines are produced in by far the largest quantities, followed by the dry whites, then the sweet to very sweet whites, the rosés, and lastly, the sparkling wines. This vast range is intended for all types of wine drinkers, from the humblest to the wealthiest, with labels of a region or part of a region (Bordeaux, Entre-Deux-Mers) designating the cheaper end of the range, and at the other end, communal (or similar) names reserved for the more expensive wines.

The most ambitious appellations are:

LEFT BANK: Sauternes, Barsac, Pessac-Léognan, Haut-Médoc, Margaux, Saint-Julien, Pauillac, Saint-Estèphe

RIGHT BANK: Saint-Emilion, Pomerol

The great wines are conspicuous by their prices, that much is obvious; however, the price is only a consequence of their organoleptic qualities, which can only reach their full matu-rity if the wine is allowed to age properly. To put it more bluntly, it may readily be argued that only lastingness enables a wine to achieve high quality, and that, whether it be the cause or the consequence of this, only the great wines have such keeping qualities.

A wine goes through a life cycle just as a person does. It is born; is young; reaches adulthood, its peak, which lasts for a few years; then gradually sinks into old age, the declining years that end in death. In humans, longevity is hereditary as well as environmental; the same may be said for wine, if we accept that its "genetic" heritage is determined by that of its parents, the vine stocks, and the environment of its gestation by soil, climate, vinification, and maturation. As with hu-mans, a wine obviously cannot reach a venerable old age un-less it is kept in perfect conditions throughout.

Looking Out for the Peak

All wine lovers seek to drink their wine when it is at its peak. Unfortunately, there is no rule of thumb for working out

DECANTING

We should distinguish between decanting as such and carafing.

The purpose of decanting is to separate the lees from the wine, whereas carafing is for young wines only. To decant, you pour the wine gently down the side of the carafe without stirring it up, leaving the lees in the bottle. Carafing means pouring the wine down the middle of the carafe so as to mix it with the air.

Should I decant?
Yes, always, with one exception: when the wine is too old or when the bouquet is so slight that it would not withstand two transfers—first from the bottle to the carafe, and then from the carafe to the glass.

Should I carafe?
Yes, always. The younger a wine, the more it will benefit from coming into contact with the air. At Château Palmer, for instance, they systematically carafe their wines, including last year's.

What to do with dry white wines
In most of these cases, the procedure is the same as for decanting, with no air mixed in. Any excess sulfur or slight reducing effect will be neutralized by carafing with mixing.

What to do with sweet wines
Sweet wines should be carafed. Some wine lovers claim that a sweet wine is always better the following day, so they pour it into a carafe the day before.

What to do with Champagne and sparkling wines
Champagne can be gently poured (obviously without mixing) into a carafe, on one condition: the carafe must first have been cooled for several hours in the refrigerator. Joseph de Venoge used to drink his Champagne out of a carafe. This custom was originally behind the shape of the Les Princes Champagne bottle, still produced for that brand name—the shape of a Champagne carafe.

In Italy, sparkling wine is often served in a carafe.

THE CHÂTEAUS

"Château wine" is a Bordeaux invention, and a recent one too, dating back only to the second half of the nineteenth century.

We know this because if we look at the 1855 classification, we see that only five growths out of seventy-eight are called "Château." And logically enough, use of the word was restricted to lords' estates upon which indeed stood a defensive castle, which had nothing to do with wine production.

The period of "furious planting" was accompanied by some furious building of new châteaus. In this way a few stately homes have legitimized the proliferation of château wines, reaching far beyond the existing buildings. In 1874 seven hundred wines were sold with a château label; twelve years later, the figure was one thousand; after the Great War, almost two thousand; and today over five thousand! The word *château* is a selling point, especially for exports. Thus, for instance, that excellent Sauternes Clos Haut-Peyraguey a few years ago became "Château Clos Haut-Peyraguey." Since 1921, a whole series of decrees have attempted unsuccessfully to curb this inflation.

---

when a wine is best drunk. For this reason, numerous books and specialist publications report on a regular basis as to how each growth is aging.

The best we can offer are a few ground rules, with plenty of exceptions. The first rule regards wines of the Right Bank and the Left Bank: those of the Right Bank reach their peak more quickly than those of the Left. The second point concerns the influence of the vintage on the aging process: since the great vintages have greater potential, they need more time to fulfill that potential. However, there is no unanimity as to

the so-called great vintages, which in fact stir up no little controversy: for instance, was 1975 a great vintage? Likewise, 1982, a "California" vintage, has no hope of aging as well as the 1961 vintage. Or again, was 1996 really a "great" year, or just a "normal" one?

Lastly, and most importantly, account must be taken of each individual wine lover's personal tastes. Someone who swears by highly developed tertiary bouquets will doubtless drink old wines, while anyone with a palate for fruity flavors will take the opposite course.

The same goes for that sacred cow, what food to serve with what wines. Here again no real consensus has ever emerged—or, to put it more precisely, panels of experts brought together to choose dishes for wines have managed to agree openly to disagree, but never yet to agree about anything specific.

In these areas we need to be careful, and humble. Let us be content to abide by the basic, universally accepted rules governing how wine should be stored, at what temperatures it should be served, and what kind of glass will bring out the best in it.

PAGES 134–35
*The final act: decanting. The wine takes a breath of fresh air
and is separated from any lees it may have deposited.*

PAGE 136
A château cellar.

THE CHÂTEAUS

Every second, twenty-four hours a day, somewhere in the world, ten more bottles of Bordeaux are being uncorked. Obviously, with such an output, any selection is going to be arbitrary. The wines described in the following pages are all excellent, each within its own category. From the pricy to the inexpensive, from the classified to the nonclassified, from the classic to the unexpected, from the memorable to the latest new addition—while they are all remarkable, needless to say, all the remarkable wines are not listed here.

Grape Variety Abbreviations

Reds	CS cabernet sauvignon	CF cabernet franc	M merlot	PV petit verdot
Whites	Se semillon	Sau sauvignon	Mu muscadelle	

Margaux premier cru classé
Château Margaux

During the eighteenth century Château Margaux was the property of François d'Aulède, whose steward Berlon was the first in the Bordeaux vineyard to separate white from red grapevines. The estate was confiscated in 1789, and later purchased, in 1810, by the marquis de la Colonilla, who had the present majestic château built. Twenty years later Margaux became the property of Count Alguado, then Count Pillet-Will and the duc de la Trémoille, to whom we owe the creation of the second wine, Pavillon Rouge. Finally, the difficult task of managing Margaux during the crisis of the seventies fell to the Ginestet family, and it took the fortune of the Mentzelopouloses of Félix Potin to set Margaux back on its triumphant course. The diversity of the soil—222 acres (90 hectares) of *croupes* of fine calcareous or clayey gravel—requires no little skill in blending the grapes to achieve the masterpiece of complexity and finesse of this world-famous wine, which came out on top of the 1855 classification. Handpicked grapes, draconian selection, new oak casks manufactured at the château—no stone is left unturned in seeking to give this wine its amazing balance of sap, velvet, nobility, and charm, which lingers on the palate as an unforgettable experience.

production area	Red: 193 acres (78 hectares); white: 30 acres (12 hectares)		33,000 cases	
grape varieties	75% CS, 20% M, 5% PV and CF			
soil	Quaternary gravel, a little clayey limestone			
maturation	New barrels			
comments	Wooden vat, no filtration			
2nd wine	Pavillon Rouge			
Vintage	**Rating**	**Peak**		
1990	10	2000	Great, rich	
1991	7	2000	Elegant	
1992	5	1997	Light type	
1993	6	2000	Broader shoulders than the above	
1994	7	2003	Tannic astringency	
1995	8	2005	Some fine, silky tannins encourage drinking	
1996	8	2005	A fine, fresh fruitiness	
1997	7	2005	Floral, fine	

Margaux deuxième cru classé
Château Brane-Cantenac

Baron Hector de Brane was nicknamed "the Napoleon of the vines" for his boldly modernist approach to winegrowing. With him as the driving force, the estate, which used to be called Gorse, and which he bought after selling Mouton (later Rothschild), became a model domaine under the new name of Château Brane-Cantenac.

As profitability and perfectionism do not always go hand in hand, the son had to put the domaine up for sale. The current fortunes of this second-growth Margaux are in the hands of Lucien Lurton, another pioneer of modern viticulture, a conquering expansionist also endowed with managerial skills and the support of his numerous children, who share his taste for hard work and a job well done. The domaine's 210 acres (85 hectares), on *croupes* on a consistently deep layer of Garonne gravel, lie at the highest point of the appellation. Tended with loving care, the vines yield an elegant, deliberately feminine wine: delicate and subtle, silky and charming, sometimes erratic but always disarming. Enologist Jacques Boissenot watches over its reputation.

production area	210 acres (85 hectares)	29,000 cases	
grape varieties	70% CS, 13% CF, 15% M, 2% PV		
soil	Deep gravel		
maturation	25% new barrels		
comments	Some weaknesses prior to the eighties		
2nd wine	Château Notton		

Vintage	Rating	Peak	
1990	8	1997	Not up to the vintage
1991	5	1997	Fine and light
1992	5	1997	Fine and light
1993	5	1997	Fine and light
1994	6	1999	Margaux-like, fine
1995	7	2003	Elegant
1996	7	2003	Finely expressed Cabernet
1997	7	2003	Characteristic, dense, 1996 developments confirmed

Margaux deuxième cru classé
Château Dufort-Vivens

The name Dufort comes from a powerful family of southwest France that planted its roots in Margaux during the fourteenth century, when it owned the greater part of the present-day appellation. Through intermarriage Dufort fell into the hands of the marchioness of Montalembert, then her nephew Viscount Vivens, who turned it into a model vineyard that he named Dufort-Vivens. Long before it was proclaimed a second growth, in 1787, Château Dufort-Vivens was rated just behind Lafite, Latour, and Margaux by ambassador to France and future U.S. president Thomas Jefferson, who was a great wine connoisseur. A few family transactions later, the property was sold to the Ginestet family (then owners of Château Margaux) who sold it in 1961 to Lucien Lurton, the proprietor of Brane-Cantenac. The vines were split up, with three parcels adjoining those of Brane-Cantenac, and the last one those of Château Margaux. The *terroir*—deep, poor Quaternary gravel— is suited to the very moderate yield of the cabernet sauvignon grape. Volume, elegance, complexity, and length on the middle palate: a great Margaux.

production area	74 acres (30 hectares)		5,000 cases	
grape varieties	82% CS, 10% CF, 8% M			
soil	Deep gravel			
maturation	50% new barrels			
comments	Has improved since 1978			
2nd wine	Domaine de Cuve-Bourse			
Vintage	**Rating**	**Peak**		
1990	8	1997	A shade under par for the vintage	
1991	5	1997	Fine, inadequate concentration	
1992	5	1997	Fine, inadequate concentratio	
1993	6	1997	Fine, inadequate concentration	
1994	7	1999	Dense	
1995	7	2003	Still unyielding	
1996	7	2003	Woody, spicy, fruity	
1997	6	2003	Light (early tasting)	

Margaux deuxième cru classé
Château Lascombes

This domaine owes its name to the knight of Lascombes, who was born in 1625. From the start of the eighteenth century, the wine built up a reputation that was borne out in its 1855 classification as a second growth. The château was built by the president of the barristers, Chaix d'Est-Ange, who defended the Suez Canal under Napoleon III. When he died, the property was divided up, and it was not until Alexis Lichine took charge of the estate in 1952 that Lascombes was revived and restored to its second-growth status. It was then purchased in 1971 by the British brewery group Bass-Charrington, which already held the Lichine trading house. Since then, the 198-acre (80-hectare) vineyard has been reviewed, and only 124 acres (50 hectares) were selected to produce the *grand vin*. The winery facilities are at the cutting edge of modern technology. Selection is rigorous, as regards both separate vinification of the widely scattered parcels and sorting of the harvest. Performed with extreme care, the blending operations lead to a wine that has great presence in the mouth. Ever loyal to its savior Lichine, Château Lascombes remains a place where the comfortably luxurious welcome is appreciated by its many visitors from all over the world.

production area	124–198 acres (50–80 hectares)		20,000 cases
grape varieties	55% CS, 40% M, 5% PV		
soil	Fine gravel		
maturation	25% new barrels		
comments	Has regained its ranking since the 1981 vintage		
2nd wine	Château Segonnes		

Vintage	Rating	Peak	
1990	8.5	2000	Concentrated
1991	5	1997	Fluid
1992	6	2000	Has substance
1993	5.5	1997	Pleasant fruitiness
1994	7	2002	Floral, interesting
1995	7	2005	Rather firm
1996	7	2005	Exuberant fruitiness, sinewy
1997	6	2004	Spicy, needs to increase its length

Margaux deuxième cru classé
Château Rauzan-Gassies

Detached from Rausan-Ségla during the Revolution, Rauzan-Gassies had the good fortune to be a model eighteenth-century vinegrowing estate. Its proprietor, M. de Rauzan, a councillor at the Parliament of Bordeaux, went for advice and for his vine plants to M. d'Argicourt, then owner of Château Margaux. Château Rauzan-Gassies obtained second-growth status under M. Viguerie's stewardship. Since 1943 the estate has been the property of the Quié family, and the size of the vineyard has remained almost unchanged since the year it was classified. The vines, on sandy gravel, are rather scattered, although the main parcel surrounds the château. Winemaking is classical and readily adjusts to the climatic variations from year to year. Between the two old Rauzan growths, despite their persistent similarity, Gassies wines are noticeably different from the Séglas in being more robust and less agreeable in character.

production area	74 acres (30 hectares)		12,000 cases	
grape varieties	40% CS, 23% CF, 35% M, 2% PV			
soil	Sandy gravel			
maturation	50% new barrels			
comments	Has long been searching for its way; recent vintages show progress			
Vintage	**Rating**	**Peak**		
1990	7	1997	Heavy, below standard for the vintage	
1991	5	1997	Elegant	
1992	4	1997	Fluid	
1993	5	1997	Adequate extracts	
1994	6	1999	Tannic	
1995	7.5	2002	Balanced	
1996	8	2004	Rich, full of promise	
1997	7	2003	Clean, straight	

Margaux deuxième cru classé
Château Rausan-Ségla

Prior to the French Revolution, the Rausan-Rauzan pair made up a single vineyard belonging to the wealthy Pierre des Mesures-de-Rausan, who owned plenty of other large vineyards as well. During the Revolution the vineyard was divided up into Rausan-Ségla and Rauzan-Gassies, both attaining second-growth status in 1855, for they had always had a reputation only just below Mouton's. Early in the nineteenth century, Baroness de Ségla added her family name to Rausan. In 1866 the last surviving descendant of the Rauzans, Baroness de Castelpers, sold Rausan-Ségla, which after belonging to the Cruses became the property of the English company Holt, which already controlled the Bordeaux wine merchant's house of Eschenhauer. The major part of the vineyard faces the château on a lean, fine gravel soil, with the northern section adjoining the vines of Château Margaux. Here the wine is made following the best traditions, using, however, cutting-edge technology—handpicked harvest, sorting, full vinification temperature control, and maturing in an air-conditioned winery. The wine is noted for its finesse and scented elegance. It is described as feminine; being delicate, it dislikes the very rainy years.

production area	111 acres (45 hectares)		11,500 cases	
grape varieties	64% CS, 30% M, 4% CF, 2% PV			
soil	Günz gravel			
maturation	50% new barrels, 50% one year old			
comments	downgraded			
2nd wine	Ségla			
Vintage	**Rating**	**Peak**		
1990	9.5	2000	Round and supple
1991	5.5	1997	Tannins still firm
1992	5	1997	Relative elegance
1993	6	1998	Fruity
1994	7	2000	Fine structure
1995	8	2003	Concentrated
1996	8	2004	Ripe tannins. Good balance
1997	7	2004	Elegant, almost sinewy

Margaux troisième cru classé
Château Cantenac-Brown

John Lewis Brown, a painter of animals and an English wine merchant's son, also related to Jacques Boyd of Boyd-Cantenac, bought this domaine near Margaux. There he built a picturesque château of English renaissance inspiration. Having more artistic talent than business acumen, he was forced to sell off the estate in two lots. Boyd was bought by a bank, and Brown became the family seat of the Lalandes, powerful dignitaries of Chartrons, who lived in style there. When Jean Lawton inherited the Brown legacy, all he could do was to make a quick sale to the du Vivier family, who in turn sold it to the Compagnie du Midi. Shortly afterward it was snapped up by Axa Millésimes. The soil is made up of fine clayey-calcareous gravel. This calcareous element is what sets apart the wine of Château Cantenac-Brown. Modern technology has done its work; the very old vines have been replanted in places, a fully stainless steel temperature-controlled fermenting room takes in the musts, and new oak barrels stand in rows in a brand new winery. Traditional parcel-by-parcel vinification produces nicely structured wines, with a depth that smoothes out over time, a roundness that needs patience.

production area	104 acres (42 hectares)		12,000 cases	
grape varieties	75% CS, 17% M, 8% CF			
soil	Fine clayey-calcareous gravel			
maturation	33% new barrels			
comments	A masculine Margaux			
2nd wine	Baron de Brane			
Vintage	Rating	Peak		
1990	9	1997	Round	
1991	5	1997	Hard	
1992	5	1997	Light	
1993	6	1999	Spicy, balanced	
1994	6	2000	Is it refined?	
1995	7	2003	Meaty and long	
1996	7.5	2003	Well constructed, lively	
1997	7	2004	Concentrated and powerful	

Margaux troisième cru classé
Château Desmirail

This part of the family heritage was Mlle. Rauzan du Ribail's dowry when she married M. Desmirail. The wines' reputation dates back to 1750, and they were classified among the third growths in 1855. In 1903 Desmirail was purchased by the Berlin banker Robert von Mendelssohn, nephew of the composer and also grandson of the Médoc poet Biarnez. After World War I, the domaine was dismantled and sold off in several lots, including the dwelling house, which took on the name of another growth, Marquis d'Alesme-Becker. The brand name and part of the vineyard were sold to Palmer. Then Lucien Lurton came on the scene. He patiently rebuilt a vineyard, annexing to it the buildings of Port-Aubin sited in the village of Cantenac, where he installed stainless steel vats and a barrel cellar. Desmirail has been revived, and now covers 30 hectares on deep Quaternary gravel divided into four parcels that are operated strictly in line with the traditions of the great Margaux growths. The new master's first vintage was 1981, which he made jointly with Emile Peynaud.

production area	74 acres (30 hectares)		5,000 cases
grape varieties	80% CS, 5% CF, 15% M		
soil	Deep gravel		
maturation	33% new barrels		
comments	Vineyard reconstituted, first vintage 1981		
2nd wine	Château Fontarney		

Vintage	Rating	Peak	
1990	9	2000	Generous
1991	5	1997	Light
1992	4.5	1997	Light
1993	5	1997	Fruity, woody
1994	6	2000	Well put together
1995	7	2003	Full
1996	7	2003	Interesting texture
1997	6	2003	Light (early tasting)

Margaux troisième cru classé
Château Giscours

Château Giscours covers 7,410 acres (3,000 hectares) of land, including a single 173-acre (70-hectare) area of vineyard. This superb estate, which has contrived to maintain its original boundaries, belonged to the Saint-Simon family before the Revolution, when it was worth a million francs. However, Giscours was purchased in 1795 by the first American to launch into the Bordeaux wine trade, and it was resold on another three occasions. There followed a dark period until 1952, when Nicolas Tari, an Algerian-born Frenchman, bought the domaine in a very dilapidated state and undertook to renovate the vineyard, the winemaking unit, and the château itself. He availed himself of the services of the top experts in viticultural research to assist him in his ambitious innovations, which included digging a 24.7-acre (10-hectare) lake with a view to improving drainage and creating a microclimate. Nicolas Tari's son Pierre, a polo player and mayor of Labarde, gave this superb site a role as a tourist and society center that suited it well. A Dutch wine merchant has recently been in charge of the property. Giscours has fallen back somewhat since the 1970s, when it produced some legendary wines, elegant, refined, balanced, full of seduction, and sustained by their perfectly ripe tannins.

production area	173 acres (70 hectares)		25,000 cases	
grape varieties	70% CS, 25% M, 3% CF, 2% PV			
soil	Gravel on sand			
maturation	33% new barrels			
comments	Recent vintages have been plagued by administrative problems			
2nd wine	Château Grand Giscours			
Vintage	Rating	Peak		
1990	8	1997	A supple 1990	
1991	5	1997	Light	
1992	4	1997	Too thin	
1993	5	1997	Supple	
1994	5	1997	Suppleness without density	
1995	6	1997	Dense, where is the elegance?	
1996	7	2003	Revival. Round, aromatic	
1997	6	2003	Fruity and delicate	

Margaux troisième cru classé
Château d'Issan

This 124-acre (50-hectare) domaine comprises a 74-acre
(30-hectare) vineyard, mostly planted with cabernet sauvignon,
which lies on a slope at altitudes of 16 to 49 feet (5 to 15 meters).
Built during the seventeenth century by Pierre d'Essenault on
the site of the medieval fort of which the water-filled moat still
remains, the château is in the massive, austere Louis XIII style.
This land has a centuries-old reputation for its wines, which
were called first Théobon, then Candale, and now d'Issan.
Its third-growth status would appear to be lower than the
reputation it enjoyed in former times. However, the French
Revolution had done its worst, and when the Cruse family
came into the estate in the aftermath of the last war, Issan was
no more than a shadow of its former self. It took many long
years to restore the vineyard, château, and outbuildings, but
Issan has now regained its former glory; each year in May,
the château attracts international musicians for concerts attended
by all the Bordeaux gentry, and the round, supple wine tries to
live up to its motto, *Regum mensis arisque deorum* (For the
table of the king and the altar of the gods).

production area	74 acres (30 hectares)		15,000 cases	
grape varieties	75% CS, 25% M			
soil	Fine gravel and clayey limestone			
maturation	25% new barrels			
comments	Elegant rather than powerful			
2nd wine	Château de Candale			
Vintage	**Rating**	**Peak**		
1990	8	2000	A genuine 1990	
1991	5	1997	Drink up	
1992	4	past	Too light	
1993	5	1999	Good development	
1994	6	2002	Well constructed	
1995	8	2005	Round, very good	
1996	8	2005	Delicious and fine	
1997	7	2005	Fruity and elegant	

Margaux troisième cru classé
Château Kirwan

In 1760, Englishman Sir John Collingwood bought the domaine of La Salle, which he later left to his daughter, who was married to an Irishman named Mark Kirwan. Kirwan was guillotined during the French Revolution, though his name lives on. When it was sold off to Mr. Shryver, Kirwan was a third growth. The Godard family bought it and in 1881 left it to the city of Bordeaux, which appointed the Schröder & Schÿler house as managers and handed over the domaine to the Guestier family. This two-way arrangement was settled by a marriage, and in 1925 Kirwan became the property of Schröder & Schÿler. The greater part of the vineyard surrounds the château, with the remaining parcels facing it. Its layer of fine gravel lies on a clayey soil that requires special growing and winemaking techniques, as the wine is highly sensitive to variation from vintage to vintage. The soil is carefully drained, the rows are widely spaced to let in the sunlight, and plenty of new oak is used for this fine, fruity wine. Substantial exporting has carried far and wide the reputation of this wine, so much so that it is better known overseas than in France itself. The intervention of enologist Michel Rolland as of 1993 has given a new lease of life to this third growth.

production area	86 acres (35 hectares) 12,000 cases		
grape varieties	40% CS, 30% M, 20% CF, 10% PV		
soil	Fine gravel		
maturation	30% new barrels		
comments	New vinification (Michel Rolland) since 1993		
2nd wine	Margaux Private Reserve		
Vintage	Rating	Peak	
1990	7	1997	Short on richness for the vintage
1991	5	1997	Light
1992	5	1997	Light
1993	6	1999	Length
1994	6	2000	Fine balance, long
1995	7.5	2005	Round, strong extracts
1996	7.5	2005	Powerful, long
1997	7.5	2005	Has character and harmony

Margaux troisième cru classé
Château Malescot-Saint-Exupéry

Malescot was proctor at the Bordeaux Parliament in the seventeenth century, and it was Count Jean-Baptiste de Saint-Exupéry, grandfather of the airman and writer Antoine de Saint-Exupéry, who gave its new name to a domaine that he extended considerably. M. Fourcade continued the expansion work, and in 1855 the wine was classified as a third growth. The next fifty years saw a procession of a dozen owners, and Malescot-Saint-Exupéry was in ruins when it was bought by Paul Zuger in 1955. The vines were replanted, the buildings restored, and the facilities renewed. The estate has now got back to classified growth status, and the labels proudly bear the arms of the Comte de Saint-Exupéry, whose motto is *Semper ad altum* (Always higher).

The wine too has returned to the tradition of a true Margaux, without falling into the fashion of less tannic wines ready to drink sooner. Here fermentation and vat times are long, and chaptalization is only done in exceptional cases. This proud, superb wine is for laying down and is well worth waiting for.

production area	74 acres (30 hectares)		11,000 cases	
grape varieties	50% CS, 10% CF, 35% M, 5% PV			
soil	Garonne and Pyrenees gravel			
maturation	25% new barrels			
2nd wine	Dame de Malescot			
Vintage	**Rating**	**Peak**		
1990	9	2000	Round and long	
1991	5	starting	A little hard	
1992	5	1997	Complex	
1993	5	1997	Red fruit	
1994	6	2000	Firmness	
1995	7	2003	Characterful charm	
1996	7.5	2004	Dense, spicy	
1997	7	2004	Very ripe tannins	

Margaux troisième cru classé
Château Palmer

This wine was enjoyed at Versailles; Richelieu adored this growth, which he would have known as Château de Gascq. Legend has it that the widow of Blaise de Gascq was forced to sell this 123-acre (50-hectare) domaine to an officer of Wellington's, Charles Palmer, whose conquering instinct was such that he snapped up whatever land came his way. But he had bitten off more than he could chew and had to sell, and in the end Château Palmer went to the Mortgage Loan Office until its repurchase by Isaac Péreire, just before it was classified as a third growth. Palmer's quality and fame were such that it should really have been made a second growth; only uninspired management by the Mortgage Office and the ravages of powdery mildew are to blame for its lower rating in 1855. The powerful Péreire family restored the vineyard and built the neo-Renaissance château that appears on the label. Since 1938 the divided property has been taken over by the nontrading company of Mälher and Sichel. The 112 acres (45 hectares) of vines, the larger portion of which enjoys perfect exposure next to the château, are planted in tight rows on fine gravel over a calcareous base. Stringent selection and careful vinification in stainless steel vats produce a wine that is full-bodied, yet not without finesse.

production area	112 acres (45 hectares)		15,000 cases	
grape varieties	55% CS, 40% M, 5% PV			
soil	Fine gravel			
maturation	40% new barrels			
comments	A model of reliability			
2nd wine	Réserve du Général			
Vintage	**Rating**	**Peak**		
1990	10	1997	Ripe tannins	
1991	6	1997	Refined	
1992	4.5	1997	Clean	
1993	6.5	starting	Tannic, long	
1994	7	2002	Finesse, elegance	
1995	7.5	2005	Round	
1996	8	2006	Grape, length	
1997	7	2005	Beautiful range of aromas	

Margaux quatrième cru classé
Château Prieuré-Lichine

This was actually a priory run by monks, the Prieuré-Cantenac, whose wine fetched a handsome price in the eighteenth century. The estate was laicized during the Revolution, and Château Prieuré achieved a fourth ranking in 1855. Then a succession of owners witnessed the decline of the estate until it was bought in 1951 by a Russian-born American, Alexis Lichine, who added his name to it. It took thirty-five years of sustained effort to restore the now Château Prieuré-Lichine to its pristine reputation. Plot by plot, Lichine bought up the vineyard, which totals 165 acres (67 hectares) of varied Margaux *terroirs* in separate parcels scattered over the area, which, combined with the blend of grapes, gives the wine its invaluable complexity. The huge fermenting rooms and ultramodern winery facilitate the production of a wine known the world over. Indeed, with his strong personality and great erudition as a wine hedonist, Alexis Lichine has engaged with natural dash and generous hospitality in a form of public relations—an advertising campaign, the envious ones call it—which was not yet common practice in Bordeaux and which has paid dividends. Alexis is no longer with us and his son Sacha has taken over. Enologist Michel Rolland was called in in 1990.

production area	165 acres (67 hectares)		25,000 cases	
grape varieties	54% CS, 2% CF, 39% M, 5% PV			
soil	Sandy gravel			
maturation	50% new barrels			
comments	Marked improvement since Michel Rolland arrived			
2nd wine	Château de Clairefort			
Vintage	**Rating**	**Peak**		
1990	9	starting	Supple	
1991	5	1997	Light	
1992	6	starting	A success for the vintage	
1993	6.5	starting	Round tannins	
1994	6	2002	Average concentration	
1995	7	2005	Fairly round	
1996	7	2005	Full and tender	
1997	6	2005	Precise (early tasting), very woody	

Margaux cinquième cru classé
Château Dauzac

During the Middle Ages, at Macau, on the site of the present
Château Dauzac, Sainte-Croix Abbey set up a *sauveté*, a farmable
area used for charitable purposes. Early in the nineteenth century
Count Lynch, who was also mayor of Bordeaux, turned Dauzac
into a large vineyard, complete with charterhouse. After its
classification in 1855, it was sold to Nathaniel Johnston who,
being something of an innovator, tried out the first antimildew
sprayings of *bouillie bordelaise* (Bordeaux mixture—lime and
copper sulfate) on his vines. Two other families followed in his
wake, and then the insurance company M.A.I.F. bought these
99 acres (40 hectares) within the Margaux appellation. The
vineyard is planted on a soil with fine *graves* going down to a
considerable depth, as witness the nearby gravel quarries, which
are still being worked. The domaine, which had been going
downhill for two generations, was crying out for renovation.
Restructuring of the vineyard and facilities was carried out, with
substantial sums of money poured in, and since the 1980s
Château Dauzac has regained its deserved place among the
fifth-ranking classified growths.

production area	99 acres (40 hectares)		15,000 cases	
grape varieties	58% CS, 5% CF, 37% M			
soil	Gravel on iron pan			
maturation	50% new barrels			
comments	Winemaker André Lurton gave it a definite boost in 1994			
2nd wine	La Bastide de Dauzac			
Vintage	Rating	Peak		
1990	7.5	1997	Start of the revival	
1991	4.5	1997	Light	
1992	4	1997	Light	
1993	6	1997	Well constructed, fruity	
1994	6.5	2000	Solid	
1995	7	2003	Dense	
1996	7	2004	Tannic, full	
1997	6	2004	Great extract	

Margaux
Château Bel Air Marquis d'Aligre

We may wonder how the panel of judges appointed to classify the great Bordeaux growths at Napoleon III's Great Exhibition contrived to overlook this wine. Doubtless this had something to do with its rarity, for during the nineteenth century this outstanding wine was not placed on the market at all: both the marquis de Pomereu and the marquis d'Aligre reserved the precious fruit of their vines to serve at their own table or to honor their many friends. One or two Parisian restaurateurs were also able to lay their hands on a few of these rare flasks, which bore a jocular if not exactly medical inscription carved into the glass opposite the château name: "Must be taken to the last drop." The present owner, Pierre Boyer, has kept to his predecessors' tradition, and with an average vine age of thirty-five years, his production is still for the happy few. The wine's supple, generous, fruity flavor reveals the harmony of the four grapes: merlot, cabernet sauvignon, cabernet franc, and petit verdot.

production area	42 acres (17 hectares) 4,500 cases		
grape varieties	35% M, 30% CS, 20% CF, 15% PV		
soil	Fine gravel		
maturation	Reused barrels		
comments	Original, old-fashioned grape blend, the opposite of flashy		

Vintage	Rating	Peak	
1990	10	1997	Smooth
1991	5	falling off	Floral
1992	5	falling off	Light
1993	6	1997	Fine, concentration?
1994	6.5	2000	Not much wine, characteristic
1995	8	2005	Concentrated
1996	7.5	2005	Supple
1997	7.5	2005	Pure, subtle, fine

Margaux
Château Siran

In the fifteenth century this domaine belonged to the *sauveté,* or rural township, of Sainte-Croix, and Sire Guilhem de Siran gave it his name. During the difficult revolutionary period, Siran belonged to comte de la Roque-Bouillac, who was forced to emigrate. His daughter kept up the heritage by marrying Count Toulouse de Lautrec, grandfather of the well-known painter. Although highly rated in the eighteenth century, Siran was passed over for the 1855 classification. Alain B. Miailhe, a descendant of a great family of wine brokers, is currently at the head of the domaine, and he has placed Siran in the same league as the classified growths. The winery facilities are modern and luxurious, as are the pink-painted outbuildings. There is a heliport over the reception hall and even a nuclear bomb shelter to protect the cellar where the wines are laid down; if ever there is a nuclear alert, this will be the last wine to go! Château Siran is a broad-shouldered wine enriched with fully ripe tannins and heady aromas, a wine made to last.

production area	57 acres (23 hectares)		14,000 cases
grape varieties	50% CS, 30% M, 8% CF, 12% PV		
soil	Gravel and sandy gravel		
maturation	35% new barrels		
comments	Worth a fifth classified growth, occasionally a fourth (1995)		
2nd wine	Château Bellegarde		

Vintage	Rating	Peak	
1990	10	starting	Suppleness
1991	5	1997	Floral fruitiness
1992	5	1997	Light
1993	6	starting	Woody, fruity
1994	6.5	2002	Woody again, concentrated
1995	8	2005	Profound
1996	7.5	2005	Dominant woodiness, needs to blend
1997	7	2006	Powerful and rich

Saint-Julien deuxième cru classé
Château Ducru-Beaucaillou

Around 1750 this wine was called Bergeron, as was its owner.
As of 1800, the estate became Ducru-Beaucaillou, the name by
which it was classified in 1855, when owned by Bertrand Ducru.
Upon his death the domaine, with 124 acres (50 hectares) of
vineyards, was finally sold to Nathaniel Johnston. This top
engineer teeming with ideas added two square towers to the
Directoire charterhouse built in 1820, then began applying the
Champagne method to the red wines of the Médoc! His steward,
not to be outdone, stumbled across the benefits of Bordeaux
mixture when, spraying a colored concoction onto the vines
to discourage pilferers, he came up with a cure for mildew!
Ducru-Beaucaillou's reputation had waned by the time the
domaine was taken over by the Borie family in 1942, after which
it regained its rank among the best second growths. Both the
vinegrowing and winemaking have benefited from the advice of
Emile Peynaud, and the wine has regained its distinguished
quality, with an expressive and flamboyant substance.

production area	124 acres (50 hectares)		15,000 cases	
grape varieties	65% CS, 25% M, 5% CF, 5% PV			
soil	Deep gravel			
maturation	50% new barrels			
comments	Winery problems in the late eighties			
2nd wine	La Croix			
Vintage	**Rating**	**Peak**		
1990	10	2000	Excellent tannins, rich	
1991	5	1997	Light	
1992	5.5	1997	Good substance	
1993	6	1997	Fruity	
1994	6.5	1997	Elegant, well constructed	
1995	8	2000	Fine tannins, dense	
1996	8.5	2006	Dense, distinguished, imperial	
1997	8	2005	Distinguished, balanced, fine	

Saint-Julien deuxième cru classé
Château Gruaud-Larose

In the early eighteenth century the knight of Gruaud, a magistrate, and his brother, the abbé de Gruaud, bought some plots of land to turn them into a vast winegrowing domaine by the name of Fonbedeau. When the knight died, his daughter, Mme de la Rose, inherited, and her husband went on to win an international reputation for this Gruaud-Larose wine, earning praise from Thomas Jefferson on his visit to the Bordeaux region. In the nineteenth century the estate was divided into two: Gruaud-Larose-Sarget and Gruaud-Larose-Fayre. It was not until Désiré Cordier, who had bought Gruaud-Larose-Sarget in 1917, was able to buy back the other property from the Faure heirs that the domaine could be reunited, taking the name of Gruaud-Larose. Finally, the Alcatel corporation became its owner, but not for long, as the Merlaut family purchased the 321-acre (130-hectare) domaine in April 1997. Everything, from the Directoire-style château and formal gardens to the winery and other buildings, is impeccable. The 203-acre (82-hectare) vineyard is planted with cabernets and merlot in a three-to-one ratio on a well drained soil of even-sized gravel. The wine is made with the help of enologist Georges Pauli, and is very rich and fruity. The scale of production is large enough to offer it at affordable prices, which contributes to its popularity.

production area	203 acres (82 hectares) 25,000 cases			
grape varieties	65% CS, 25% M, 5% CF, 5% PV			
soil	Gravel on limestone and iron pan			
maturation	33% new barrels			
comments	Slow developer for a Saint-Julien			
2nd wine	Sarget de Gruaud-Larose			
Vintage	Rating	Peak		
1990	9	1999	Round	
1991	6	1997	Concentrated for the vintage	
1992	5	1997	Light	
1993	5.5	1999	Well constructed	
1994	6.5	2000	Silky tannins	
1995	7	2004	Finesse, fruity, balance	
1996	7.5	2005	Subtlety, elegance	
1997	7	2005	Noble and charming	

Saint-Julien deuxième cru classé
Château Léoville Barton

Léoville and Langoa Barton are inseparable, although each has its own personality. They have a shared history, and the same owner, and there is only one château, Langoa, for both properties. The long history of the Barton family began in 1722, when Irishman Thomas Barton came to settle in Bordeaux to trade in wine. His grandson, Hugh, in 1786 founded with Daniel Guestier the wine merchant's house of Barton & Guestier and decided to buy some vines. He missed out on Lafite but acquired ownership of Château Langoa in 1821. Six years later, he bought a part of Léoville, a vast estate that had been divided among the descendants of Alexandre de Gascq. Ronald Barton, who inherited both domaines, did his utmost to uphold the prestige they had gained from their classification as second and third growths in 1855. Upon his death in 1986 his nephew, Anthony Barton, took charge of this valuable heritage. The two châteaus form a single production unit, although their output is kept strictly apart. The wine has kept its typically Barton style: the aristocratic charm of a naturally distinguished and dependable wine, made to last, with Langoa slightly suppler than Léoville.

production area	116 acres (47 hectares)		20,000 cases
grape varieties	72% CS, 8% CF, 20% M		
soil	Gravel on clay		
maturation	50% new barrels		
comments	Reliable and well behaved		
2nd wine	Lady Langoa		

Vintage	Rating	Peak	
1990	10	2000	Round, elegant
1991	4.5	1997	Light
1992	5	1997	Average density
1993	6	2000	More powerfully built than the above years
1994	7	2003	Fruit and tannins
1995	7.5	2005	Meaty
1996	7.5	2006	Round, with elegance
1997	7	2005	Dependable, classic, successful

Saint-Julien deuxième cru classé
Château Léoville Las Cases

The great Léoville vineyard belonged to Alexandre de Gascq, but after the Revolution it was divided up among his three heirs. In 1900 Gabriel de las Cases sold his share, and Théophile Skavinski took thirty years to reorganize what is now Château Léoville Las Cases. He handed it down to his descendants, the Delons.

The château was a building shared with Léoville Poyferré, but the vineyard, next door to Latour, was enclosed within walls and entered by a monumental gate surmounted by a majestic lion. The 240-acre (97-hectare) vineyard is planted on deep gravel with the four Médoc grapes. Wine is the lion king here, and a splendid winery is devoted to its care, with marble, air conditioning, and luxury décor. Michel Delon, the current director, goes all-out for quality by using the most expensive state-of-the-art methods: small yields, stringent sorting of the harvest, draconian hygiene, reverse osmosis, strict selection, and new barrels. At the end of the day, this is an outstanding wine at an outstanding price. Las Cases enthusiasts keep it for about fifteen years before discovering, within a profound and generous growth, so much harmony of finesse and elegance.

production area	240 acres (97 hectares)		30,000 cases	
grape varieties	65% CS, 13% CF, 17% M, 5% PV			
soil	Gravel on iron pan			
maturation	50 to 100% new barrels			
comments	A second growth that is becoming a first			
2nd wine	Clos du Marquis			
Vintage	**Rating**	**Peak**		
1990	10	**2005**	Superlative	
1991	7	**2000**	One of the best 1991s	
1992	7	**1999**	One of the best 1992s	
1993	7.5	**2002**	Superb structure, great fruitiness	
1994	8	**2005**	High concentration	
1995	8.5	**2005**	Meaty	
1996	9	**2007**	The Léoville Las Cases of the century	
1997	8.5	**2005**	Strict selections, a safe bet for the vintage	

Saint-Julien deuxième cru classé
Château Léoville-Poyferré

On the death of Blaise de Gascq, the lord of Léoville, his vast domaine was divided up into three portions. One of these came to Hugh Barton in 1826, and the remaining land was shared between Jean de Las Cases and his cousin, the wife of the baron of Poyferré. M. Lalande bought Poyferré in 1866, leaving it to his daughter, Mme Lawton. In 1921 Léoville Poyferré changed owners for the last time. The Cuveliers, wine merchants already in possession of Château Le Crock at Saint-Estèphe, bought it along with Château Moulin, a rich bourgeois growth of Saint-Julien. Of the Léoville threesome, Poyferré made the least of the promise of its *terroir:* a 198-acre (80-hectare) vineyard, a Garonne gravel soil on a clay base, and cabernet sauvignon grapes of a fine age. Didier Cuvelier has finally obtained from his family the vital capital funds required to improve the production equipment, and brought the famous enologist Michel Rolland in. The wine has recovered some of its panache and can now compete for excellence with its two Saint-Julien cousins.

production area	198 acres (80 hectares)		25,000 cases	
grape varieties	65% CS, 2% CF, 25% M, 8% PV			
soil	Gravel on clay			
maturation	50% new barrels			
comments	New winery and arrival of Michel Rolland in 1994			
2nd wine	Château Moulin Riche			
Vintage	**Rating**	**Peak**		
1990	10	2000	A great success, generous	
1991	5	1997	Elegant	
1992	4.5	1997	Light	
1993	5.5	1997	Supple	
1994	7	2002	Plump	
1995	7.5	2004	Balanced	
1996	7.5	2004	Full and long	
1997	7	2005	Perfect tannins, meaty	

Saint-Julien troisième cru classé
Château Lagrange

When Count Cabarrus bought this vineyard in 1796, it was already appreciated by connoisseurs. He expanded it, adding onto the elegant eighteenth century style mansion a tower in the style of Tuscany! Château Lagrange later belonged to John Lewis Brown, who sold it to Count Duchatel, the first man in Bordeaux to install earthenware pipes one meter underground to drain his land. The estate then covered 741 acres (300 hectares). The wine was given a third-growth rating in 1855, at which time it belonged to a minister of Napoleon. There followed a number of owners before Manuel Cendoya, who failed to survive the depression of the 1930s, and had to sell off a substantial proportion of his property piecemeal to his neighbors. The wine became poor. In 1984 the powerful Japanese group Suntory bought the remaining 388 acres (157 hectares). Reinstating Château Lagrange was a task entrusted to local experts, whose proven methods, with substantial financial backing, have given this estate a new lease of life. The wine has recovered its Médoc style, and the cabernet sauvignon grape outshines the merlot to achieve a balanced and interestingly complex structure. The domaine is managed by Marcel Ducasse, whose firm character leaves its stamp on these long-lived wines.

production area	280 acres (113 hectares)		25,000 cases	
grape varieties	66% CS, 27% M, 7% PV			
soil	Fine gravel on limestone			
maturation	50% new barrels			
comments	1985, revival of Lagrange, a manly Saint-Julien			
2nd wine	Les Fiefs de Lagrange			
Vintage	Rating	Peak		
1990	10	2000	Powerful	
1991	5	1997	Fruity, supple	
1992	4.5	1997	Fruity, supple	
1993	6	1999	Round	
1994	6.5	2002	Powerfully built	
1995	7	2005	Very tannic	
1996	7.5	2005	Perfect tannins, well balanced	
1997	7	2006	Powerful, tannic	

Saint-Julien quatrième cru classé
Château Beychevelle

The Duke of Epernon, a great French admiral, came into Beychevelle upon his marriage to the heiress to the Foix-Candale estate. During the eighteenth century the property was purchased by the marquis of Brassier, who had the present château built on the site of the old medieval fort, surrounded by superb gardens ornamented with century-old trees: it was known as "the Versailles of the Médoc." Beychevelle kept its naval associations when it subsequently belonged to a privateer owner, M. Conte. At the time of the 1855 classification Beychevelle was the property of Guestier the wine merchant before coming to the Achille-Fould family in 1874. After a hundred and ten years in that family, Beychevelle was bought in 1984 by the insurance company G.M.F., which pumped in the necessary resources to revive the growth to its former glory, for it had long been going downhill. The vineyard is an extensive one, with 210 acres (85 hectares) in several parcels on a large gravel soil, spread over a domaine that covers some 618 acres (250 hectares). The backbone grape, cabernet sauvignon, is blended with 28 percent merlot, with cabernet franc and petit verdot making up the rest. With tight controls on yields, long maceration times, and new oak, everything has been done to give extra build and muscle to a charming, dainty wine, capable of winning over even the uninitiated.

production area	210 acres (85 hectares)		25,000 cases	
grape varieties	60% CS, 8% CF, 28% M, 4% PV			
soil	Deep gravel			
maturation	50 to 100% new barrels			
comments	A fourth growth that can't help thinking it is a second growth			
2nd wine	Amiral de Beychevelle			

Vintage	Rating	Peak	
1990	9	1997	Round, average body
1991	5	1997	Easy
1992	4.5	1997	On the thin side
1993	5.5	1997	Supple and round
1994	6	1999	Fruity, balanced
1995	6.5	2005	Firm tannins
1996	6.5	2004	Light for the vintage
1997	7	2004	Distinctive, classy

Saint-Julien quatrième cru classé
Château Branaire

On entering the territory of Saint-Julien, on the hill to the left, Château Branaire, in a very pure Directoire style, comes into view. This elegant abode was built by Louis Duluc, together with the winery and an orangery, on the land of Braneyre that he had bought after the death of the last Duke of Epernon. In 1855 the Duluc growth was given a fourth growth-rating, and in 1860 it was sold to Gustave Ducru, who added his name to that of Branaire-Duluc, which was subsequently abbreviated for all practical purposes to Branaire-Ducru. The estate later fell to four members of the Ducru family in succession, and their crowns of nobility still adorn the four corners of the Château Branaire label. In 1952 Jean Tapie, an Algerian-born Frenchman who was related to the Tari family of Giscours, bought up this fine 111-acre (45-hectare) domaine, a mosaic of parcels here and there adjoining most of the top growths of the commune. In 1988 a group of investors bought a 50 percent stake in the company and set about modernizing the operation. With a gravel soil on an iron pan base, a blend of cabernet sauvignon, merlot, and petit verdot produces sensible yields. Vinified in ideal conditions, this deliciously elegant wine has a spicy vanilla flavor, with a touch of chocolate caramel.

production area	111 acres (45 hectares) 16,000 cases		
grape varieties	75% CS, 22% M, 3% PV		
soil	Gravel on iron pan		
maturation	50 to 75% new barrels		
comments	New, demanding owners since 1988		
2nd wine	Château Duluc		
Vintage	**Rating**	**Peak**	
1990	9	1997	Round
1991	5	1997	Light
1992	5	1997	Fruit
1993	6	1997	Well constructed
1994	6.5	2000	Plump
1995	7	2005	Astringent tannins
1996	7.5	2005	Smooth tannins, rich
1997	7	2005	Fruity, good tannins, balanced

Saint-Julien quatrième cru classé
Château Saint-Pierre

This domaine was called Sérançan until the baron of Saint-Pierre gave his name to it in 1767. After 1832, complicated successions would separate the vineyard from the manor house and create two different brand names, Saint-Pierre-Bontemps-Dubary and Saint-Pierre Sevaistre. This division noticeably downgraded the wines, which had been given fourth-growth status under both names.

Château Saint-Pierre's fortunes took an upturn in 1982 when Henri Martin, already proprietor at Château Gloria, appeared on the scene. He bought the house, the vineyard, and the brand name from their various owners and had the estate reunified as it appeared on the old maps. Under a single label, he restored Château Saint-Pierre to its natural place among the classified growths. When Martin died, his son-in-law Jean-Louis Triaud continued the growth's improvement. The vineyard extends over several plots totaling 42 acres (17 hectares), on large gravel. Cabernet sauvignon makes up the lion's share, leaving only 20 percent merlot and 10 percent cabernet franc. The vines are of a respectable age, and vinification encourages long extracts, producing a deep-colored, powerful, meaty wine.

production area	42 acres (17 hectares)		8,000 cases	
grape varieties	70% CS, 10% CF, 20% M			
soil	Gravel on clayey limestone			
maturation	50% new barrels			
comments	Estate reconstituted and taken over in 1982 by Henri Martin (Château Gloria)			
Vintage	**Rating**	**Peak**		
1990	10	1997	Tannic, round	
1991	5	1997	A good 1991	
1992	5	1997	Fruity	
1993	5.5	1997	Well built for the vintage	
1994	6	2002	Fruity	
1995	7.5	2004	Tannic, balanced	
1996	7.5	2003	Vigorous, superb tannins	
1997	7	2004	In the spirit of 1996	

Saint-Julien quatrième cru classé
Château Talbot

We can only wonder why this domaine bears the name of a
famous English high constable, but what we do know is that in
1855 Château Talbot belonged to the marquis d'Aux de Lescout.
After passing it on to his children and grandchildren, the
domaine was sold at a public auction to M. Claverie. In 1918
Désiré Cordier bought it, a year after buying Gruaud-Larose.
Today, Jean Cordier's daughters watch over the destinies of
this huge 247-acre (100-hectare) estate. The land is made up
of fine Günz gravel on an asteriated limestone base. Malbec
complements the traditional four Bordeaux grape varieties, with
a patch of sauvignon and semillon set aside for the house white,
Château Talbot Caillou Blanc. The care with which the estate is
maintained and its spotlessness remind one of the residence of
some extremely wealthy nabob with a passion for winegrowing.
In fact Château Talbot has always been the Cordier's family
residence. The wine is full-bodied, but elegant nevertheless, with
a highly developed bouquet of aromas. Another of its strong
points lies in its even quality and its equal suitability for long
keeping and for drinking when young.

production area	247 acres (100 hectares)		38,000 cases	
grape varieties	66% CS, 3% CF, 2% Malbec, 24% M, 5% PV			
soil	Fine gravel on limestone			
maturation	40% new barrels			
comments	Suitable for drinking young			
2nd wine	Connétable de Talbot			
Vintage	**Rating**	**Peak**		
1990	9.5	2000	Excellent, full, complex	
1991	5	1998	Balance?	
1992	4.5	1998	Fast developer	
1993	5.5	1998	Beef and tannins	
1994	7	2002	Dense, excellent	
1995	7	2003	Tannins need to blend	
1996	7.5	2004	Plump, ripe tannins	
1997	7	2004	Blended and distinguished elegance	

Pauillac premier cru classé
Château Lafite-Rothschild

Nicolas, of the third generation of Ségurs, nicknamed the "Prince of the Vineyards," inherited from Lafite, among others. Ruined, his grandson was forced to sell it. It was auctioned off as "the best Médoc wine and producing the best Bordeaux wine"; a turbulent period ensued. However, steward Goudal saved the vineyard, and at the auction of 1868 Baron James de Rothschild paid a princely sum for a vineyard that he is said to have bought because it bore the same name as the street where he owned a bank! He died without ever setting eyes on it. Baron Eric de Rothschild today has the great responsibility of running the vast 247-acre (100-hectare) domaine and maintaining the first of the first growths at the peak of its reputation. He combines a strictly traditional and a luxuriously modern outlook; in the château precinct he has had Ricardo Bofill design a circular-columned winery that makes it easier to handle the casks. This mythical, inaccessible wine did, after all, call for a temple. Revered and coveted by wealthy fanatics of 140 different countries, it only really reveals itself to those who believe in it or deserve it. Then, it offers a blazing moment of unspeakable delight.

production area	247 acres (100 hectares)		25,000 cases	
grape varieties	70% CS, 20% M, 5% CF, 5% PV			
soil	Gravel on limestone			
maturation	New barrels			
comments	Eclipse from 1960 to 1974. Legendary vintages: 1975, 1982, 1986			
2nd wine	Carruades de Lafite-Rothschild			
Vintage	**Rating**	**Peak**		
1990	9	starting	Body and fruit	
1991	5	1997	Firm tannins	
1992	5	1997	Pleasant aromatic complexity	
1993	6	2002	Meaty, fruity	
1994	6.5	2006	Spicy, tannic cabernet sauvignon wine	
1995	8	2005	Complex and meaty	
1996	9	2005	The best of the appellation	
1997	8	2006	Probable, again, the best of its appellation	

Pauillac premier cru classé
Château Latour

The present round tower was built in 1860, whereas the square tower from which the estate takes its name was part of a fortress that the English and French fought over during the Hundred Years War (1337–1453). We also note that the two nations carried their jousting over to the commercial field, as the domaine changed countries on a number of occasions. In 1705 the estate already extended over 74 acres (30 hectares), and Alexandre de Ségur became its owner upon his marriage. He left it to his son Nicolas, the "Prince of the Vineyards." It was the English, who were fond of the Bordeaux "claret," who made Château Latour's reputation, but the estate remained the property of a French family until 1962. In that year financial problems forced the descendants of the Ségurs to sell a majority holding to the British groups Pearson and Harvey of Bristol, until François Pinault, chairman and CEO of the Printemps store, purchased the 153 acres (62 hectares) for 720 million francs— one up for France! The twenty years of management at Latour by Jean-Paul Gardère have been crucial, as he has established his reputation as a winegrowing genius and molded the distinctive style of this dependably great first growth. The ancient vines grow in view of the river and in very large gravel on a clay base. Château Latour, a powerful, imposing, austere, and unshakable wine, will pay dividends for anyone patient enough to wait for it.

production area	116 acres (47 hectares)		18,000 cases
grape varieties	78% CS, 17% M, 5% CF-PV		
soil	Large gravel		
maturation	New barrels		
comments	Longest-lived		
2nd wine	Forts de Latour		

Vintage	Rating	Peak	
1990	10	2005–2010	The greatest of the vintage (?)
1991	6	starting	Very good 1991, rich
1992	6	starting	Low acidity, concentrated for the vintage
1993	6.5	2000	Balanced
1994	7	2004	At the top of the 1994s
1995	8	2006	Profound, the tannins need to develop
1996	8	2007	Classic, dense, long
1997	7	2006	Light for a Latour

Pauillac premier cru classé
Château Mouton Rothschild

Early in the eighteenth century Joseph de Brane was in charge of the Mouton vineyard, and in 1830 Baron de Brane sold Brane-Mouton to Isaac Thuriet, a banker. In 1853 Thuriet sold it to Nathaniel de Rothschild (on the English side), who never set foot on the estate but just wanted to have a wine to offer his guests that bore his own name. In 1855 Mouton was rated a second growth. Philippe de Rothschild was the great man at Mouton; he imposed château bottling, invented the annual illustrated label, and won the ultimate accolade by raising Mouton to official first-growth status in 1973. The vineyard sits on the Pouyalet plateau. Here the gravel is poor and very thick. The cabernet sauvignon vines reign supreme; they are very old—proof of quality—and renewed by planting. In recent years, a plot has been set aside for making a white wine that is as unusual as a five-legged sheep (or *mouton*). Château Mouton-Rothschild is a flamboyant wine; for a cabernet sauvignon, it is astonishingly fruity. The finesse of its tannins is well known, and it is said to have the famous "capsule taste."

production area	185 acres (75 hectares)		25,000 cases	
grape varieties	80% CS,10% CF, 8% M, 2% PV			
soil	Gravel on iron pan			
maturation	New barrels			
comments	The fruity, supple Pauillac			
Vintage	Rating	Peak		
1990	10	2005	Concentration, richness	
1991	5	starting	Complex nose	
1992	5	1997	Complex nose	
1993	6.5	2000	Dependable, very fruity	
1994	7	2004	Superb extract	
1995	8	2005	Plump, fruity, explosive	
1996	7.5	2005	Lacking its usual stature	
1997	7	2005	Very fruity, beautiful length	

Pauillac deuxième cru classé
Château Pichon-Longueville

The history of the very old Pichon family in the Médoc dates back to the seventeenth century. Bernard de Pichon had two sons: François, who founded the branch of the barons of Parempuyre, and Jacques, who founded the branch of the barons of Longueville. In 1694 Jacques married Thérèse des Mesures-de-Rauzan, who had inherited the Enclos de Rauzan at Saint-Lambert to which her husband's name, Pichon-Longueville, was attached. The estate lasted until 1840, when it had to be split among two sons and three daughters, with a detached portion being given the name Pichon-Longueville-Comtesse de Lalande after the last surviving daughter. Pichon-Baron was bought up in 1935 by the Bouteiller family. In 1987 it was bought by the Axa Millésimes group and managed by a shareholder, Jean-Michel Cazes, also the manager of Château Lynch-Bages. The larger part of the 111-acre (45-hectare) vineyard surrounds the château and is very close to the Pichon-Comtesse vines. The neighbor on the other side is Latour. Given the investment that has been made in recent years, it is not surprising to find at Château Pichon inky wines with a marvellously structured concentration.

production area	111 acres (45 hectares)		13,000 cases	
grape varieties	80% CS, 20% M			
soil	Gravel on iron pan			
maturation	60% new barrels			
comments	Revival as of the 1988 vintage			
2nd wine	Les Tourelles de Longueville			
Vintage	Rating	Peak		
1990	10	1997	Concentrated	
1991	5.5	1997	Good for the vintage	
1992	5	1999	Highly successful	
1993	7	2000	Good extract, full-bodied, rich	
1994	6.5	2002	Tannic	
1995	7	2007	Very powerful extracts	
1996	7.5	2005	Distinguished tannins, balanced	
1997	7	2006	Plump, great extract	

Château Pichon-Longueville-Comtesse de Lalande

This domaine, detached in 1840 from its neighbor Pichon-Baron, is the portion the countess Virginie de Lalande received from her father, Baron Joseph de Pichon-Longueville. In 1841 the countess had a château built by the architect Duphot and ran the estate herself. The Comtesse de Lalande's descendants sold Pichon-Comtesse to Édouard Miailhe in 1925. In 1978 his daughter, May-Eliane de Lencquesaing, took over management of the property as Virginie de Lalande had done before, with energy, competence, and a gift for communicating. The château has preserved all its former glory and period furniture, and a reception hall extended by a terrace with a panoramic view has been added. The vineyard is tended like a garden, the winemaking facilities have been renewed, and a wonderful underground aging cellar 36 feet (11 meters) long and an air-conditioned storage building have been built. The wine of Pichon-Longueville-Comtesse de Lalande, in which the merlot grape has its share alongside the other three Bordeaux varieties, is haloed with a deep color. Its powerful aroma, its distinguished roundness, and elegance are attractive from the earliest years of its long life.

production area	153 acres (62 hectares)		30,000 cases	
grape varieties	45% CS, 12% CF, 35% M, 8% PV			
soil	Gravel on clay and iron pan			
maturation	50% new barrels			
comments	A Pauillac Saint-Julien!			
2nd wine	Réserve de la Comtesse			
Vintage	Rating	Peak		
1990	8	1997	Not up to the vintage	
1991	5	1997	Good for 1991	
1992	5	1997	Light	
1993	6	1997	Rounder	
1994	7	2000	Fruity and fine	
1995	7.5	2005	One of the good ones of the vintage	
1996	7.5	2005	Vigorous, full	
1997	7	2005	Fine, almost light	

Pauillac quatrième cru classé
Château Duhart-Milon-Rothschild

It is said that Duhart was the name of a pirate who owned this land in the seventeenth century, Milon being the name of a nearby village. Duhart-Milon was the only Pauillac wine to be classed fourth growth. The close proximity to the Lafite vineyards inspired the French branch of the Rothschilds to buy up Duhart-Milon in 1962, and add their own name to the marque. The domaine was then entirely replanted, as it was necessary to pull up three-quarters of the vinestocks to drain the soil owing to the presence of low, wet ground immediately to the north. In addition, the vineyard's proximity to the moors and trees increases the risk of frost in spring.

When replanting took place, mostly cabernet sauvignon vines were planted, as is only normal for Pauillac. They cover 148 acres (60 hectares) on fine *graves*. The young vines are held back by some very hard pruning, thereby reducing yields per unit acreage, as at Lafite. Vinification and maturing also follow the practices of Lafite. The wine from these young vines is amazingly dense and deep in color, and connoisseurs are keeping a keen eye on how this Rothschild offspring with a promising future turns out.

production area	148 acres (60 hectares)		12,000 cases	
grape varieties	65% CS, 7% CF, 28% M			
soil	Gravel on limestone			
maturation	40% new barrels			
comments	Vineyard replanted in 1970. A wine for laying down			
2nd wine	Moulin de Duhart			

Vintage	Rating	Peak	
1990	8.5	2002	Round
1991	5	1997	Tender
1992	5	1997	Fruity
1993	6	starting	Balanced, spicy
1994	6	2003	Harsh tannins
1995	6.5	2005	The tannins ought to blend
1996	7	2005	Concentrated, spicy
1997	6	2005	Spicy, sinewy

Pauillac cinquième cru classé
Château d'Armailhac

Two hundred and fifty years ago, Dominique Armailhac bought some land, a few patches of vines on the edge of the Mouton plateau. In 1855 A. d'Armailhac was the owner, and the wine named after him was given a fifth-growth ranking. That same year he brought out an excellent book entitled *Vinegrowing, Winemaking and Wines in the Médoc.* On reading this, we see that there was nothing d'Armailhac did not know about the art of vinegrowing and winemaking. A relation of the d'Armailhacs, the count of Ferrand, took over the property until Philippe de Rothschild bought it in 1933—a logical enough move, since these vines were just next door to the Mouton-Rothschild vineyard to the northwest, spreading southward as far as the vines of Pontet-Canet. This wine changed names on a number of occasions, something unique in the Médoc. In 1956 it was called Château Mouton Baron Philippe, and, as of 1975 it took the name of Château Mouton Baronne Philippe. In 1979, the wine ought to have been labeled Château Mouton Baronne Pauline; this was not possible, though Philippe de Rothschild insisted on having "In homage to Pauline" inscribed on it; finally, in 1989, coming full circle, it reverted to its original name of Château d'Armailhac. This Pauillac is a good example of how masculine this appellation can be. It is made and matured with the same care as its neighbor Mouton-Rothschild, if not in the same luxury.

production area	124 acres (50 hectares)		20,000 cases	
grape varieties	50% CS, 23% CF, 25% M, 2% PV			
soil	Gravel and sand on iron pan			
maturation	50% new barrels			
comments	Serves as a link between Mouton-Rothschild and Pontet-Canet			
Vintage	**Rating**	**Peak**		
1990	10	starting	Supple, full-bodied	
1991	5	1997	Light	
1992	4.5	1997	Fine, fruity, lean	
1993	6	starting	Well balanced	
1994	6.5	1999	Well built	
1995	7	2001	Round	
1996	7.5	2002	Fine yet dense	
1997	6.5	2003	Sinewy finesse, some lightness?	

Pauillac cinquième cru classé
Château Batailley

This wine's name is thought to come from a battle fought against the English during the Hundred Years War. In the eighteenth century Batailley belonged to the Saint-Martin family. It came by marriage to Rear-Admiral De Bedout. Upon his death, the property was purchased by Daniel Guestier, who expanded the vineyard, rebuilt the master's house, and had 12 acres (5 hectares) of delightful grounds designed by Napoleon III's landscape gardener, Barillet-Deschamp. After 1867, with the rise in wine prices, a Parisian, M. Halphen, bought up Batailley, which he sold in 1929 to the brothers Marcel and Francis Borie, who shared the domaine between them. Marcel kept the château, outbuildings, and the heart of the vineyard, while Francis took what is now called Haut-Batailley. Currently Marcel Borie's son-in-law, Emile Castéja, is in charge of the 136-acre (55-hectare) estate, located southwest of Pauillac. Sold far and wide thanks to the dynamic sales force of the family merchant's business, Borie-Manou, this fifth growth has lived up to its ranking. Made with 70 percent cabernet sauvignon, the wine refuses harshness, emphasizing mellowness on the flesh of a very ripe fruit with which the merlot grape blends harmoniously.

production area	136 acres (55 hectares)		23,000 cases
grape varieties	70% CS, 25% M, 5% CF		
soil	Gravel		
maturation	50% new barrels		
comments	A traditional, manly Pauillac		
Vintage	**Rating**	**Peak**	
1990	9	starting	Fruity and supple
1991	5	1997	Easy
1992	5	1997	Somewhat fruity
1993	6	1999	Successful, long
1994	5.5	1999	Full-bodied for the vintage
1995	7	2003	Rich
1996	7	2003	Beefy
1997	6	2003	Round without greatness

Pauillac cinquième cru classé
Château Clerc-Milon

It was the Clerc family that owned this domaine when it became a fifth growth under the 1855 classification, Milon being a small village in the vicinity. When it was bought at the turn of the century by a Pauillac notary, Jacques Mondon, the property had been split up among the Clerc heirs. The wine was then being sold under the triple-barreled name of Château Clerc-Milon-Mondon, reverting to its previous name when it was purchased by Baron Philippe de Rothschild, who already owned Mouton and Château d'Armailhac. Thereafter, Clerc-Milon followed Baron Rothschild's usual practice in getting the best out of the *terroir*—restoring the vineyard by adapting vinestocks to suit the soil, for a distinctive cabernet sauvignon wine that needs to be rich, full-bodied, and long-lived, by following closely in the footsteps of his illustrious elder brother.

The Clerc-Milon label offers a stylized example of the kind of art that adorns the large collection of drinking vessels that can be seen at the Musée de Mouton. The twelfth-century German marriage cup, filled with wine for a ceremony solemnizing the bride and groom's mutual commitment, preceded the "Dancing Jesters" shown here, copied from a piece of jewelery that once belonged to Catherine of Russia.

production area	74 acres (30 hectares)		14,000 cases	
grape varieties	70% CS, 10% CF, 20% M			
soil	Gravel on iron pan and sand			
maturation	2-year-old barrels			
comments	Estate purchased in 1970, restructured within ten years			
1990	10	1997	Full-bodied, ripe	
1991	4.5	1997	Light	
1992	5	1997	A 1991 with more accomplished tannins	
1993	5.5	starting	Tannins and fruit	
1994	6	2000	Good volume	
1995	7	2004	Round, long	
1996	7	2004	Tannic, distinctive Pauillac	
1997	6	2005	Dense and firm	

Pauillac cinquième cru classé
Château Grand-Puy Ducasse

Grand-Puy is a place name designating a domaine that was divided into two sections for M. Déjean to give to his son and daughter. When M. Ducasse bought one of them, it was named Grand-Puy Ducasse, and the other property was called Grand-Puy Lacoste. To complicate matters even further, until it reached fifth-growth status, the wine of Grand-Puy Ducasse was known as Château Artigues-Arnaud, and only changed to its new name upon receiving this distinction. The Duroy de Suduirauts, who inherited Grand-Puy Ducasse, kept it in the family for two centuries. In 1971 the vineyard, down to 25 acres (10 hectares), and the decrepit installations were taken over by the Bordeaux firm of Mestrezat, and then by the Paribas group in 1987. Extension and renovation were the watchwords as this great wine in decline was set back on track. Now it is a 99-acre (40-hectare) estate divided into three plots at some distance from each other. The wine takes advantage of this diversity in blends that give it a fine color, a rich bouquet, and a build in keeping with its appellation and its ranking. The château and the buildings, a sober eighteenth-century horseshoe arrangement, open out onto the quays at Pauillac.

production area	99 acres (40 hectares)		14,000 cases	
grape varieties	62% CS, 38% M			
soil	Siliceous gravel			
maturation	30% new barrels			
comments	New lease of life as of the 1991 vintage			
2nd wine	Château Artigues-Arnaud			
Vintage	**Rating**	**Peak**		
1990	7.5	1997	Elegant	
1991	5	1997	Clean	
1992	6	starting	One of the best of the vintage	
1993	6	1999	Well constructed, fruity	
1994	6	2000	Balanced, tannic	
1995	7	2004	Elegant and well constructed	
1996	7	2004	Solid, tannic	
1997	6	2004	Harmonious, good extracts	

Pauillac cinquième cru classé
Château Grand-Puy Lacoste

Halfway between Bages and Artigues lies Château Grand-Puy Lacoste, constructed in 1850 butting up against the old house built in 1737. Like many others, the growth was the brainchild of the great bourgeois of Bordeaux, starting with the attorney Saint-Guiron and a parliamentarian, Maître Lacoste, who gave his name to the château. Following the long reign of the Duroy de Suduirauts and relatives, the property was bought in 1932 by Raymond Dupin, who made wines there that are remembered to this day. In 1978 the estate passed into other equally capable hands when taken over by Jean-Eugène Borie of Château Ducru Beaucaillou. The vines are planted on the well-known Bages plateau, on which the greatest vinegrowers, including Château Latour, own plots. The vineyard extends over about 124 acres (50 hectares) around the château, where generous *graves* give life to cabernet sauvignon and merlot vines of a respectable age, a guarantee of quality. Traditional winemaking, placed at the service of a Pauillac that is itself traditional, upholds the longstanding reputation of this slightly masculine, always powerfully clad wine.

production area	124 acres (50 hectares)		16,000 cases	
grape varieties	75% CS, 25% M			
soil	Gravel			
maturation	33% new barrels			
2nd wine	Lacoste Borie			
Vintage	Rating	Peak		
1990	10	1997	Supple	
1991	5	1997	Light	
1992	5	1997	Light	
1993	6	starting	Good extraction	
1994	7	2000	Dense	
1995	7.5	2003	Powerful	
1996	8	2004	Vigor, complexity	
1997	7.5	2005	Classic, powerful	

Pauillac cinquième cru classé
Château Haut-Bages Libéral

When it achieved fifth-growth status in 1855, Haut-Bages belonged to M. Henry, and shortly afterward it became the property of a wine broker, M. Libéral, who also owned the Château du Tertre at Margaux. Three other proprietors followed until the fifties, when the domaine fell into the hands of the Cruse family, who already owned Pontet-Canet and Issan. Haut-Bages Libéral then recovered its great wine qualities, which had fallen off. It drew the interest of the group that already owned Chasse-Spleen, and which bought up the château and restored it to its former position. The vineyard has developed from 23 acres (9 hectares) in 1970 to 69 acres (28 hectares) today, and produces four times more wine than it did a century ago. It has two sections, one adjacent to the main Latour vineyard, the other comprising two parcels on the Bages plateau. A notable absentee from the grape blend is cabernet franc, while the proportion of cabernet sauvignon is high, at 80 percent. Made using traditional methods, the wines have shown a marked improvement thanks to the careful attention of Claire Villars, who is carrying on her mother's efforts to make this a gilt-edged Pauillac.

production area	69 acres (28 hectares)		14,000 cases	
grape varieties	80% CS, 20% M			
soil	Sandy gravel on clayey limestone			
maturation	40% new barrels			
comments	A Pauillac with a smile			
2nd wine	Chapelle de Bages			
Vintage	**Rating**	**Peak**		
1990	9	1997	Supple	
1991	5	1997	Light	
1992	4.5	1997	Light	
1993	5	1997	Fruity	
1994	6.5	2002	Beefy, sensuous	
1995	6.5	2005	Dense	
1996	7	2005	Ripe tannins, cheerfully fruity	
1997	6	2005	Becoming well-built and balanced	

Pauillac cinquième cru classé
Château Haut-Batailley

Haut-Batailley came about when Château Batailley was divided up between two heirs of the Borie family. The two shared a common history until 1942, when Marcel Borie, then his daughter, Madame Castéja, came into part of the vineyard of Château Batailley plus the winery buildings. Haut-Batailley has no château in the architectural sense. There is, however, rising amid vines, a tower: the Tour d'Aspic, built thanks to one Mlle Averous in devotion to Our Lady of Lourdes. The Tour d'Aspic watches over a 54-acre (22-hectare) vineyard in several parcels, with the gravel soil on a limestone base. Sixty-five percent cabernet sauvignon, 25 percent merlot, and 10 percent cabernet franc go into the blend. The wines are made in traditional style, with no filtration. Château Haut-Batailley is suppler and finer than its sibling, and some find it has a family resemblance to its next-door neighbors, the Saint-Juliens.

production area	54 acres (22 hectares)		8,000 cases	
grape varieties	65% CS, 25% M, 10% CF			
soil	Gravel			
maturation	33% new barrels			
comments	A supple Pauillac			
2nd wine	Château La Tour d'Aspic			
Vintage	Rating	Peak		
1990	9	1997	Supple	
1991	4.5	1997	Light	
1992	5	1997	Short	
1993	5	1997	Easy, round	
1994	5.5	1999	Discreet body	
1995	6.5	2003	Ripe tannins	
1996	7	2003	A delicate Pauillac	
1997	6.5	2004	Balanced, round	

Pauillac cinquième cru classé
Château Lynch-Bages

The knight Drouillard purchased the domaine in 1728, and planted vines. He left it to his sister, who was married to an Irish Catholic emigrant, Thomas Lynch. In 1824 the Lynch family, which also owned Château Dauzac, sold what was known as "the Lynch growth" to the Swiss wine merchant Sébastien Jurine.

Having become Lynch-Jurine, the growth was classed fifth growth and sold again, this time to M. Cayrou, who gave it the name it was to keep. When it was bought by Jean-Charles Cazes, Lynch-Bages covered only 91 acres (37 hectares). Within three generations, the Cazes family put all its talent and know-how into making the estate a spectacular comeback in both enological and commercial terms. The Pauillac *terroir* was not alone responsible for this success; grandmaster Jean-Michel Cazes reigns over 198 acres (80 hectares) of old vines, where the rules are very strict regarding yields. The wine is made in the traditional style, but vat times are limited so as to get the wine to peak earlier while still keeping its excellent aging potential. A fantasy wine, with a velvety black color, a fragrance of peonies, and a soft, voluptuous body.

production area	198 acres (80 hectares)		30,000 cases	
grape varieties	75% CS, 10% CF, 15% M			
soil	Gravel			
maturation	50% new barrels			
comments	A fifth growth as good as a second growth			
2nd wine	Château Haut-Bages Averous			
Vintage	**Rating**	**Peak**		
1990	9.5	1997	Smooth	
1991	6	1997	Perfect extract for the vintage	
1992	6	1997	Perfect extract for the vintage	
1993	6	1997	Fruity, supple, spicy	
1994	6.5	2000	An amplified version of the above	
1995	7	2005	Highly tannic	
1996	7	2004	Frank; complexity?	
1997	6.5	2005	Plump, full	

Pauillac cinquième cru classé
Château Pontet-Canet

This domaine bears the name of a locality added to that of Jean-François Pontet, who purchased the property in 1750 and held on to it until it received its fifth growth classification. The next owner was Herman Cruse. For over a century the Cruses expanded the vineyard, extending the buildings and adding extensive grounds. In 1975 Pontet-Canet was bought up by Guy Tesseron, a Cognac man whose wife's maiden name is Cruse. This truly vast domaine includes 185 acres (75 hectares) of vines on high ground rising to 98 feet (30 meters), which enables it to have underground cellars reminiscent of Champagne. In the winery, alongside the gleaming stainless steel temperature-controlled vats, they have kept the concrete vats of the fifties and the old oak vats. Gentle sorting and pressing processes have helped to bring to fame a wine that was well known in former times owing to the large quantities it was produced in; for instance, it is the favorite wine of the International sleeping car company. It now bases its reputation on the distinctive character of a great Pauillac, its sturdy tannins tempered with elegant suppleness.

production area	185 acres (75 hectares)		22,000 cases	
grape varieties	62% CS, 32% M, 5% CF			
soil	Gravel on limestone and iron pan			
maturation	40% new barrels			
comments	Needs following very closely as of the 1996 vintage			
2nd wine	Les Hauts de Pontet			
Vintage	Rating	Peak		
1990	9.5	2000	Ripe tannins	
1991	5	1997	Fine	
1992	4.5	1997	Lean although tannic	
1993	6	starting	Meaty, fruity	
1994	7	2003	One of the best of the vintage	
1995	7.5	2005	Complex	
1996	7.5	2005	As successful as the 1995	
1997	7	2006	Concentrated, long	

Saint-Estèphe deuxième cru classé
Cos d'Estournel

The eye is struck and the memory marked by the pinnacle turrets of Cos d'Estournel, which have something Chinese and something Indian about them. The somewhat eccentric Louis-Gaspard d'Estournel built this very personal château to store his wine in. His love of wine was equaled only by his love of Arab horses: he would send it by sea as barter for stallions intended for English mares. The unsold wines, back from India, acquired connotations of dreams and travel. This incorrigible innovator even attempted to introduce the syrah grape into the Médoc! His precarious financial position eventually forced him to sell Cos d'Estournel to an English millionnaire called Martyns. After a few more careful owners, this fine 173-acre (70-hectare) estate in one piece fell to the Ginestet and Prats families. The cabernet sauvignon grape is the major ingredient, planted at the top of the gravelly hillocks, while the merlot vines are planted in places where limestone rises to the surface. Bruno Prats watches over the restrained yields and severe selections in a traditional but customized winemaking process that produces a meaty wine in which the unaggressive tannins have the edge on a velvety fruitiness. A very distinguished second growth.

production area	173 acres (70 hectares)		27,000 cases	
grape varieties	60% CS, 38% M, 2% PV			
soil	Gravel on limestone			
maturation	50 to 100% new barrels			
comments	Smooth, harmonious roundness, very reliable			
2nd wine	La Pagode de Cos			
Vintage	Rating	Peak		
1990	10	2000	Supple, harmonious	
1991	7	2000	Well-constructed	
1992	6	1997	Round for the vintage	
1993	6.5	1999	Round, fruity	
1994	7.5	2003	Tannic, round	
1995	8	2005	Concentrated, a great wine	
1996	8	2006	Even better than the great 1995?	
1997	7.5	2006	Concentrated, full-bodied, round	

Saint-Estèphe deuxième cru classé
Château Montrose

Until 1815, this was no more than a field of wild shrubs and pink heather; hence the name, meaning pink mountain, given to the château that Etienne-Théodore Dumoulin had built facing the river. He had decided that the exposure of this moorland and its gravelly soil would be suitable for vinegrowing. He cleared the ground, planted his vineyard, and gradually built the winery buildings and accommodation for his staff. Château Montrose covered 77 acres (31 hectares) when it rose to second-growth status. When Dumoulin died, his heirs sold the estate to M. Dollfus, who carried on its creator's work with some notable improvements. Upon being bought by the Hostein family, Montrose came to Louis-Victor Charmolüe by marriage. His descendants took over and now Jean-Louis Charmolüe works the 168 acres (68 hectares) of vines that gently slope down toward the river, where in the olden days casks of wine were loaded onto ships. Everything at Montrose is impeccably well organized, and the wine is made in keeping with the traditions of the appellation—powerful, austere, and manly, it is not overcooperative in its youth and only reveals its finesse to those who can wait to discover it in its prime.

production area	168 acres (68 hectares)		20,000 cases	
grape varieties	65% CS, 10% CF, 25% M			
soil	Gravel on marly clay			
maturation	40% new barrels			
comments	A manly Saint-Estèphe for keeping			
2nd wine	La Dame de Montrose			
Vintage	**Rating**	**Peak**		
1990	10	2000	Concentrated	
1991	5.5	1997	Fruity	
1992	4.5	1997	Dry and lean	
1993	5.5	2000	Balanced, fruity	
1994	7	2002	Round tannins, complex	
1995	7.5	2005	Plump, round	
1996	7.5	2006	Tight-knit, long	
1997	7.5	2007	A great Montrose	

Saint-Estèphe troisième cru classé
Calon-Ségur

This is the northernmost château of the Saint-Estèphe appellation, and one with a long history. The noble house of Calon was purchased from the lords of Lesparre by the Gasqs. In the eighteenth century Nicolas de Ségur reigned over the estate; this famous viticultural specialist, who operated a number of vineyards of repute, used to say, "I make wine at Lafite and at Latour, but my heart is in Calon." This heart now features on the labels of this wine. However, at the close of the ancien régime, his son, a compulsive gambler, gambled away the family heritage. Calon-Ségur was auctioned off to M. Dumoulin, then resold to M. Lestapis and classed as a third growth. In 1894 the wine merchants Hanappier and Capbern-Gasqueton bought the estate with Edouard Capbern-Gasqueton as its administrator. Until his recent death, he was the very first grand master of the famed Commanderie du Bontemps de Médoc. The current vineyard, set within walls, lies on low ground adjacent to the château.

While showing the vigorous quality of the *terroir,* the wine of Calon-Ségur has not always lived up to its third-growth ranking, but has occasionally done even better (1966, 1982). The most recent vintages are outstanding.

production area	148 acres (60 hectares)		25,000 cases	
grape varieties	65% CS, 15% CF, 20% M			
soil	Gravel on ferruginous limestone			
maturation	40% new barrels			
comments	A charmer of a Saint-Estèphe. Revival since 1994			
2nd wine	Marquis de Ségur			
Vintage	**Rating**	**Peak**		
1990	9.5	2000	Ripe tannins	
1991	5	1997	Supple, easy	
1992	4.5	1997	Light	
1993	5	1997	Balanced	
1994	6.5	2002	A richer, better built 1993	
1995	7.5	2005	Perfectly balanced, rich	
1996	7	2005	Full, fruity	
1997	6.5	2005	Spicy, characteristic of the appellation	

Saint-Estèphe
Haut-Marbuzet

Here is a Médoc château that owes nothing to property handed down in the family or to financial means. What Hervé Duboscq bought in 1952 was a life interest in 16 acres (6.5 hectares) of neglected vines. Of course the soil was good, but this civil servant from the Gers *département* of southwest France, who lived for his passion for wine, was to perform with his son the feat of restoring a 50-hectare estate whose wine was to achieve a huge success, all in the space of ten years. A fine example of a father-and-son team working together, both enthusiastic and ambitious. It is no miracle if the wine of Haut-Marbuzet is bought (either at the château or by mail order) by hedonists from every background. Henri Duboscq looks after his vines and is a virtuoso performer when it comes to careful winemaking and aging in new barrels. His wine, which some find too commercial, is intended to be harmonious and attractive, voluptuous and pleasing even when still young. Not so very bourgeois, this growth made for immediate, unreserved enjoyment is irresistible all the same!

production area	124 acres (50 hectares)		25,000 cases	
grape varieties	50% CS, 40% M, 10% CF			
soil	Gravel on limestone			
maturation	New barrels			
comments	Henri Duboscq, master winemaker, grand master of the cellar			
Vintage	Rating	Peak		
1990	10	2000	Complex, long	
1991	5	1997	Full-bodied for the vintage	
1992	6	1997	Successful extraction	
1993	7	1997	Empyreumatic	
1994	7	1997	The merlot sings	
1995	7.5	2000	Harmonious	
1996	7.5	2002	Fine maturity	
1997	7.5	2003	Round, original, seductive	

Saint-Estèphe
Pez

The Pez vineyard has existed since the fifteenth century; with Calon, it is the oldest in Saint-Estèphe. Jean de Briscos, M. Ducos, and Jean de Pontac were the first to work it, and Pez remained in the Pontac family (creators also of Haut-Brion) until the Revolution. Other owners followed: the Lawtons, the Vivier du Fays, and finally, in 1920, Robert Dousson's grandfather, Jean Bernard. Lastly in 1995, the domaine was purchased by Roederer Champagne. It is said that the surface area of Pez has not varied in three centuries and still covers "80 *journals*"— i.e., 57 acres (23 hectares). The vineyard is on a hillock whose altitude varies between 59 and 39 feet (18 and 12 meters). The very thick *graves* rest on a clayey-calcareous base. Cabernet grapes are the main ingredient of the blend, with moderate yields. Traditional winemaking techniques are used, faithful to wooden vats but with a cooling system. The wine is barrel-aged and never filtered. In this way the wine of Pez is characterful and virile, seeking not to be subtle or likable but to showcase the frankness of the *terroir,* with power and density.

production area	57 acres (23 hectares)	15,000 cases	
grape varieties	44% M, 43% CS, 10% CF, 3% PV		
soil	Gravel		
maturation	33% new barrels		
comments	This vineyard was in exactly the same spot three centuries ago		
2nd wine	La Salle de Pez		

Vintage	Rating	Peak	
1990	10	2000	Round, fruity
1991	5	1997	Supple
1992	4.5	1997	Light
1993	5	1997	Concentration?
1994	6	2002	Broad-shouldered
1995	7.5	2005	Full-bodied, beefy
1996	7.5	2005	Round, ripe tannins
1997	7.5	2005	Spicy and complex

Moulis
Château Chasse-Spleen

This domaine has the prettiest name in the Médoc, all at
once romantic and healthily medical! It is said that the idea of
chasse-spleen (getting rid of those nineteenth century blues)
owes something to Odilon Redon, the painter who illustrated the
works of Charles Baudelaire and who lived in the neighboring
château, Peyrelebade. The long history of this famous estate
begins in 1560 with the Gressier family, who were farmers and
later owners of the place. It came by marriage to the Castaings,
who restored the vineyard and had the present château built.
In 1905 a Bremen wine merchant bought the property and
gave it its international standing. World War I forced the sale
of this German possession, and Chasse-Spleen was auctioned
off to the Lahary family, who resold it in 1976 to a group
led by M. Merlau. His daughter, Bernadette Villars, was an
impeccable manager. An enterprising perfectionist, she ran
Chasse-Spleen with admirable mastery and had a passion for
its wine, which she wanted to be classical and well built, but
with a charming fruitiness. She was cut down in her prime by
an accident, and her daughter Claire took over. Chasse-Spleen
has upheld its bred-in-the-bone prestige among the great
successful bourgeois growths.

production area	180 acres (73 hectares)		36,000 cases	
grape varieties	60% CS, 35% M, 5% PV			
soil	Clayey calcareous gravel			
maturation	40% new barrels			
comments	Possesses the qualities of a classified growth			
2nd wine	L'Oratoire de Chasse-Spleen			
Vintage	Rating	Peak		
1990	10	1997	Full-bodied	
1991	5	1997	Merlot wine	
1992	5	1997	Charming	
1993	6	1999	Tannic, spicy	
1994	6.5	2001	Woody, manly	
1995	7	2005	Even manlier	
1996	7	2005	Round	
1997	6.5	2006	Full, round. For keeping	

Moulis
Château Poujeaux

During the nineteenth century, the Castaing family owned several châteaus at Poujeaux. One of them became Chasse-Spleen; two others were bought in 1920 and 1957 by the Theil family. Since 1981, Philippe and François Theil have watched over the operations of this fine estate covering an unbroken stretch of 124 acres (50 hectares), on a sandy gravel soil where cabernet and merlot vines grow in equal numbers. Winemaking in the modern facilities is inspired by Peynaud, and careful maturing contributes to the success of a wine that is becoming steadily more elite. Well built, with tannins that are fine but present from its early years, Château Poujeaux has a velvety texture and a bouquet that give it a full roundness. It is impossible not to quote in connection with this great classified bourgeois growth the story of Baron Elie de Rothschild, who, at a dinner given by former President Pompidou of France, mistook Château Poujeaux 1967 for a Château Lafite. Was the taster just obsessed with his own wine, or does Poujeaux have a royal twin? A cousin at any rate, due to the likeness between the two soils, confirmed by geological analysis.

production area	124 acres (50 hectares)		30,000 cases	
grape varieties	50% CS, 40% M, 5% CF, 5% PV			
soil	Gravel and sand on iron pan			
maturation	50% new barrels			
comments	A model of reliability			
2nd wine	Château La Salle de Poujeaux			
Vintage	Rating	Peak		
1990	10	2000	Round tannins	
1991	5	1997	Full-bodied	
1992	5.5	1997	Fruity	
1993	6.5	1997	Round, supple, powerful	
1994	6.5	2000	Well built, round	
1995	7	2005	Fine maturity	
1996	7	2005	Round, delicious tannins	
1997	6.5	2005	Ripe and long	

Haut-Médoc troisième cru classé
Château La Lagune

On the road of the Châteaux, La Lagune is the first classified growth you come to after leaving Bordeaux. The Seguineau family, in the eighteenth century, had the present château built, a fine charterhouse with harmonious proportions. The troubled times of the French Revolution saw a whole series of owners one after the other, and it was only through the good offices of M. Pistou that the domaine earned its third place in the 1855 rankings and a foreign market for its wines. Disaster struck in the twentieth century, with the vineyard down to 10 acres (4 hectares) in 1933. It was only when Georges Brunet arrived in 1957 that La Lagune made a spectacular recovery. Four years later, Brunet sold the revived estate to the Ayala Champagne house. The vineyard now covers 173 acres (70 hectares) in one block, rising to a height of 52 feet (16 meters), and the winery, a model of order and cleanliness, houses a score of stainless steel vats and numerous new barrels. The wine comes from thirty-year-old vines planted on a soil of very fine *graves,* and has a distinctive style characterized by its attractive, velvety roundness.

production area	173 acres (70 hectares)		29,000 cases
grape varieties	60% CS, 10% CF, 20% M, 10% PV		
soil	Mindel gravel		
maturation	90% new barrels		
comments	Very dependable		
2nd wine	Château Ludon Punies Agassac		

Vintage	Rating	Peak	
1990	9	1997	Supple, ripe
1991	5	1997	Simple
1992	4.5	1997	Light
1993	5.5	1997	Easy but successful
1994	6	2000	Broad-shouldered
1995	7	2003	Ripe grapes
1996	7	2004	Beefy and round
1997	6.5	2004	Anise-flavored, balanced

Haut-Médoc cinquième cru classé
Château Belgrave

In 1855 Château Belgrave was classed under the name of Coutenceau, although the actual building, constructed in 1740 by a member of the English royal family, was already called Belgrave. In the nineteenth century Bruno Devez, and then Marcel Alibert, earned the domaine a reputation with their highly regarded wine. But during the 1920s Belgrave kept changing hands and lost its prestige. The heirs of M. Gurgès sold the property to the French Bank of Agriculture, which farmed the business out to the Dourthe-Kresman firm of wine merchants. Large sums were invested in the revival of Belgrave and its single 131-acre (53-hectare) plot of vines. The château was restored, the fermenting room and winery were renovated, and new barrels were brought in. Château Belgrave has made a fine recovery and now does justice to its ranking as a classified growth. It is a generous, elegant, perfectly balanced wine. On the corks, which bear the Belgrave stamp, the crown and ferret recall the royal origins of the man who had the château built as a shooting lodge.

production area	131 acres (53 hectares)		22,000 cases	
grape varieties	40% CS, 20% CF, 35% M, 5% PV			
soil	Gravel on limestone			
maturation	50% new barrels			
comments	Estate completely rebuilt during the 1980s			
2nd wine	Diane de Belgrave			
Vintage	**Rating**	**Peak**		
1990	8	1997	Supple	
1991	5	1997	Minor vintage, balance achieved. Nice and fruity	
1992	5	1997	Minor vintage, balance achieved. Nice and fruity	
1993	5.5	1997	Supple and round	
1994	6	starting	More powerfully built, ripe grapes	
1995	7	2003	Extensive extracts	
1996	7	2003	Tannic, fruity	
1997	6.5	2003	A good, balanced Belgrave	

Haut-Médoc cinquième cru classé
Château Camensac

When Camensac was classified in 1855, it was the property of the Popp family, who later sold it to M. de Tournadre. Then the Cuveliers marked their period of ownership by planting a vineyard to make white wine, not unusual in the Saint-Laurent area during the nineteenth century. Camensac's fortune was hard hit by successive troubles, and when the estates was bought by the Forners, who came from Spain and were wine producers in Rioja, it needed a lot of work. To begin with, 161 acres (65 hectares) of vines were replanted. Next in the renovation program came the outbuildings, followed by the château itself, a fine charterhouse located on a hillock affording an extensive view over the vineyards as far as Saint-Julien. The replanted vines have now reached the age required for producing a choice wine, and by applying to the letter winemaking methods largely inspired by Emile Peynaud, Château Camensac is once more a full-bodied, fruity, and reliable wine.

production area	161 acres (65 hectares)		25,000 cases	
grape varieties	60% CS, 20% CF, 20% M			
soil	Fine gravel on iron pan			
maturation	40% new barrels			
comments	Mechanical harvesting during the 1980s; revival as of 1992			
2nd wine	La Closerie de Carmensac			
Vintage	**Rating**	**Peak**		
1990	7	1997	Round	
1991	4.5	1997	Short	
1992	4.5	1997	Light	
1993	5	1997	Has finesse	
1994	6.5	starting	Ripe	
1995	7	2002	Balanced, characteristic	
1996	7	2002	Fresh, fruity	
1997	6.5	2002	Clean and elegant	

Haut-Médoc cinquième cru classé
Château Cantemerle

Singing blackbirds (hence the name, *Chante-merle*) enjoy the grassy spaces of the grounds around the château, through which runs a refreshing babbling brook. The archives document that the vines have been in existence since 1570. Until 1892, Cantemerle belonged to the De Villeneuve family. Three years before it joined the ranks of the great wines, Cantemerle had been the scene of experiments into the effects of sulfur in combating powdery mildew. At the turn of the century the wine merchant Théophile Dubos bought the domaine, which remained in the family until problems of joint possession led it to sell in 1980. A purchasing syndicate, the S.M.A.B.T.P., entrusted its management and a monopoly on production to the Cordier firm, which owned the classified growths Gruaud-Larose, Talbot, and other vineyards. Cordier's experience and the skill of Georges Pauli, a strong personality, bore fruit. The surface area of the vineyard was doubled to 163 acres (66 hectares), in three sections. The wine reflects the variety of soil types, the equal shares of the two main grape varieties, the careful winemaking, and the long maturation in barrels of a certain age. This dense, sappy wine with its subtle aromas goes for finesse, not for strength.

production area	163 acres (66 hectares)		27,000 cases	
grape varieties	35% CS, 23% CF, 40% M, 2% PV			
soil	Fine and sandy gravels			
maturation	30% new barrels			
comments	Much of the vineyard too young			
2nd wine	Baron Villeneuve de Cantemerle			
Vintage	**Rating**	**Peak**		
1990	8	1997	Graceful	
1991	5	1997	Supple, distinguished	
1992	4.5	1997	Light	
1993	6	starting	Agreeably fruity	
1994	6.5	2000	Charming	
1995	7	2002	Supple and fine	
1996	7	2002	Supple and fine	
1997	7	2002	Excellent Cantemerle, delicate	

Haut-Médoc
Château Sociando-Mallet

They say in the Médoc that for the vine to produce good wine, it needs its roots dug deep into the *graves* and its leaves to be within sight of the river. Both these conditions obtain at Château Sociando-Mallet, where the vineyard slopes gently down toward the Gironde. The site and the all-round view decided Jean Gautreau, then a wine merchant at Lesparre, to purchase this domaine in 1969. The estate had already seen its heyday when owned by M. Sociando in 1633, then by the great lawyer Brochon, then Madame Mallet, who added her name to Sociando's. After a succession of sales, all that remained were 12 acres (5 hectares) of vineyard and some tumbledown buildings. Having to start again from scratch was part of the appeal of the place for Gautreau. Now the vineyard covers a single 124-acre (50-hectare) plot and the buildings are functional, with a spanking new winery. The wine has rewarded these efforts, taking each vintage as it came till it reached its current acknowledged roundness. Like Gautreau, it is broad-shouldered, agreeable, and easy to get on with.

production area	124 acres (50 hectares) 25,000 cases		
grape varieties	60% CS, 25% M, 10% CF, 5% PV		
soil	Gravel on clayey limestone		
maturation	80 to 100% new barrels		
comments	Often rated as a third growth		
2nd wine	La Demoiselle de Sociando		

Vintage	Rating	Peak	
1990	10	2005	Concentrated
1991	6	starting	Delicate
1992	5	1997	Fine
1993	6	2000	Full, spicy
1994	7	2003	Tannic
1995	8	2005	Complex
1996	8	2006	Concentrated, well built, long
1997	7.5	2005	Spicy, masterful extract, highly successful

Médoc
Château La Tour-de-By

A vineyard is documented at Roque-de-By in the sixteenth century, owned by a Pierre Tizon; he was succeeded by the count of Grammont, whose family held the domaine until the Revolution. The present château was built in 1876 by M. Rubichon, who also gave it its new name, La Tour-de-By. Overlooking the Gironde, this tower was a lighthouse erected on top of an old mill. In 1910 Rubichon sold the property to Julien Damoy, a well-known figure in the food industry, who planted nothing but merlot in his vineyard. Upon his death, a certain Kaskoreff bought the domaine, selling it again in 1965 to the three current owners, Messrs Cailloux, Lapalu, and Pagès. Under their guidance, cabernet sauvignon has regained its vital role in making distinctive, balanced Médocs. Marc Pagès is manager of this vast operation, which extends over 180 acres (73 hectares), with its biggest vineyard at a height of 49 feet (15 meters), on the hillock where stands the famous tower. The facilities have been renovated, and the semiunderground winery still uses wood alongside stainless steel. The great age of the vines contributes to the success of this wine.

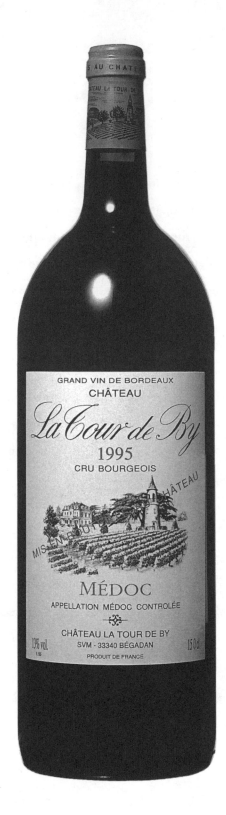

production area	180 acres (73 hectares)		45,000 cases	
grape varieties	58% CS, 36% M, 4% CF, 2% PV			
soil	Gravel			
maturation	20% new barrels			
comments	Large output, impressively dependable			
2nd wine	Château La Roque-de-By			
Vintage	Rating	Peak		
1990	10	1997	Well built, full	
1991	5	past		
1992	4	past		
1993	5	1997	Fruity, floral	
1994	5.5	1997	Round	
1995	7	2000	Ripe tannins	
1996	7	2002	Powerful and fruity	
1997	6	2002	Supple, round, and long	

Médoc
Château Les Ormes Sorbet

During the sixteenth century the domaine of Coucques belonged to Louis de Genouillac; it passed in 1852 to M. Sorbet. For over a century, the Boivert family has redeveloped the vineyard, which now covers 52 acres (21 hectares), on parcels where the calcareous bottom soil is of marine origin, full of fossilized *couquèques* (named after the region). The well-exposed vineyard is planted with twice as much cabernet sauvignon as merlot, giving the wine a rich body and its universally acknowledged distinctive Médoc character. Jean Boivert lovingly tends this small estate. The grapes are handpicked, and the wine, made carefully with a preference for long fermenting times and barrel-aged in costly oak from Tronçais Forest blossoms with finesse and elegance, develops over the years tertiary aromas that age very well. This being so, it is hardly surprising that Château Les Ormes Sorbet should garner high praise in specialist guides, and be found at the tables of connoisseurs.

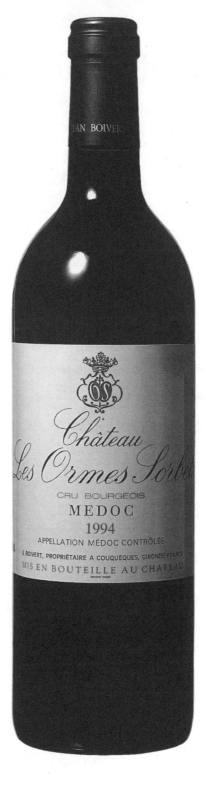

production area	52 acres (21 hectares)		12,000 cases	
grape varieties	65% CS, 30% M, 2% CF, 2% PV, 1% carmenère			
soil	Gravelly sand			
maturation	33% new barrels			
comments	Authenticity and dependability			
2nd wine	Château de Conques			

Vintage	Rating	Peak	
1990	10	2000	Round, rich
1991	5	advanced	Light
1992	4.5	advanced	Even lighter
1993	7	2000	Complex, full
1994	6.5	2000	Precise
1995	7	2002	Fine, elegant
1996	7	2005	Cabernets perfectly ripe
1997	6.5	2003	Long and supple

Médoc
Château Rollan de By

Qualities apparently required to become a winegrower in the Médoc include an artistic talent, some managerial experience, and a passionate character. To this Jean Guyon, the head of a big interior decoration firm in Paris and recent proprietor of Rollan de By, would add solid financial credentials. His taste for good wine led him in 1989 to fulfill a wild dream, to buy a Bordeaux vineyard—no little feat in an age dedicated to immediate profitability. His vineyard at first occupied 5 acres (2 hectares), followed by another 15 acres (6 hectares). Without giving up his earlier business, a vital source of funds, he settled into his new job with all the conviction and creativity of the keen newcomer. With good advice, his innovations fitted in neatly with the traditions of the Médoc, and promotion to bourgeois growth status crowns his acknowledged achievement. Like its maker, the wine also has a very strong personality. It is a jewel that he has fashioned at great cost to satisfy his passion, a precious, seductive, one man's wine, at once likable and serious.

production area	37 acres (15 hectares)		7,500 cases	
grape varieties	70% M, 20% CS, 10% PV			
soil	Gravel and sand			
maturation	New barrels			
comments	A bourgeois growth vinified like a first growth			
2nd wine	Château Fleur-de-By			
Vintage	Rating	Peak		
1991	5.5	1997	Spicy, woody	
1992	5	1997	Supple	
1993	6	starting	Strong extraction	
1994	7	2000	Woody, textured	
1995	7.5	2001	Powerful and rich	
1996	7.5	2002	Original, empyreumatic aromas	
1997	7.5	2003	Big success. Rich and long	

Médoc
Château Tour-Haut-Caussan

The Courrian family, who had been in the Médoc since the seventeenth century, bought the Tour-Haut-Caussan vineyard in 1877. The tower in question is in fact a windmill that was built in 1734. Philippe Courrian had it restored, and can still use it to grind his grain. This windmill commands a hummock, on which lies one of the three parcels that make up this 40-acre (16-hectare) vineyard. The Laignan plot is planted with merlot vines on a clayey calcareous soil and potensac with cabernet sauvignon on ferruginous Garonne gravel. Philippe Courrian, a perfectionist, never backs away from the demands involved in creating a great wine. The handpicked grapes are sorted; the careful vinification varies according to the vintage, with no filtration; the wine is matured in wood; and fining is done with fresh egg whites. All these things, plus the winemaker's talent, mean that Château Tour-Haut-Caussan combines finesse, complexity, and keeping qualities.

production area	40 acres (16 hectares)		10,000 cases	
grape varieties	50% CS, 50% M			
soil	Clayey-calcareous gravels			
maturation	33% new barrels			
comments	An exemplary winegrower			
2nd wine	Château Landette			
Vintage	**Rating**	**Peak**		
1990	10	2000	Round	
1991	5	finishing	Fruity	
1992	5	finishing	A watercolor	
1993	6	1999	Meaty	
1994	6	2000	Round	
1995	7	2005	Rich	
1996	7	2005	Sumptuous cabernets	
1997	6	2004	Beautiful extract, will become balanced in time	

Pessac-Léognan premier cru classé
Château Haut-Brion

Five centuries have passed since the birth of this prestigious château; it was on April 23, 1525, that Jean de Pontac married the daughter of the mayor of Libourne, whose dowry came in the form of the vineyard of Haut-Brion. The French writers Montaigne and La Boétie were witnesses at the marriage. The supremacy of the wines of Haut-Brion was established through the help of English and American wine lovers. In London, the Pontacs opened a sort of wine bar, which soon became fashionable. In France, the wine was served at the king's table. During the Revolution, Haut-Brion belonged to the mayor of Bordeaux, the comte de Fumel, who was later guillotined. Confiscated and returned to his heirs, the domaine was then bought by French statesman Charles Maurice de Talleyrand on the advice of Marie-Antoine Carême, his famous chef. Having more of a gift for diplomacy than for wine, he sold Haut-Brion to the Larrieus, who swore by this wonderful wine. Their efforts were crowned with success when it was classified as a first growth, the only Graves to emulate the very best of the Médocs. In 1935 a New York financier, Clarence Dillon, bought the 113 acres (45.9 hectares) of Château Haut-Brion. His son Douglas was ambassador in Paris, and his daughter Joan married Prince Charles of Luxemburg. On becoming a widow, she married again, to the Duke of Mouchy. Today, along with enologist J. B. Delmas, they watch together over this legendary wine, a miracle of harmony, balance, elegance, and smoothness.

production area	Red 101 acres (43.2 hectares)		16,000 cases	White 6.7 acres (2.7 hectares)	800 cases
grape varieties	45% CS, 37% M, 18% CF			37% Sau, 63% Se	
soil	Gravel on clayey sand			Gravel on clayey sand	
maturation	New barrels			New barrels	
comments	A fabulous, legendary 1989, the best of the vintage			Nonclassified growth	
2nd wine	Le Bahaus du Château Haut-Brion				

Vintage	Rating	Peak			
1990	10	starting	Finesse and length		
1991	6	1997	Narrow-shouldered	The best white Graves	
1992	5	1997	Good extraction	Best drunk between 5 and 10 years old	
1993	7	2000	A full-blooded 1991	All the vintages are remarkable	
1994	8	2002	Smooth, 1989 style	The 1994 especially, better than the 1995	
1995	8	2003	Very fine tannins		
1996	8	2005	Unostentatiously full	The 1996 outstandingly fresh	
1997	7.5	2006	Huge success for the vintage. The best, along with Lafite	Outstanding success in white as well. The best of the appellation	

Pessac-Léognan cru classé (R & W)
Château Bouscaut

During the seventeenth century this vineyard was known by the name of Haut-Truchon. Two centuries later, the Chabanneau family were to restructure the vineyard, drain the soil, and build a modern fermenting room. The next owners, the Places, increased the popularity of their wines by taking in show-business personalities at Bouscaut. Unfortunately the seventeenth-century château was devastated by fire twice in the space of two years, the first fire started by the singer Gilbert Bécaud, who was trying to cook himself a sirloin steak over some vine shoots! In 1962 a group of American investors carried on improving the domaine, which they then sold to Lucien Lurton in 1979. Château Bouscaut is in capable hands. From the terrace you can see right across the 111-acre (45-hectare) vineyard, which extends in a single stretch as far as the N113 highway. The soil is made up of Pyrenees gravel on an iron pan base. The merlot grape accounts for over half of the red vines, with 35 percent cabernet sauvignon and lesser quantities of cabernet franc and malbec. In the 20 acres (8 hectares) given over to white wine, there is 70 percent semillon and 30 percent sauvignon. Red Château Bouscaut is a full-blooded, beefy wine. The white wines are both lively and plump.

production area	Red 91 acres (37 hectares)		10,000 cases		White 20 acres (8 hectares)	2,500 cases
grape varieties	55% M, 35% CS, 5% CF, 5% Malbec				70% Se, 30% Sau	
soil	Pyrenees gravel, sandy clay					
maturation	35% new barrels				40% new barrels	
comments	The merlots are peculiarly hard					
2nd wine	Château Valoux					
Vintage	**Rating**	**Peak**				
1990	7	**1997**	Not a great 1990			
1991	4.5	**1997**	Light, too light		Best drunk at 3 years old	
1992	5	**1997**	Light, too light		Can be kept	
1993	5.5	**starting**	Satisfactory extract		Can be kept	
1994	6	**1999**	Concentration?		Can be kept	
1995	7	**2002**	Fine merlots, but . . .			
1996	7	**2002**	Solid		Drinkable now	
1997	6	**2003**	Balanced, good tannins; improving		Fresh, elegant, just beginning	

Pessac-Léognan cru classé (R & W)
Château Carbonnieux

This very old vineyard had belonged to the Carbonnieux since 1234. From 1519, the Ferron family owned the vineyard and the château, which then had twelve towers. In 1740 the domaine was sold to the Benedictines of Sainte-Croix, who improved the vineyard and sold their produce to the four corners of the globe. They even contrived to get round the laws of the Koran by shipping to the rich Muslims of Constantinople a white wine labeled "Mineral water from Carbonnieux in Guienne"! The monks were turned out in the turmoil of the Revolution, and Carbonnieux was sold off as a national asset. There followed half a dozen different proprietors until 1956, when Château Carbonnieux became the family seat of the Perrins, just back from Algeria, with long experience in winegrowing and restoring vines and buildings. The present-day château has kept the same old configuration of four pavilions and two towers.

The 193-acre (78-hectare) vineyard, the most extensive of all the classified Graves growths, planted on deep *graves* covering a clay base, slopes gently down to the northeast. The vines produce nearly as much white wine (deliciously scented) as red wine (firm and straight).

production area	Red 101 acres (41 hectares) 25,000 cases			White 91 acres (37 hectares) 20,000 cases		
grape varieties	60% CS, 7% CF, 30% M, 3% PV-Malbec			65% Sau, 34% Se, 1% Mu		
soil	Gravel on clay			Gravelly clay		
maturation	33% new barrels			33% new barrels		
comments	A light style of Pessac-Léognan			New vinification since 1983		
2nd wine	La Tour Léognan			La Tour Léognan		
Vintage	**Rating**	**Peak**		**Rating**	**Peak**	
1990	9	1997	Complex	8	1997	Fresh, sinewy
1991	4.5	1997	Lean	5	1997	Fluid
1992	4.5	1997	Light	7	1997	Floral
1993	5.5	1999	Good extract	6	1997	Nice and fruity
1994	6	2001	Beefy	7.5	1997	Powerful
1995	7.5	2002	Harmonious, successful	7	2000	Fine
1996	7	2002	Fine, light	6.5	2000	Incisive and light
1997	6	2002	Not very complex	7	2001	Spicy, fine, charming

Pessac-Léognan cru classé (R & W)
Domaine de Chevalier

This is the only classified growth that does not carry the indication "château." The Domaine de Chevalier, formerly "Chibaley," in no way suffers from it, and holds its standing more than honorably, since its white wine is twice the price of its red, which commands the same prices as the second growths of Médoc, if not higher! The domaine had been turned into a pine forest until it was bought by the Ricard family in 1865. Jean Ricard replanted a 91-acre (39-hectare) vineyard, including 10 acres (4 hectares) of white vines. Gabriel Beaumartin, his son-in-law, was to carry on his work, spending lavish sums on the domaine, which he called his *danseuse* (an expensive sideline, like a paramour). Chevalier then reverted to Claude Ricard, who applied to his wines the same artistry he had given to becoming a virtuoso pianist. When he was forced to sell the domaine to Olivier Bernard, the two-men together continued in their quest for perfection. Proven, strict methods applied to an outstanding *terroir* produce rare, complex, secretive wines that are not delivered up to the wine tasters until the years required for their slow development have passed.

production area	Red 86 acres (35 hectares)		10,000 cases		White 10 acres (4 hectares)		1,500 cases	
grape varieties	65% CS, 30% M, 5% CF				70% Sau, 30% Se			
soil	Surface gravel on clay				Surface gravel on clay			
maturation	50% new barrels				25% new barrels			
comments	Straight, true, for keeping				For keeping			
2nd wine	Esprit de Chevalier				Esprit de Chevalier			
Vintage	Rating	Peak			Rating	Peak		
1990	9	2002	Powerful		9	2000	Full	
1991	6	1997	Good extract		9	1997	Pure	
1992	6	1997	Astringent		8	1997	Elegant	
1993	7	1999	Well built		7	1997	Supple	
1994	7	2000	Elegant		7	2003	Fruity	
1995	7	2003	Fine tannins		8	2004	Rich	
1996	7.5	2003	Straight, full-bodied		8	2004	Natural distinction and vigor	
1997	7	2004	Full-bodied, plump		8	2005	Complex and rich	

Château Couhins-Lurton

André Lurton added his own name to that of Couhins in order to distinguish between his vineyard and the one belonging to the French national agronomy research institute, INRA, when Château Couhins was divided in two. Wine has been made here for over two centuries, but the vines nearly disappeared during the 1960s, when the proprietor, Madame Gasqueton, who had been left the domaine by her uncle Hanappier, stated her intention to pull up the vines. André Lurton saved the vineyard when he took over its tenancy in 1967. In 1992 he had the good fortune to buy the château and the winery, enabling him to reconstitute the classified growth. Couhins-Lurton is among the rare single-grape classified growths, and sauvignon reigns supreme on the deep clayey *graves* suitable for white vines. The wine, fermented in barrels in an air-conditioned winery, remains on the lees for nearly a year, and regular lees stirring gives it a full body. Although made entirely with the sauvignon grape, Château Couhins-Lurton will happily withstand the ravages of time; in fact, its density and fermentation mean that it can be cellared for several years, during which time it gains in complexity without losing its aromatic freshness.

production area	15 acres (6 hectares)		3,000 cases
grape varieties	100% Sau		
soil	Sandy gravel		
maturation	45% new barrels		
comments	One of Bordeaux's rare varietal wines		
2nd wine	Château Canteban		

Vintage	Rating	Peak	
1990	10	starting	Well built, rich
1991	5	1997	Floral
1992	5.5	1997	Fine
1993	6	2000	Characteristic of the grape variety
1994	8	2003	A great wine
1995	8	2003	Elegant, classic
1996	8	2003	Finesse and length
1997	7.5	2003	Fine, sharp, sinewy, modern

Pessac-Léognan cru classé (R)
Château de Fieuzal

French writer La Rochefoucauld (1613–1680), who owned Château de Fieuzal, proclaimed his taste for fine wine in his *Maximes:* "I personally hold sobriety to be a form of impotence." When he died, de Fieuzal fell into oblivion. It regained its reputation at the end of the nineteenth century, when it became Pope Leo XIII's favorite wine. Before World War II, Abel Ricard was the master of the house. After his death during the war, the domaine was left to go to seed until taken over by his daughter in 1945. Together with her companion, Erik Bocké, she undertook to revive de Fieuzal, which ended up being a model estate. Since 1974 the latest proprietor, Georges Nègrevergne, has expanded the vineyard and modernized the winery. Vinification is done using traditional methods, except for the high fermentation temperature. The 99-acre (40-hectare) vineyard is in three sections on a soil of thin and thick layers of white gravel.

The blending of cabernet sauvignon (65 percent) and merlot (25 percent) grapes—together with some cabernet franc and petit verdot—produces dense, robust, but distinguished wines. Five hectares of white vines produce a powerful white, marked by the sauvignon, fermented in barrel, but not classified.

production area	Red 86 acres (35 hectares)		11,000 cases		White 12 acres (5 hectares) 1,000 cases
grape varieties	65% CS, 25% M, 5% CF, 5% PV				50% Sau, 50% Se
soil	Thin gravel				Thin gravel
maturation	60% new barrels				New barrels
comments	Very reliable, powerful				Nonclassified growth; outstanding vintages: 1993–94
2nd wine	Abeille de Fieuzal				Abeille de Fieuzal
Vintage	**Rating**	**Peak**			
1990	10	2000	Rich, ripe		Wines strongly marked by the sauvignon grape
1991	4	1997	Light		Peak: 5 years old
1992	5	1997	Good balance		
1993	6	2000	Firm		
1994	6.5	2002	Powerfully built		
1995	7	2002	Serious extract		
1996	7	2003	Close knit		
1997	6.5	2004	Meaty and full-bodied		Full-bodied (stirred), round

Pessac-Léognan cru classé (R)
Château Haut-Bailly

Several families presided over the destinies of Château Haut-Bailly until its purchase in 1872 by Alcide Bellot des Minières, who had trained as an engineer and became a vine enthusiast whose original experiments earned him a great deal of publicity; his own wine's reputation went up considerably as a result. When he died, Haut-Bailly was sold to M. Malvezin, who was also to innovate, by pasteurizing his wines! The domaine then passed through several owners' hands as the vineyard dwindled to no more than a dozen hectares. In 1955 the Sanders family launched a campaign to save the growth, adding another 69 acres (28 hectares) of vines and a winery worthy of them. The current proprietor, Jean Sanders, has two passions: his wine and his airplane. In 1998, Robert Wilmers, an American, purchased Haut-Bailly. Jean Sanders became the manager of his former property. Seen from above, the single expanse of vines, planted at one-meter intervals in both directions, is said to be a fine checkerboard, with a secondary road running through the middle. The vineyard is on a high hillock. The soil is made up of Günz gravel of Pyrenean origin (excellent for the vine) on a compact and watertight iron pan base (bad for rainwater runoff). The wine of Haut-Bailly is dense and attractive, with a richly fruity bouquet and tender, silky flavors.

production area	69 acres (28 hectares)		11,000 cases
grape varieties	65% CS, 25% M, 10% CF		
soil	Pyrenees gravel on iron pan		
maturation	50% new barrels		
comments	A classic of the appellation, very reliable		
2nd wine	La Garde Haut-Bailly		

Vintage	Rating	Peak	
1990	9.5	starting	Full-bodied, rich
1991	no Haut-Bailly		Declassified to second wine
1992	4.5	1997	Plump for a 1992
1993	7.5	2000	Well built, amazing
1994	6.5	2000	Flowing
1995	7	2004	Well built, fruity
1996	8	2004	Well balanced, fine, exemplary, sober
1997	7	2004	Not as good as 1996

Pessac-Léognan cru classé (R)
Château La Mission Haut-Brion

In 1550 these lands, "*22 journals* of vines" and a few outbuildings, were no more than a tenant farm attached to Haut-Brion. When Olive de Lestonnac bought them, she made a gift of them to the mission fathers of Saint Vincent de Paul in 1630. A chapel was built, and the lazarists' wine was highly thought of by Cardinal Richelieu, who drank it in immoderate quantities at the French court. The estate was laicized in the turmoil of the Revolution. After fetching an extravagant price, it subsequently changed hands three times over before coming to the Woltner family, who added onto it the neighboring land of La Tour Haut-Brion. Modern technology—underground winery, steel vats with temperature control—was introduced to the La Mission as early as 1926. In 1983 La Mission turned back the clocks, as the property was merged with Haut-Brion, having been purchased by the duke and duchess of Mouchy. Surrounded by residential blocks, the three sections of the 51.6-acre (20.9-hectare) vineyard, on very large, very deep *graves,* have not changed in a century. La Mission wine is very different from Haut-Brion—a mystery of the union of earth and vine, whose offspring is always unique. This one is black in color, with a smoky fragrance, a strapping body, and a manly temperament. Its rarity keeps its admirers keen.

production area	51.6 acres (20.9 hectares)		7,500 cases	
grape varieties	48% CS, 45% M, 7% CF			
soil	Thick gravel on sandy clay			
maturation	New barrels			
comments	Sweet, powerful roundness			
2nd wine	La Chapelle de la Mission Haut-Brion			

Vintage	Rating	Peak	
1990	10	starting	Smooth
1991	6	1997	Short ending
1992	5	1997	Delicate
1993	6	2000	Balsamic, smoky
1994	7.5	2005	Full
1995	8	2005	Explosively fruity
1996	8	2005	A masculine "Mission"
1997	7	2006	Well built; fine tannins

Pessac-Léognan cru classé (R & W)
Château Latour-Martillac

When Alfred Kressman bought this domaine, in 1929, the wine was sold as Château Latour. To avoid any confusion, he renamed it Latour-Martillac. The name comes from a tower located at the entrance to the property that had been the staircase of a twelfth-century fort. Latour-Martillac has been handed down from father to son in the Kressman family. The modernization of the winemaking premises and restructuring of the vineyard have obviously gone ahead without undermining family traditions. Thus the gold-and-sable stripes on the label have not changed since their famous first appearance at Buckingham Palace in 1936, for the coronation of George VI. As for the vineyard, with its 25 acres (10 hectares) of white grapes, it still has its 85 percent sauvignon and 15 percent semillon. The white wines of Latour-Martillac are therefore highly regarded, offering an outstandingly complex range of aromas and a rich sappiness that asserts itself with age. The red wine too is made from old vines, built around cabernet sauvignon, its major component, and merlot, with some old cabernet franc, malbec, and petit verdot stock. It is a colorful wine, and its very tannic youthful frame becomes supple in time, blending into some very flattering tertiary aromas.

production area	Red 69 acres (28 hectares)		11,000 cases		White 25 acres (10 hectares)		1,500 cases
grape varieties	59% CS, 35% M, 2% CF, 2% PV, 2% Malbec				85% Sau, 15% Se		
soil	Gravel, sand, clay on limestone				Gravel, sand, clay on limestone		
maturation	35% new barrels				50% new barrels		
comments	Different vinification as of the 1988 vintage				New vinification as of the 1986 vintage		
2nd wine	Lagrave-Martillac						
Vintage	**Rating**	**Peak**			**Rating**	**Peak**	
1990	10	2000	Crystallized, long		8	1997	Full-bodied
1991	4.5	1997	Vines frozen		5	1997	Aromatic
1992	5	1997	Light		5	1997	Fine, light
1993	5.5	1997	Not very concentrated		9.5	1999	Complex
1994	6	1999	Spicy, characteristic		7.5	1999	Concentrated
1995	7	2002	Concentrated		7	2001	Aromatic
1996	7	2003	Extensive extract		7.5	2002	Rich and well balanced
1997	6.5	2004	Anise flavored, maximum extract		7	2002	Full-bodied, round

Pessac-Léognan cru classé (W)
Château Laville Haut-Brion

When Henri Woltner bought La Tour Haut-Brion, almost at the same time as La Mission Haut-Brion, the southern end of the vineyard, planted on fine clayey gravel, struck him as not being quite suitable for red wines. On the other hand, the south-facing rich gravel soil appeared ideal for white wine varieties. So he dug up the cabernet and the merlot and planted a 9-acre (3.7-hectare) plot with 70 percent semillon, 27 percent sauvignon and 3 percent muscadelle. The result was a success, and the Laville Haut-Brion white wine won a place in the 1953 classification. In 1983 the estate was taken over by the Clarence-Dillon SA firm—that is, by Haut-Brion. The wines are barrel-fermented and matured in new wood. This is a rare and very expensive wine whose 14,500 bottles annually are in great demand among wealthy wine lovers. Some describe this superbly full-bodied, unctuous wine, with a smooth bouquet that will stay fresh for many years as a dry Sauternes in some years, and its similar grape blend and rich concentration do indeed justify such a description.

production area	9 acres (3.7 hectares)		1,100 cases	
grape varieties	70% Se, 27% Sau, 3% Mu			
soil	Clayey gravel			
maturation	New barrels			
comments	Ageworthy, full-bodied, rich; nothing else quite like it			
Vintage	Rating	Peak		
1990	10	starting		
1992	5	1997	Fluid	
1993	6	2000	Harmonious but limited	
1994	8	2004	Very rich	
1995	7	2002	Needs to blend	
1996	8	2005	1994 style, superb	
1997	7	2005	Unctuous, full	

Pessac-Léognan cru classé (R & W)
Château Malartic-Lagravière

When Pierre Malartic purchased the Lagravière domaine at Léognan in 1803, he added his own name to it. In 1850 it was bought up by the widow of Arnaud Ricard, a capable woman who extended the vineyard to 47 acres (19 hectares). André Ridoret married a Ricard girl and took charge of the estate from 1929. The Ridorets were sailors, and it is their three-master, the *Marie-Elisabeth*, that we see in profile on the Château Malartic-Lagravière label. In 1947 a Ridoret married Jacques Marly, who was to operate the domaine until 1990, in which year Laurent Perrier Champagne bought them out. In 1996 the property again changed hands, with Bruno Marly staying on to ensure continuity. The vineyard is planted on a soil combining gravel, limestone, and clay. The red wine stock includes 50 percent cabernet sauvignon, 25 percent cabernet franc, and 25 percent merlot, while the whites are almost exclusively restricted to sauvignon. Red Château Malartic-Lagravière is deeply colored and develops a pleasant fruity and spicy bouquet, sustained by the strong presence of tannins, which take time to blend. The white wine reveals an amazingly powerful and sinewy sauvignon that comes alive with a variety of complex aromas.

production area	Red 37 acres (15 hectares)		6,000 cases		White 10 acres (4 hectares)		1,200 cases
grape varieties	50% CS, 25% CF, 25% M				85% Sau, 15% Se		
soil	Deep gravel on clay				Deep gravel on clay		
maturation	50% new barrels				50% new barrels		
comments	Finesse rather than power				Strongly marked by the Sauvignon grape		
2nd wine	Sillage de Malartic				Sillage de Malartic		
Vintage	**Rating**	**Peak**			**Rating**	**Peak**	
1990	7.5	1997	A fluid 1990		7	1997	Round
1991	4.5	1997	Vines frozen		5	1997	Well constructed
1992	5	1997	Supple ·		5	1997	Fine
1993	6	1997	Body?		9	starting	Rich, powerful
1994	7	2002	Meaty, successful		8	1997	Fairly dense
1995	7	2002	Stiff tannins		7	1997	Sappy
1996	7	2003	Distinguished, well balanced		7	1999	Fresh and lively
1997	7	2004	Balanced, distinct		6	2000	Fine without affectation

Pessac-Léognan cru classé (R & W)
Château Olivier

The château itself is no impostor, being a twelfth-century fortress. Windows were opened into it to lend a less forbidding appearance to this massive building, with its round towers and waterfilled moat. In 1663 Marie de Lasserre, a Protestant who was the daughter of the lord of Olivier, married Baron de la Brède and bestowed on him the Olivier domaine as her dowry. The only daughter of that marriage was Montesquieu's mother. The Eschenauer firm had the tenancy of the property for many years, but since 1981 M. de Bethmann has taken over the running of Château Olivier himself. The 494-acre (200-hectare) estate includes 74 acres (30 hectares) of red vines, 10 acres (4 hectares) of white. On the higher ground, the soil is made up of Günz gravels similar to those of the Médoc. The three traditional varieties find their full expression here. Farther down, the soil contains more clay and is more suitable for white wines. Under the master's demanding eye, the red wine has gained in concentration and nobility; its initial austerity becomes more refined over a period of years. As for the white, which is also classified, it has the attractive fruitiness of sauvignon, while its backbone grape, semillon, ensures its development. To this is added a mischievous dash of muscadelle.

production area	Red 74 acres (30 hectares) 8,000 cases			White 10 acres (4 hectares) 5,500 cases		
grape varieties	51% CS, 8% CF, 41% M			44% Sau, 48% Se, 8% Mu		
soil	Gravel and clayey limestone			Gravel and clayey limestone		
maturation	40% new barrels			50% new barrels		
comments	The vineyard suffers from its young age			The vineyard suffers from its young age		
2nd wine	Réserve d'Olivier du Château Olivier			Réserve d'Olivier du Château Olivier		
Vintage	Rating	Peak		Rating	Peak	
1990	8.5	1997	Balanced	7	1997	Round
1991	5	1997	Sinewy	5	1997	Light
1992	5	1997	Rounding out	5	1997	Sinewy
1993	5.5	1999	Still sinewy	6	1997	Well balanced
1994	6	2000	Dense	6	starting	Floral
1995	7	2003	Concentrated	6	2000	Closed; wait
1996	7	2004	Nice tannins	7	2000	Spicy, woody
1997	6	2004	Average complexity	6	2001	Nicely characteristic

Pessac-Léognan cru classé (R)
Château Pape Clément

Pape Clément's history dates further back than that of any other Bordeaux growth, and we are certain of the details since it involves an eminently important figure: Pope Clement V. In 1299, on his appointment as archbishop of Bordeaux, Bertrand de Goth received an estate with a vineyard and woods at Pessac from his brother. Six years later he was elected the first Avignon pope. Next to souls, wine was his main concern, and the financial revenues of the archbishopric did well out of it: Clement V had no compunction about selling his wines during his numerous journeys afield. He tended the vineyard, making sure that the grapes were harvested by married couples! Upon his death, the domaine took the name of Pape Clément and remained church property until the Revolution, when it was sold off as a national asset. When Paul Montagne bought Pape Clément from the Maxwells, the vineyard was devastated in a hailstorm. He then devoted his efforts to reviving the domaine, and since 1983 his son Léo and son-in-law Bernard Magrez have been reaping the fruits of his labors. The château and winery have been renovated, and the vineyard covers 80 acres (32.5 hectares). Cabernet sauvignon and merlot play a balanced duet in this symphony of a generous wine with a seductive bouquet.

production area	Red 74 acres (30 hectares)		10,000 cases	White 6 acres (2.5 hectares)	300 cases
grape varieties	60% CS, 40% M			45% Sau, 45% Se, 10% Mu	
soil	Sandy gravel on limestone			Sandy gravel on limestone	
maturation	70% new barrels			New barrels	
comments	The 1981 and 1982 vintages suffered owing to contamination of the winery			Nonclassified growth	
2nd wine	Le Clémentin du Pape Clément				

Vintage	Rating	Peak		
1990	10	1997	Powerful	
1991	4.5	1997	Short	
1992	5	1997	Limited	Sold in very small quantities
1993	6	1996	Not full-bodied	
1994	7	2000	Well balanced	A delicate, floral wine, for drinking at 5 years of age
1995	7.5	2003	Full and rich	
1996	8	2005	Complexity, roundness, length	Remarkable
1997	7.5	2005	Fine and ripe tannins	Fresh, light, pure, true. For 2000

208

Pessac-Léognan cru classé (R)
Château Smith Haut-Lafitte

In 1720 George Smith bought the property that had been operated under the name Lafitte since 1549, giving the name Smith Haut-Lafitte to the vineyard located on a hummock covered with fine, deep Günz gravel. In 1856 the mayor of Bordeaux, Sadi Duffour-Debergier, became the new owner, and his nursing of the vines earned him a purely honorific gold medal. The estate was taken over by the Louis-Eschenauer firm in 1958.

A substantial injection of capital improved operating conditions, and a vast underground winery was built with space for over two thousand barrels. In 1990 Daniel Cathiard took over the domaine, where he introduced a new direction in the working of the vineyard—with tight controls on yields—and in the winery, with strict practice the order of the day. Forty-four hectares of vines, mostly cabernet sauvignon, were allocated to red wine, and 27 acres (11 hectares) of sauvignon for nonclassified white. These wines, from vines in their prime and fermented in optimum conditions, are attracting the attention of the specialist media, always on the lookout for competitive wines in the race for excellence.

production area	Red 109 acres (44 hectares)		20,000 cases	White 27 acres (11 hectares)	5,000 cases
grape varieties	55% CS, 35% M, 10% CF			100% Sau	
soil	Fine gravel			Fine gravel	
maturation	50% new barrels			50% new barrels	
comments				Nonclassified growth	
2nd wine	Les Hauts de Smith				

Vintage	Rating	Peak		
1990	9	1997	Velvety	
1991	5	1997	Astringent	
1992	4.5	1997	Light	Very good white wine, vinified with the sauvignon
1993	7	1997	Tannic	flavor for drinking at 4 years old.
1994	7	1997	Ripe	The 1995 and 1996 vintages are superb.
1995	7.5	2003	Round	
1996	7.5	2004	Complex, fine tannins	
1997	7	2004	Difficult, yet perfectly successful vintage	1997 is as handsome as previous years. For drinking fairly soon (2–3 years)

Pessac-Léognan
La Louvière

During the fifteenth century La Louvière was home to a
Bordeaux poet, Jehan de Guilloche. His grandson married one
Mademoiselle de Roquetaille, and the estate remained in the
de Roquetaille family until 1618. At that time it was bought
by Father Armand de Gascq, who left it to the Carthusians,
and they cultivated the vines until the Revolution. In 1791
La Louvière was sold off to the Mareilhac family, who had the
current château built, attributed to Victor Louis. The superb
grounds romantically cast their reflection in a lake, and La
Louvière recently became a listed site. In 1965 André Lurton
bought La Louvière, giving it the wherewithal to produce a
growth that would not be out of place among the best wines of
the appellation. High output is an extra advantage in getting a
worldwide audience for the excellent Pessac-Léognan wines.
In the vast, unbroken vineyard, 82 acres (33 hectares) are given
over to red wine, and 37 acres (15 hectares) to white. The red
La Louyière wines are fruity, beefy, and models of dependability.
The elegant, delicate whites develop a luxurious bouquet.

production area	Red 82 acres (33 hectares)		18,000 cases	White 37 acres (15 hectares)		7,500 cases
grape varieties	64% CS, 30% M, 3% CF, 3% PV			85% Sau, 15% Se		
soil	Gravel			Gravel		
maturation	50% new barrels			50% new barrels		
comments	Not classified, but on a par with the classified growths. Fine wines, delicate rather than powerful					
2nd wine	L de La Louvière					
Vintage	Rating	Peak				
1990	9	starting	Round			
1991	5	1997	Sharp tannins			
1992	5.5	1997	Fine extract for the year			
1993	6.5	1997	Powerful, full-bodied	Distinguished, reliable white wine, distinctively		
1994	6.5	1999	Very well constructed	sauvignon, for drinking at around 4 years old		
1995	7	2003	Strong extract			
1996	7	2004	Concentrated, powerful			
1997	6.5	2005	Strong extracts	The 1997 vintage is fine and pure. For drinking at 2–3 years old		

Graves
Clos Floridène

AOC Graves is the only appellation in France with a name
that refers to the geological nature of the soil. The area used to
extend as far as Bordeaux, but since 1987 the top end of the
appellation has gone its own way, calling itself Pessac-Léognan.
The legitimacy of this separation may be questioned when one
tastes a Clos Floridène, whose vines (65 miles, or 40 km, outside
Bordeaux) are planted on a rather special soil, similar to AOC
Barsac: the renowned red sands on a limestone base. These
clayey sands are very suitable for white wine grapes, and Denis
Dubourdieu—often nicknamed the "Pope of white wines," as
he operates as consultant enologist for a number of classified
Pessac-Léognan growths—deploys all his artistry in this Clos,
which is actually a real enclosure, surrounded by walls. Needless
to say, he uses the techniques he has championed, a certain
"burgundianization" of Bordeaux white wine making procedures,
including fermenting and maturing in wood and lees stirring
(bâtonnage), but no malolactic fermentation. A white Clos
Floridène—for there is a red too—is round and full-bodied
(but not too), with good length. It can and must age if the
semillon is to give its full expression.

production area	66 acres (12 hectares), and 12 acres (5 hectares) of red		6,000 cases	
grape varieties	50% Se, 30% Sau, 20% Mu			
soil	Red sand on limestone			
maturation	30% new barrels			
comments	Dry white AOC Graves n° 1			
2nd wine	Le Second de Floridène			

Vintage	Rating	Peak		
1990	10	1997	Rich	
1991	7	1997	Light, sinewy, distinguished	
1992	6	1997	Meaty semillon	
1993	7	1997	Exuberant sauvignon	
1994	7.5	starting	Grapy, polished, reserved	
1995	8	1999	Meaty, elegant	
1996	8.5	2000	Powerful, concentrated	
1997	7.5	2000	Fine and delicate aromas	

Sauternes premier cru supérieur classé
Château d'Yquem

Built on a mound that rises to 246 feet (75 meters), this château has preserved several of the enclosure walls of the twelfth-century fort purchased in 1592 by the Sauvage family. Joséphine Sauvage married Compte Louis-Amédée de Lur-Saluces, and for three centuries, Yquem remained under Lur-Saluces ownership. Even the Revolution was powerless against this heritage, which was not held to be feudal property. Since the death of Marquis Bertrand de Lur-Saluces in 1968, his nephew Alexander, comte de Lur-Saluces, has upheld the aura of glory that illuminates the worldwide reputation of Château d'Yquem. The 247-acre (100-hectare) vineyard is tended like a garden. Each and every operation is special, with attention to every detail—selective picking of the grapes, overripened to a turn and duly botrytized, pressing and barrel fermentation, followed by maturation for three and a half years, with twice-weekly topping up. The bottom line is, one glass of Château d'Yquem per vine! Yquem is the absolute, quintessential Sauternes, a symphony of aromas, an elixir of golden fluid that in its glass prison retains its infinite youth while taking on an amber gleam. It is a unique beverage to be tasted with devotion, gourmandise, and sensuous delight.

production area	247 acres (100 hectares)	8,000 cases	
grape varieties	80% Se, 20% Sau		
soil	Gravel and sand on limestone		
maturation	New barrels, three years maturing, four years between harvesting and marketing		
comments	Many wine lovers place its peak at twenty years of age		
Vintage	Rating		
1990	10	A legendary Yquem	
1991	8	Small harvest	

Sauternes premier cru classé
Château Clos Haut-Peyraguey

In 1879, the uppermost section of Château Peyraguey was sold to a pharmaceutical chemist called Grillon, and took on the name Clos Haut-Peyraguey without forfeiting its first-growth classification. The remaining section became Lafaurie-Peyraguey. In 1914 the domaine was purchased by Eugène Garbay and Fernand Ginestet. Jacques Pauly, an heir to the Garbay estate, has been the lucky owner since 1948. The 40-acre (16-hectare) vineyard, just across the road from Lafaurie-Peyraguey, comprises two parcels, one rising to 236 feet (72 meters) facing Château d'Yquem, the other following on from the vines of that same château. The soil is a combination of gravels and sand on a clay base. The grape mix is a typical Sauternes blend, with mostly semillon, seconded by 15 percent sauvignon and 2 percent muscadelle. The harvest, which involves several successive sortings, tends to pick the semillon when "fully rotten," but the sauvignon when only well ripened, so as not to lose any of its aromas. Finesse rather than power is what characterizes the wine of Clos Haut-Peyraguey. Its delicacy makes it a wine for those who like their Sauternes aromatic, fresh, and light.

production area	40 acres (16 hectares)		2,500 cases	
grape varieties	83% Se, 15% Sau, 2% Mu			
soil	Sandy gravel			
maturation	25% new barrels			
comments	Classical			
Vintage	Rating	Peak		
1990	10	2000	Rich, botrytized	
1991	5.5	1997	Light, fine	
1992	5	1997	Light, fine	
1993	5	1997	Light, fine	
1994	6.5	2000	Botrytized and fat	
1995	7	2003	Even fuller than 1994	
1996	8	2005	Very fine botrytis	
1997	8	2005	Excellent as always	

Sauternes premier cru classé
Château Guiraud

This growth was classified in 1855 under the name of Bayle. M. Solar sold it in 1862 to the Bernard family, who in turn sold it to Paul Rival. Château Guiraud again came up for sale in around 1970 and was without a buyer for roughly ten years, while the property and its reputation went into decline. In 1981 a Canadian-born ship owner's son, Hamilton Narby, put this situation to rights when he bought this vast 296-acre (120 hectare) domaine. Everything was rather dilapidated, but a substantial injection of funds revived the fortunes of Château Guiraud. Located above Sauternes, the single 247-acre (100-hectare) stretch of vineyard lies on a gravel-clay soil and slopes down toward the river Ciron, which collects rainwater and ensures the morning mists that encourage botrytis. Plenty of sunshine was the other positive factor on which Hamilton Narby staked his ambitions, using Château d'Yquem as a model. With such aspirations and such confidence, it should come as no surprise that Château Guiraud is improving every year. Characterized by the sauvignon grape (35 percent), the wines are sinewy and fruity, and derive their good aging qualities from their semillon.

production area	247 acres (100 hectares)		8,000 cases	
grape varieties	65% Se, 35% Sau			
soil	Gravelly clay			
maturation	45% new barrels			
comments	New owner since 1981. Remarkable wines since 1983			
2nd wine	Le Dauphin de Ch. Guiraud			

Vintage	Rating	Peak	
1990	10	2005	Balanced, powerful
1992	5	1997	Light, sauvignon flavor
1993	4.5	1997	Too light
1994	6.5	2000	Botrytized
1995	7.5	2002	Full-bodied and botrytized
1996	8	2004	Generous, overripened
1997	8	2006	A great Guiraud

Sauternes premier cru classé
Château Lafaurie-Peyraguey

As is common in the Sauternes, this château is an ancient fort, with crenellated walls, corner towers, and a keep still standing. The buildings were obviously reorganized during the eighteenth century by M. de Pichard, president of the Bordeaux Parliament (and also owner of Château Lafite), who was guillotined during the Revolution. When the national assets were being sold, it was bought by M. Lafaurie, who added his name to it. The growth became famous, being particularly favored by the king of Spain. In 1864 Lafaurie's widow sold the property to a minister, Duchâtel. His heirs sold it to Farinel and Grédy at a time when the estate had already been separated from what was to become Clos Haut-Peyraguey. Finally the Ets Cordier firm purchased Château Lafaurie-Peyraguey in 1913 and expanded the vineyard to its present-day 99 acres (40 hectares).

Enologist Georges Pauli has contrived to harness modern enological and technological resources to traditional methods to produce a high-quality first growth. The semillon gives it finesse, complexity, and lastingness, while the sauvignon and muscadelle contribute liveliness and attractive aromas of fruit and flowers.

production area	99 acres (40 hectares)		7,000 cases	
grape varieties	90% Se, 5% Sau, 5% Mu			
soil	Pyrenean gravel			
maturation	40% new barrels			
comments	Fine vinification since the 1980s			
2nd wine	La Chapelle de Lafaurie			
Vintage	**Rating**	**Peak**		
1990	10	1997	Rich and balanced	
1991	5	1997	Easy	
1992	5	1997	Light	
1993	5	1997	Fine, light	
1994	6.5	starting	Supple, crystallized fruit	
1995	7.5	2002	Botrytized, full-bodied	
1996	8	2003	Supple, balanced	
1997	8	2004	Fresh; not as full-bodied as others	

Sauternes premier cru classé
Château La Tour Blanche

The only white tower here is the one on the label. It gets its name from Jean Saint-Marc-de-Latourblanche, treasurer general to Louis XVI, who died at Bommes in 1784. Château La Tour Blanche received a first-growth classification in 1855, when the chamber of commerce placed it at the top of the first growths, just behind the "superior" Château d'Yquem. At the time it belonged to someone named Focke, who died shortly afterward, and the estate was sold off. The buyer was Daniel Osiris, and when he died in 1907 he disclosed in his will that he was making a gift of his domaine to the state, provided it was used to set up an agricultural college. This was done in 1911. Ever since, this domaine has been used to teach young trainee viticulturists, who lend a hand with all the tasks in the vineyard, fermenting house, and winery. Jean-Pierre Jausserand, the brilliant director of both the college and the château itself, has given the wines of Château La Tour Blanche the stimulus they needed to recover their high standing. The growth is constantly improving and asserting its personality. Its ambition is evident from these rich, harmonious wines with their lingeringly seductive aromas.

production area	77 acres (31 hectares)		6,000 cases	
grape varieties	77% Se, 20% Sau, 3% Mu			
soil	Gravel, sand on clay			
maturation	New barrels			
2nd wine	Mademoiselle de Saint-Marc			
Vintage	Rating	Peak		
1990	10	2000	Round	
1991	5		Frozen	
1994	6	2000	Plummy	
1995	7.5	2002	Full, crystallized, botrytized	
1996	7.5	2003	Rich	
1997	8	2005	Creamy, aromatic	

Sauternes premier cru classé
Château Rabaud-Promis

The first half of the domaine's name comes from Marie Peyronne de Rabaud, who married Arnaud de Cazeau in 1660. The Rabaud vineyard remained a Cazeau heirloom until 1819. When the growth was classified in 1855, the owner was Gabriel Deyme. In 1903 the property, then owned by the Drouilhet de Sigalas family, was divided into two parts, one of which was sold to Adrien Promis and given his name, the other being named Rabaud-Sigalas. Both estates kept their first-growth classification. In 1950, the then owner of Rabaud-Promis, Pierre Ginestet, sold it off to its present owner, the Lanneluc family, who have placed Philippe Dejean in charge. Eighty-two acres (33 hectares) of vines in a single stretch of vineyard cover a south-facing hillock topped by the chateau itself.

On a gravelly soil containing plenty of clay, the semillon vines dominate among the three Sauternes grape varieties. Picking the grapes is a long, drawn-out affair, and the wines are separated by sorting and by plot before being fermented in the barrel. A cryo-extraction system is used. In recent years Rabaud-Promis wines have stood out in wine tasting sessions thanks to their fine, lingering bouquet. A wine with amazing concentration and great nobility.

production area	82 acres (33 hectares)		5,000 cases
grape varieties	80% Se, 18% Sau, 2% Mu		
soil	Clayey gravel		
maturation	30% new barrels		
comments	Rabaud-Promis is where cryo-extraction was researched		
Vintage	**Rating**	**Peak**	
1990	10	starting	Powerful and lively
1991	5	1997	Easy
1992	5	1997	Light
1993	5.5	1997	Average body
1994	6	2000	Rain
1995	7	2003	Botrytized
1996	7	2003	Balanced
1997	6	2003	Less botrytized than others

Château Rayne-Vigneau

Originally called Vigneau in the seventeenth century, the estate was given a first-growth classification in 1855, at which time it belonged to Baroness de Rayne. In 1860 she left it to Gabriel de Pontac; he passed it on to his nephew Albert, who christened it Rayne-Vigneau. This growth covered itself in glory at the Great Exhibition of 1867, in a blind tasting in which the panel of judges picked out Château Rayne-Vigneau 1861 as the best Sauternes, ahead of a Rhineland wine. Following M. de Pontac, his son-in-law, the Viscount of Roton, took over the management of the property. An inquisitive and cultured man, he made a great hobby of researching the minerals he discovered in the soil of his vast estate. In this way he built up an impressive collection of fossils, semiprecious stones, and rock crystals. The 195-acre (79-hectare) vineyard was sold in 1961 to Paul Raoux, but the château and the grounds remained the property of the De Roton family. Since 1971 the domaine has been taken over by a non-trading company run by J.-P. de la Beaumelle. Rayne-Vigneau, which has everything it takes to be successful—*terroir,* climate, modern facilities—has improved considerably in recent vintages. It already has distinction and finesse. What we now expect of it are more richness and brilliance.

production area	195 acres (79 hectares)		6,700 cases	
grape varieties	75% Se, 23% Sau, 2% Mu			
soil	Sandy gravel			
maturation	50% new barrels			
comments	Quality improves at the end of 1980			
2nd wine	Clos l'Abeilley			
Vintage	**Rating**	**Peak**		
1990	10	starting	A model of balance	
1991	5	1997	Light	
1992	5	1997	Lively	
1994	6	1997	Fluid and fine	
1995	6.5	2000	Elegant botrytis	
1996	7	2001	Attractively balanced	
1997	8	2003	The best since 1990; might become superior	

Sauternes premier cru classé
Château Rieussec

This domaine belonged to the monks of Langon until it was sold as a national asset during the Revolution. As the years passed and successive generations took over, Rieussec was transformed, expanded, and reorganized. In 1855 M. Mayne had the satisfaction of seeing his wine classified as a first growth. After changing hands on a number of occasions, Rieussec was bought in 1971 by Albert Vuillier, who held onto it for ten years or so. Then the domaines belonging to Rothschild, also owner of Château Lafite, took over the destiny of this vast 185-acre (75-hectare) estate, bringing their perfectionist methods to bear. This single vineyard gives pride of place to the semillon grape, with only 18 percent sauvignon and 2 percent muscadelle. The soil—gravel, clay, or sand on an iron pan base—is so poor that it has to lie fallow for five years before replanting. The vinification and maturing processes have been adapted to suit the tastes and resources of the new purchaser. Already, wine specialists and tasters of all nationalities are noting how Rieussec, once full-bodied and concentrated but occasionally heavy, is now nobler and richer, with finesse and elegance.

production area	185 acres (75 hectares)		10,000 cases	
grape varieties	80% Se, 18% Sau, 2% Mu			
soil	Gravel, sand on iron pan			
maturation	50% new barrels			
comments	Full-bodied, becomes colored as it develops. This does not affect the wine			
2nd wine	Clos Labère			
Vintage	**Rating**	**Peak**		
1990	10	2000	Full-bodied and balanced	
1991	5.5	1997	Frozen vines	
1992	5	1997	Floral	
1994	7.5	2000	Full-bodied, distinctive, voluptuous	
1995	8	2002	Opulent, botrytized	
1996	8	2005	Rich, full-bodied, lavish	
1997	8.5	2006	Exceptional wine in every respect	

Sauternes premier cru classé
Château Sigalas Rabaud

The portion belonging to Henry Drouilhet de Sigalas took this name of Sigalas Rabaud to distinguish it from the other plot detached from Château Rabaud and purchased by M. Promis. The two properties kept the title of first growth that Château Rabaud had earned in the 1855 classification. The Lambert des Granges family owns Château Sigalas Rabaud; thus the domaine has stayed in the family, as one of the Sigalas girls had married the marquis de Lambert des Granges in 1930. Since 1995, the Ets Cordier firm have been in charge of the Sigalas tenancy, and their demand for quality was soon to influence production. The 35 acres (14 hectares) of vineyard are on a west-facing slope, and most of them are given over to the semillon grape, with only 15 percent sauvignon, on a clay-gravel soil. The wine is made and matured in vats, not in the wood, applying the theories of Count Emmanuel de Lambert with regard to very sweet wines. Strength and alcoholic content are not sought-after qualities, and these very fine wines have a powerful floral bouquet to both the nose and palate and a subtle seductiveness.

production area	35 acres (14 hectares)		2,500 cases
grape varieties	85% Se, 15% Sau		
soil	Clay-gravel		
maturation	60% new barrels		
comments	Ets Cordier in charge of winemaking as of 1994		

Vintage	Rating	Peak	
1990	10	1997	Elegant, fine
1991	5.5	1997	Frozen vines
1992	5	1997	Light
1994	6	1997	Lemony, woody
1995	7.5	2000	The finest botrytis
1996	8	2003	Finesse and power
1997	8.5	2005	The perfect botrytization (plus elegance)

Sauternes premier cru classé
Château Suduiraut

The old manor house was burned down upon the instigation of the Duke of Epernon, and the superb present-day château was built around 1670, and set off with a French garden designed by André Le Nôtre. The label carries the marking "cru du Roy" (the king's growth), a remnant of the family name of its former owner, or maybe—we are not sure about this—an allusion to a bounty bestowed on Suduiraut by Louis XIV. Be that as it may, this sweet wine, and the places where it is made, are certainly fit for a king. In fact, the reputation of this growth, given a first-growth rating in 1855, has never been in question. After the phylloxera epidemic, the vineyard, replanted to be trained on wire by E. Petit de Forest, grew to reach its present area of 222 acres (90 hectares). The Fonquernies bought this immense domaine in 1940 and administered it jointly with Madame Frouin and cellarmaster M. Pascaud. The latter remained in control when Axa Millésimes took over ownership. With 80 percent semillon and 20 percent sauvignon, the grape mix is rather similar to that used for Château d'Yquem. Yields and vinification are controlled with a very firm hand. One is awed by the magnificence of this wine, which reaches new heights in its special cuvée (or blend), "crême de tête." Its complexity and delicate aromas, the perfect balance of its supple, sappy, and fresh qualities, are the miracle of a great sweet wine.

production area	222 acres (90 hectares)		10,000 cases	
grape varieties	80% Se, 20% Sau			
soil	Sandy gravel			
maturation	50% new barrels			
comments	The Axa Millésimes corporation took over in 1992. Needs watching closely			
2nd wine	Castelnau de Suduiraut			

Vintage	Rating	Peak	
1990	10	1999	Full and fine
1994	7	2003	Botrytized
1995	8	2005	In the spirit of 1988, 1989, 1990
1996	8	2005	Close to the above
1997	7.5	2004	Very rich, almost heavy

Sauternes deuxième cru classé
Château Filhot

In 1709 the property was bought by the Filhots, a noble family known back in the fifteenth century in Guyenne. When it was sold off as a national asset at the time of the French Revolution, some severe frosts ruined the vineyard, and in 1806 Joséphine de Filhot, marquess of Lur-Saluces, recovered the family heritage for a very reasonable price. Her husband, chamberlain to Napoleon I, also obtained a loan to restore the vineyard. The fame of the Filhot growth was such that it made the 1855 classification at a time when their son, Romain-Bertrand de Lur-Saluces, was in charge of the domaine. He added two wings to the eighteenth-century château. The buildings occupy 5 acres (2 hectares) of the 815 of the domaine overall. The vineyard, which has varied in size over the centuries, currently extends over a single 148-acre (60-hectare) stretch, with the nearby forest increasing the likelihood of frost. The Château Filhot has been headed since 1974 by Count Henri de Vaucelles. The vineyard and winemaking processes receive careful, conventional management. The growth is appreciated for its delicacy, its very aromatic fruitiness, and a pleasing, elegant, and yet generous lightness.

production area	148 acres (60 hectares)		1,000 cases	
grape varieties	50% Se, 45% Sau, 5% Mu			
soil	Gravel on limestone			
maturation	In vats, or short stay in preferably new wood			
comments	Extraordinary wines: 300 cases of "big frost wine" in 1985, in 1990 a special sorting for an outstanding Sauternes			
Vintage	**Rating**	**Peak**		
1990	10	2000	Sumptuous	
1991	5	1997	Sinewy	
1992	4.5	1997	Dilute, rains	
1993	4	past		
1994	6	2000	Sinewy and fruity	
1995	7	2002	Sinewy, fruity, and botrytized	
1996	7	2003	Perfect sugar/acid balance	
1997	6.5	2003	Fine, without being airy	

Sauternes deuxième cru classé
Château de Malle

This magnificent domaine has belonged for five centuries to the same de Malle family. At the beginning of the 17th century, Jacques de Malle, president of the Bordeaux Parliament, had built this superb, classical château together with the Italian grounds, both of which are listed historic monuments. In 1702, Jeanne de Malle married Eutrope-Alexandre de Lur-Saluces. Thus it came about that the Lur-Saluces became the lords of Malle before being so at Yquem. Pierre de Bournazel, who was a direct descendant of the Lur-Saluces, was the last master of Malle. Since his sudden death in 1985 his wife, Countess Nancy de Bournazel, has been in charge of the domaine, carrying on from where her husband left off.

The 62-acre (25-hectare) vineyard is planted on a siliceous base covered by sand and fine clay-gravel soil. After the big freeze of 1956, it was replanted with 75 percent semillon, 23 percent sauvignon, and 2 percent muscadelle vines. The grapes are harvested by selective sorting by grape variety and by plot. This richly unctuous wine reflects the nobility of the house; it is seductive without being arrogant, and is subtly and discreetly charming.

production area	62 acres (25 hectares)		5,000 cases	
grape varieties	75% Se, 23% Sau, 2% Mu			
soil	Clay-gravel and sand			
maturation	Vats and casks			
comments	The wine, always with the same finesse, became more full-bodied as of the (highly successful) 1986 vintage			
2nd wine	Château de Sainte-Hélène			
Vintage	**Rating**	**Peak**		
1990	10	1997	Fine, complex, long	
1991	5.5	1998	Floral	
1994	6	starting	Finely botrytized	
1995	7	2001	Complex, full	
1996	7.5	2003	Fruit, botrytis, wood, finesse	
1997	7	2003	The classic fruitiness of Malle	

Sauternes
Château de Fargues

The château was built in 1306 by Cardinal Raimond-Guilhem de Fargues, a nephew of Pope Clement V, on the site of an old fortress. This ancient building with its massive outline has survived the ravages of time, but remains a testimony to the warring past of the Sauternes region. The Lur-Saluces family, of the old nobility, had owned it since the marriage of Pierre de Lur with Isabeau de Montferrand in 1472. So Fargues figures among the heritage of the Lur-Saluces, over three centuries before Yquem. The small vineyard, which is also of a respectable age, extends over 32 acres (13 hectares). The success of Fargues's sweet wine is recent and is of course linked to its owner's reputation. During the 1970s it made a name for itself in the monographs of the famous writer on wine, C. Féret, and has become a great favorite of a few well-informed wine lovers.

When we remember that Fargues is treated with the perfectionist methods that have mostly taken their inspiration from those applied at Yquem, we understand how, although not classified, this wine has its unconditional enthusiasts. It has the dazzling qualities of a great Sauternes: seductive bouquet, fine sparkle, and a fine long life.

production area	32 acres (13 hectares)	1,000 cases
grape varieties	80% Se, 20% Sau	
soil	Gravel on clay-gravel	
maturation	New barrels	
comments	Exceptional nonclassified wines. Reach their best at eight years of age. The 1990 vintage achieves perfection. Note the duration of barrel aging: at least three years. The wine is thus marketed four years after the harvest.	

Sauternes
Château Gilette

At Preignac, the Médeville family has been making Sauternes for over two centuries. There was Numa, then Joseph, René, and now Christian Médeville, who at Château Gilette and Château Les Justices have been carrying on the family tradition of always doing better. Les Justices, a vineyard covering 21 acres (8.5 hectares), produces an exquisite Sauternes with extravagant flavors of flowers, fruit, and honey, which is sold after two years in the cellar. With Château Gilette, we come to the outstanding wine, in a kind of Médeville Sauternes museum. Here a tiny 11-acre (4.5-hectare) domaine is reserved for an extremely long-lived nectar, a sweet wine that only comes into is own after having been kept for years in inert vats, something quite unique in the case of a great wine. Twenty years old, isn't that the best age? It is at least the age of the marvellous bottles that Christian and Andrée Médeville propose—in tiny quantities moreover, as quantities are limited and takers many. It is a curiosity to be tasted with emotion and respect. We find in it the melted savors of the past. As writer André Gide has put it, "Patina is the reward of masterpieces."

production area	11 acres (4.5 hectares)	600 cases
grape varieties	90% Se, 8% Sau, 2% Mu	
soil	Gravelly sand on limestone	
maturation	Twenty years in a concrete vat (!)	
comments	Absolutely unique. The youngest vintage on sale is the 1976. 1976, 1975, and 1967, currently on offer, are worth 10 out of 10, the incomparable 1970 9.5 out of 10, if we are very hard to please. For drinking now, or in ten, twenty, or thirty year's time!	

Barsac premier cru classé
Château Climens

During the sixteenth century Jean Climens gave this domaine his name, and later it belonged to the Roborel family. In 1802 Eloi Lacoste began his skilfull reign over Climens, which was given a first ranking in the 1855 classification. In the late nineteenth century it was taken over by the Gounouihous, who maintained its high reputation. Problems in handing down the estate placed it in a difficult situation, however, until Lucien Lurton bought it up for two of his ten children, Brigitte and Marie-Laure. Everything was then undertaken to restore this first-growth Barsac to its confirmed reputation.

The estate's 72 acres (29 hectares) form an extended rectangle one kilometer long, which overlooks Barsac from a height of 66 feet (20 meters). The soil is made up of red sands and gravel on a fissured calcareous base. The semillon grape has pride of place at Climens, being best suited to botrytization by the noble rot, encouraged by late harvesting. The wine is made in casks and aged in wooden barrels for two years. Only the juice from the first pressings goes into Château Climens, as it has to stay at a peak of sweet and delicate concentration. This great and distinguished Barsac offers a spectacular display of aromas and is remarkably long-lived.

production area	72 acres (29 hectares)		3,000 cases	
grape varieties	100% Se			
soil	Red sands, Mendel gravel on limestone			
maturation	35% new barrels			
comments	Ages extremely well			
2nd wine	Les Cyprès de Climens			

Vintage	Rating	Peak	
1990	10	after 2000	Powerful and rich
1991	6	now	Fine
1994	6	1998	Fine
1995	7.5	2003	Botrytized
1996	8	2004	Rich and full-bodied
1997	8	2005	Already complex

Barsac premier cru classé
Château Coutet

The architecture of Château Coutet tells us about its military past during the Hundred Years War. It was restored during the sixteenth century, and Gabriel de Filhot, president of the Bordeaux Parliament, purchased the estate in 1788. Filhot was guillotined during the French Revolution, and Coutet then became part of the vast winegrowing empire of the Lur-Saluces, who already owned Yquem, Filhot, Malle, Fargues, and others. In 1922 an industrialist from Lyons, M. Guy, bought the property. One of his daughters married Edmond Rolland, who masterfully governed the estate until 1977. The property was then bought up by Marcel Baly, an industrialist from Strasbourg, for whom the making of a quality wine has been a constant concern, together with the reputation of Château Coutet. Ninety-four acres (38 hectares) of old vines surrounded by walls, from the three ritual grape varieties, grow on various soils covering a plain of asteriated limestone. The wine of Château Coutet is very fruity and ages admirably well. In outstanding years a special selection of wine from the first pressings produces the precious and unaffordable Cuvée Madame, an unbelievably unctuous Barsac with endlessly lingering aftertastes.

production area	94 acres (38 hectares)		8,500 cases	
grape varieties	75% Se, 23% Sau, 2% Mu			
soil	Fine gravel, sand			
maturation	40% new barrels			
comments	The quintessential Coutet: Cuvée Madame—1,200 bottles in outstanding years			
2nd wine	La Chartreuse de Château Coutet			
Vintage	Rating	Peak		
1990	10	2000	Elegant, perfect	
1994	7	2000	Supreme finesse	
1995	8	2003	Complex	
1996	8	2004	Elegant, lively, rich	
1997	8.5	2005	Dry fruit with white flesh; powerful	

Barsac deuxième cru classé
Château Caillou

Continuity presides over the destiny of Château Caillou. After belonging to the Sarraute family throughout the nineteenth century, it was then bought up by Joseph Ballen, the grandfather of the current owner, Mme Bravo. Classified as a second growth in 1855, the domaine has kept the acreage of its vineyard unchanged around its small château, a charming manor house with two pinnacle turrets. The 32-acre (13-hectare) vineyard extends over a flat stretch of sandy *graves* on a limestone bottom soil. Semillon is the largely dominant grape variety, set off by a dash of 10 percent sauvignon. The fermenting room has been modernized over the years. The wine ferments in small 177-cubic-foot (50-hectoliter) stainless steel vats, and a new type of horizontal press makes it possible to press limited amounts with a light touch. This classified Barsac growth has remained loyal to extended barrel aging, however, and has kept to a traditional style. If the year has been unfavorable, Jean-Bernard Bravo, a demanding artist, takes a firm line; there was no Château Caillou in 1972, 1974, or 1984. Outstanding years are marked by an exceptional wine, fermented in casks and called Private Cuvée. Château Caillou reveals a delightful bouquet of plums and flower honey.

production area	32 acres (13 hectares)		3,000 cases	
grape varieties	90% Se, 10% Sau			
soil	Sandy gravel on limestone			
maturation	20% new barrels			
comments	Surface area unchanged since the 1855 classification. Recent family problems have affected the winemaking.			
2nd wine	Château Haut-Mayne			

Vintage	Rating	Peak	
1990	10	2005	Powerful and rich
1991	5	1997	Fluid
1992	5	1997	Light
1993	4.5	1997	Thin
1994	5.5	starting	Vines frozen. Candied rather than fine
1995	7.5	2002	Botrytized and fine
1996	5	2002?	Unbalanced
1997	5	?	Unbalanced

Barsac deuxième cru classé
Château Doisy-Daëne

This château has kept the name of M. Daëne, who was the owner of Doisy at the time of the 1855 classification. After M. Dejean, it was Georges Dubourdieu who bought the vineyard in 1924, when it covered only 10 acres (4 hectares). This acreage was increased thanks to his son, Pierre Dubourdieu, who ran the business until 1945. The 37-acre (15-hectare) vineyard is divided into two plots, one next to Doisy-Védrines to the southeast, the other touching on Doisy-Dubroca. In former times these three entities belonged to a single estate. The soil is red and gravelly, on fissury limestone. The vinestocks are planted in the following proportions: 75 percent semillon, 20 percent sauvignon, and 5 percent muscadelle. The harvest takes place in numerous successive selective pickings, and the grapes are pressed very slowly and vinified following a well-researched method. The wine ages in new casks and is filtered before bottling in sterilized bottles. Pierre Dubourdieu and his son, the enologist Denis Dubourdieu, refuse to be set in traditional ways and have no hesitation in trying out interesting experiments. As sweet wines go, Doisy-Daëne has more finesse than power; it is a lively, highly perfumed wine of the purest elegance.

production area	37 acres (15 hectares)		4,000 cases	
grape varieties	75% Se, 20% Sau, 5% Mu			
soil	Red sand on limestone			
maturation	33% new barrels			
comments	More finesse than power			
Vintage	Rating	Peak		
1990	10	1997	Rich and complex	
1991	6	1997	Fruity, lingering fragrance	
1994	7	starting	Botrytized, floral, full-bodied for Doisy-Daëne	
1995	7.5	2001	Full-bodied and botrytized	
1996	8	2003	Finesse, richness, length	
1997	8	2004	Close or equal to 1996	

Barsac deuxième cru classé
Château Doisy-Dubroca

Reference is made to this estate back in the late sixteenth century. At the turn of the nineteenth, the highly reputed wines of Doisy are quoted among the best of the Barsacs, and they were duly counted among the second growths in the 1855 classification. Shortly after this, the property was split into three when the owner died. When Henri Gounouilhou, then owner of Château Climens, married the daughter of the Dubroca household, she brought him the smallest of the three sections of Doisy. In this way Doisy-Dubroca and Climens were linked and were purchased in 1971 by Lucien Lurton. In 1992 his elder son, Louis Lurton, was given responsibility for Doisy-Dubroca, the smallest classified growth of the Barsacs. This 8-acre (3.3-hectare) vineyard is surrounded by the two other Doisy vineyards. Planted around the château itself, the vines—all semillon—grow on a layer of red sand and gravel on a fissured limestone base. Climate and *terroir* here combine to give this little vineyard all the qualities required to make a Sauternes or Barsac of excellent stock. The renovation of the winery in 1995 has made it a great deal easier to make the wine in casks, followed by barrel aging for eighteen to twenty-four months. The wines of Doisy-Dubroca are elegant, fine, and smooth.

production area	8 acres (3.3 hectares)		600 cases
grape varieties	100% Se		
soil	Red sand on limestone		
maturation	35% new barrels		
comments	The second wine was only introduced in 1994		
2nd wine	La Demoiselle de Doisy		

Vintage	Rating	Peak	
1990	10	starting	Crystallized fruit and honey
1991	5	1997	Extra light
1994	7	2000	Barsac type
1995	7.5	2003	Round
1996	7.5	2003	Botrytized in spirit
1997	7	2003	Fine and balanced

Barsac deuxième cru classé
Château Doisy-Védrines

The knights of Védrines left their name to this estate, of which they were lords. As for Doisy, for a long time it was the fief of the Daëne family. Doisy-Védrines is currently owned by Pierre Castéja. Located on a plot neighboring the two other Doisy estates, the vineyard covers a single 62-acre (25-hectare) plot, on poor soils of shallow, fine *graves,* covering an asteriated limestone plateau. Semillon accounts for 80 percent of the vine blend, complemented with 17 percent sauvignon and 3 percent muscadelle. Here winemaking procedures are in line with conventional, traditional practice. Only two pressings are kept each day, the third being discarded. Fermentation takes place in casks in the customary way, and the wine then spends a lengthy period in the wood. Given the very special circumstances in which the noble rot appears, and which do not satisfactorily obtain every year, Pierre Castéja passes over certain vintages altogether. In this way, 1984, 1987, and 1991 were all years with no Château Doisy-Védrines. It is a good-looking wine in which the noble botrytis makes its presence felt, richly sweet and soft, with plummy aromas that linger on and on.

production area	62 acres (25 hectares)		1,500 cases
grape varieties	80% Se, 17% Sau, 3% Mu		
soil	Red sand on limestone		
maturation	75% new barrels		
comments	Classical and serious		
Vintage	**Rating**	**Peak**	
1990	10	starting	Fruity, balanced
1992	5	starting	Light
1993	5.5	starting	Fruity, fresh, short
1994	6.5	2000	Well-constructed, botrytized
1995	7	2003	Plummy, botrytized
1996	7	2003	A great fruity wine
1997	8	2005	Great, rich wine; sumptuous

Château de Myrat

Until the mid-nineteenth century, Myrat was part of the Cantegril estate, which belonged to the lord of Cantegril, who married a Myrat girl. This Myrat growth, which was classified second growth, had some enthusiastic devotees, particularly in Great Britain. It disappeared altogether for a time, producing nothing at all in the years after 1975. Its owner, the comte de Pontac, was going through a difficult period; he had the vines pulled up rather than lease them to a tenant farmer or see the quality of the wines go down. So today we are seeing this estate take on a new lease of life. The single plot of 54 acres (22 hectares) of vineyard have been replanted, with 88 percent semillon, 8 percent sauvignon, and 4 percent muscadelle. It is clay-calcareous soil on a fissured limestone bottom soil. The wine is fermented in casks and well aged before being château bottled. It is still rather soon to gain an overall impression of several vintages, but Jacques de Pontac makes no secret of his ambition to give Myrat the panache of former days with the qualities of the best Sauternes and Barsacs of today. His *terroir* and his expertise augur well for his success.

production area	54 acres (22 hectares)		3,000 cases
grape varieties	88% Se, 8% Sau, 4% Mu		
soil	Clay-calcareous on limestone		
maturation	40% new barrels		
comments	Wine from young vines, fine rather than full-bodied		

Vintage	Rating	Peak	
1990			Vines too young
1991	4.5	1997	Distinctive, botrytized
1992	5	1997	Light
1993	6	starting	Fine, fluid
1994	7	2000	Botrytized
1995	6.5	2002	Botrytized, peculiarly developed
1996	8	2003	The best since replanting, full-bodied, rich
1997	8	2004	Full-bodied, rich, like 1996

Barsac deuxième cru classé
Château Nairac

This château bears the name of an illustrious family of Protestant merchants, who left their mark on the economy of Bordeaux in the eighteenth century. The most famous of them all was Paul Nairac, a shipowner. It was around this time that the château was built, a superb traditional house, the work of architect Mollié, a disciple of Victor Louis. During the Revolution the Nairac family went into exile in the Netherlands and Mauritius. Following a succession of owners, one of whom planted red vines, the estate took over again its traditional vineyard just before 1914. Finally, in 1971, Nairac was bought up by Nicole Tari (the daughter of the Taris of Giscours) and her husband, Tom Heeter. She is now the sole proprietor of Nairac, and her son, Nicolas, shares the running of the estate with her. The 42-acre (17-hectare) vineyard extends over a gravel soil planted with 90 percent semillon, 6 percent sauvignon, and 4 percent muscadelle. At harvest time there are innumerable selective pickings. The wine is made in new barrels with close attention to every detail. The results are invariably brilliant, for there is no Nairac in years when the conditions are considered to have been anything less than ideal for producing the eagerly awaited nectar, which reveals its perfection after ten years: dense, woody, in full bloom, and magnificent.

production area	42 acres (17 hectares)		2,200 cases
grape varieties	90% Se, 6% Sau, 4% Mu		
soil	Gravel on limestone		
maturation	66% new barrels		
comments	Small production of a Barsac for laying down, drawn from a very stringent selection process		

Vintage	Rating	Peak	
1990	10	2000	Powerful, complex
1991	6	1997	Fruity
1992	7	1997	Full-bodied
1993	5.5	1997	Delicate, plummy
1994	7	2003	Balanced, sinewy
1995	7.5	2003	Fine, classical
1996	7.5	2004	Fruity and botrytized
1997	7.5	2006	Very botrytized; powerful

Saint-Emilion premier grand cru classé A
Château Ausone

Ausonius is the name of a Latin poet who is said to have lived in this place so conducive to meditation. Built on the remarkable site of a rocky hillside, this château, the only one in Saint-Emilion that predates the Second Empire, is surrounded by 18 acres (7.3 hectares) of old vines planted in terraced rows up the steep hillside. The farm tools are horse-drawn, and the precious grapes are handpicked, then sorted on a conveyor belt before being destemmed and vinified in small wooden vats. Merlot and cabernet franc play a balanced duet in the famed symphony of a rare, refined wine that shares top ranking for this appellation with Cheval Blanc. The estate is co-owned by the two branches of the family, who share the running of it— an explosive situation, which ended up in the courts. One of the co-owners, Madame Dubois-Chalon, is seeking to sell her 50 percent stake; the other co-owner, Alain Vauthier, has just taken it over. So Château Ausone will be kept at the high level required by this wine, whose subtle bouquet is followed by its delicate, naturally distinguished body and elegance that stays without weakening over the years, particularly if it has been aged in the cool underground galleries that form the cellars of the château where it was born.

production area	18 acres (7.3 hectares)		2,000 cases	
grape varieties	50% M, 50% CF			
soil	Calcareous-clay and molasse			
maturation	New barrels			
comments	Very weak wines from 1967 to 1975			
Vintage	**Rating**	**Peak**		
1990	10	2002	Perfect tannins	
1992	5	1997	Narrow-shouldered	
1993	6.5	2000	Round and full	
1994	6	2001	Full-bodied, well built	
1995	7.5	2005	Round	
1996	8	2006	Powerful, fruity, round	
1997	8.5	2008	The first of the appellation; a wine for laying down	

Saint-Émilion premier grand cru classé A
Château Cheval Blanc

The destiny of this former *métayage* farm of Figeac has been a prodigious one indeed. In 1832 M. Ducasse bought 37 acres (15 hectares) of vineyards that were running wild, together with a tumbledown building. But the estate was to stay in the same family right up to the present day, with improvements following on from each other logically and to great effect. A further 54 acres (22 hectares) rounded off this single stretch of vineyard. A small château was built, the soil was drained, and in 1853, for the first time, the wine was labeled Cheval Blanc.

Was this a reference to French King Henry IV's white horse? No matter, the stallion was a thoroughbred all right, sailing over every hurdle and winning victory after victory. Although passed over for the 1855 classification, revenge was sweet a century later, in 1955, when it was proclaimed *premier grand cru classé A* alongside Ausone. A family member, Jacques Hébrard, took over the reins of Cheval Blanc, which, in its triumphal march forward, reached the prices of the top Médocs. The miracle of a success story like this is due to a white horse, and to the wine itself—a sublimated expression of cabernet franc (60 percent) in a harmonious blend with merlot and a bunch or two of malbec. This is a charmer that never lets you down. It is seductive when still young, engaging when fully matured, and still delightful in difficult years.

production area	91 acres (37 hectares)		10,000 cases
grape varieties	60% CF, 37% M, 2% malbec, 1% CS		
soil	Gravelly, sandy on clay		
maturation	New barrels		
comments	Drinkable young. The last word in cabernet franc		
2nd wine	Le Petit Cheval		

Vintage	Rating	Peak	
1990	10	starting	Archetypal
1992	5	1997	
1993	6	1997	Fairly round
1994	7	2001	Very fruity
1995	7.5	2003	Round
1996	8.5	2004	The best of the appellation
1997	8	2005	The finesse of the Cheval blanc, plus the roundness of the Merlot

Saint-Emilion premier grand cru classé B
Château L'Angélus

The Angelus proudly rings out to every echo its recent promotion to *premier grand cru classé* status in 1996, a well-deserved promotion as part of the ten-year review for a château that has done everything possible to achieve the demanding heights of quality leading to renown. In 1909 Maurice de Bouärd de la Forest, who in his youth had emigrated to America, inherited a 32-acre (13-hectare) property that produced wines sold by the name of Mazerat. In 1924 he bought the next-door enclosure, which was called L'Angélus because from it you could hear the bells of all three neighboring churches. His sons decided to use its attractive name for the whole estate. By then the third generation was in charge—Hubert de Bouärd, the enologist, and Jean-Bernard Grenié, looking after the administrative side. The single plot of 64 acres (26 hectares) faces south at the foot of a well-exposed hill. Traditional winemaking techniques are studiously followed, with a lengthy stay in the vat. Cellaring is divided between aging in new oak and developing the wine's distinctive fruitiness in vats. This clever combination produces an attractive, deep-colored, rich, velvety wine characterized by its great charm and harmony.

production area	64 acres (26 hectares)		10,000 cases	
grape varieties	50% M, 45% CF, 5% CS			
soil	Clay-siliceous and calcareous			
maturation	70 to 100% new barrels			
comments	Drinkable young but keeps a long time. Classified first growth since 1996			
2nd wine	Le Carillon de l'Angélus			

Vintage	Rating	Peak	
1990	10	2000	Sumptuous
1992	5	1999	One of the best of a difficult vintage
1993	6	2000	Colored and full
1994	8.5	2007	A model of success
1995	8.5	2007	Classical
1996	8.5	2007	Exemplary, concentrated
1997	8	2008	Tannic, to be kept

Saint-Emilion premier grand cru classé B
Château Beauséjour

For over a hundred and fifty years, Château Beauséjour has been in the Troquart family, whose current descendants bear the name of Duffau-Lagarosse. In 1847 the Beauséjour estate was divided into two neighboring properties, which took the name of each of the owners (Beau-Séjour Bécot). The Duffau-Lagarosse heirs formed a nontrading company, and ever since they have been operating a single stretch of 17 acres (7 hectares) of vineyard on the Saint-Martin plateau, where the soil is calcareous clay on a limestone bottom soil. At 60 percent, merlot is the dominant grape, with 25 percent cabernet franc and 15 percent cabernet sauvignon. The vineyard's excellent exposure leads to extremely rich musts with exceptional sugar content. The merlots and the two cabernet varieties are made into separate wines, which helps to modulate the fermenting process of each, as well as blending. Steward Jean-Michel Dubos ensures the smooth running of the estate with exacting passion.

The wine is rich and powerfully built, with lingering flavors, and takes time to reveal its ripe fruitiness around unaggressive tannins.

production area	17 acres (7 hectares)		3,500 cases	
grape varieties	60% M, 25% CF, 15% CS			
soil	Clay on limestone			
maturation	New barrels			
comments	A great, discreet, very dependable wine			
2nd wine	Croix de Mazerat			
Vintage	Rating	Peak		
1990	10	starting	Harmony, power	
1991	4	1997	Very light	
1992	6	2000	Tannic	
1993	5.5	2000	Velvety	
1994	7	2002	Concentrated	
1995	7.5	2003	Serious, rich	
1996	7	2003	Vigorous, tannic	
1997	6.5	2004	Meaty, round tannins	

Saint-Emilion premier grand cru classé B
Château Beau-Séjour Bécot

Created in the eighteenth century, the Beauséjour vineyard is split into two properties, one of which, since being purchased in 1969 by Michel Bécot, has been called Beau-Séjour Bécot, so as to avoid any confusion with the other Beauséjour (Duffau). Since that time, the estate has been entirely overhauled, and Bécot has poured money into it. Among other things, he has expanded the property northward and now has 40 acres (16 hectares) of vines over a 66-foot (20-meter) drop toward the southwest. Here merlot is the king of the grapes, with the two cabernets sharing the remaining 30 percent. Calcareous clay soils cover an asteriated limestone base. The winery is equipped with state-of-the-art enhancements, with shiny stainless steel vats and ancient galleries dug out of the stone underneath, to form ideal cellars. Buyers of the young wines can have them aged there in the best possible conditions. The estate was unfairly downgraded, but reinstated to its former ranking in 1996, as a tribute to the success and dependable quality of these generous, harmonious, and well-constructed wines.

production area	40 acres (16 hectares)		8,000 cases	
grape varieties	70% M, 25% CF, 5% CS			
soil	Clay-calcareous on limestone			
maturation	50% new barrels			
comments	Declassified, reclassified, nothing affects this very dependable wine			

Vintage	Rating	Peak	
1990	10	2000	Round
1992	5	1997	Light
1993	6	1997	Fruity, supple
1994	7	2000	Well constructed
1995	7.5	2005	Concentrated
1996	7	2005	Strong and tannic
1997	6.5	2005	Fine, elegant

Saint-Emilion premier grand cru classé B
Château Belair

It used to be called Canolle, a mispronunciation of the owner's
name; he was Seneschal Knolles, who during the Hundred Years
War accepted the surrender of the valiant Frenchman Bertrand
Du Gesclin during the English occupation. The Knolles family
settled in France and acquired ownership of Belair, as it came
to be called, through a marriage with the baron de Marignan.
Already in 1851 the wine had a brilliant reputation, placing it at
the top of the first growths of Saint-Emilion. In 1916 the domaine
was sold to E. Dubois-Challon, who already owned Ausone.

The two estates are adjacent and as at Ausone, the bottom
soil of the plateau had for centuries been worked by quarries,
which extracted stone for the extensive building work in and
around Bordeaux. This is how the wine of Belair comes to
be stored in superb cellars located under the vines that produced
it. Although the Dubois-Challons have concentrated more
particularly on Ausone, Château Belair has everything that it
takes to stay hot on the heels of its illustrious neighbor, with
almost twice the acreage of vineyard. There has been much
talk of the sinewy, subtle, and distinguished wine of Belair
these last few years.

production area	32 acres (13 hectares) 4,500 cases		
grape varieties	65% M, 35% CF		
soil	Clay-calcareous and molasse on limestone		
maturation	60% new barrels		
comments	Marked improvement as of the 1988 vintage		
Vintage	Rating	Peak	
1990	10	2000	Tannic, round
1992	5	1997	Fruity
1993	6	1999	Round
1994	6.5	2003	Fine tannins
1995	7.5	2003	Elegant
1996	7.5	2003	Harmonious, delicate, frank
1997	7	2004	Elegant lightness

Saint-Emilion premier grand cru classé B
Château Canon

King's privateer Jacques Kanon, having made his fortune on the high seas, bought up some vines at Saint-Martin, which he worked until 1770. However, tiring of his landlubber's existence, off he went for distant climes, selling his estate to a Libourne wine merchant, R. Fontémoing. After a further three buyers, the estate was bought in 1919 by the Fournier family, at which point it became Château Canon. Henriette Fournier took things in hand, and her strict, demanding methods and unbending character forged her reputation as a great lady of wine, taking Château Canon to the enviable ranking of *premier grand cru classé* in 1958. Her grandson Eric stepped brilliantly into her shoes, but in 1996 the Vertheimer family, of Coco Chanel fame, which already owned Rausan-Ségla, bought up the Canon joint possession. John Kolasa, the man in charge of making the wines, had the fermenting room rebuilt, adding two new wooden vats and restoring those that were only a few years old.

Château Canon wine is recognizable by its almost black color, its concentration, and its power. It is absolutely vital to wait patiently and give it the time it needs to reveal its full range of spicy aromas and its full-bodied fruitiness.

production area	44 acres (18 hectares)		6,500 cases	
grape varieties	55% M, 45% CF			
soil	Clay-calcareous, siliceous			
maturation	50% new barrels			
comments	Went through a bad patch from 1994 to 1996			
2nd wine	Clos J. Kanon			
Vintage	**Rating**	**Peak**		
1990	10	2002	Tannic, complex	
1992	5	1997	Lean	
1993	6	1997	Supple, lacks concentration	
1994	5	1997	Not very agreeable, lacks concentration	
1995	6.5	1999	Improving	
1996	7	2002	Light textured, harmonious, polished	
1997	6.5	2003	The domaine hasn't returned to its previous high level	

Saint-Emilion premier grand cru classé B
Clos Fourtet

The label has not changed and does not use the word *château,* although a large residence was built there before the French Revolution. On the other hand, the walls of the medieval *Campfourtet,* or "little camp," still survive and justify the name *Clos,* which means enclosure. The 47-acre (19-hectare) vineyard grows on a thin layer of clay soil on a limestone base. This subsoil has been excavated from time immemorial to extract the stone, creating monolithic cellars in the process, in which the wine is held in cool, damp conditions all the year round. In the seventeenth century the estate belonged to the Rulleau family. Two other owners followed until the Clos was sold by Fernand Ginestet in 1918. In 1948 he exchanged it for the shares held by François Lurton in the Château Margaux corporation. Until recent years the Clos Fourtet growth slumbered; it woke up when the drive and energy of the new generation of Lurtons took over, and is now one of this appellation's more reliable wines. Its style, once classical and slow to mature, is now more attractive and easier to age, and hence drinkable earlier.

production area	47 acres (19 hectares)		4,500 cases
grape varieties	72% M, 22% CF, 6% CS		
soil	Clay-calcareous		
maturation	80 to 100% new barrels		
comments	Noticeable improvement since the late 1980s		
2nd wine	Domaine de Martialis		
Vintage	**Rating**	**Peak**	
1990	9	1997	Supple
1991	4.5	1997	Light
1992	5	1997	Fruity
1993	5.5	1997	Start of concentration
1994	6	2001	Ripe fruit
1995	7	2003	Classical, successful extract
1996	7	2004	Concentrated, meaty
1997	6.5	2004	Full and savory

Saint-Emilion premier grand cru classé B
Château Figeac

A second-century Gallo-Roman villa during the Middle Ages, the château belonged the Duke of Decazes. It was burned down and rebuilt under Henry IV of France. Around 1810, Figeac was a huge estate that was doing well and enjoying a fine reputation, but the negligence of several owners led to its breakup. Cheval Blanc, its former *métairie,* was to emerge from these catastrophic sales. This left 99 acres (40 hectares) in poor condition, which were bought by the Manoncourt family. After the frost of 1956 Thierry Manoncourt, an agricultural engineer, plunged with great gusto into reviving this growth drawn from a soil type like none other in Saint-Emilion, where the gravel is 23 feet (7 meters) deep, a figure that was confirmed when new cellars were dug out. The stock of vines is distinctive for this particular appellation due to the high proportion of the two cabernets (two-thirds), with the merlot grape making up the rest. This feature has led to Figeac being called the closest thing to a Médoc among the growths of this appellation. The cabernets make it a long-lived, austere wine, tempered by the fruity roundness of the merlot. The blending of the three grapes is consummated during cellaring, resulting in a powerful, sappy wine, wrapped in the spicy, slightly smoky flavors of ripe fruit.

production area	99 acres (40 hectares)		12,500 cases	
grape varieties	35% CS, 35% CF, 30% M			
soil	Gravel, sand, molasse			
maturation	New barrels			
comments	Needs sunshine to ripen the cabernets			
2nd wine	La Grange Neuve de Figeac			
Vintage	Rating	Peak		
1990	10	2000	A model	
1992	5	1997	Ripeness?	
1993	6	1997	Fruity	
1994	7	2000	Meaty, lively	
1995	7.5	2005	Imposing, fruity, violent	
1996	7.5	2006	Supple, fresh, lingering	
1997	7	2007	Firm, straight	

Saint-Emilion premier grand cru classé B
Château La Gaffelière

Among the ancestors of Count Malet de Roquefort was a Viking who settled at Roquefort Castle. At the end of the Hundred Years War, a Malet de Roquefort would marry a daughter of the Leroy family, who brought him La Gaffelière as her dowry. The estate remained in the family, but for a long time the progress of this place steeped in history was curbed by its ancestral ways. While respectful of tradition, the current lord and master, Léo Mallet de Roquefort, has brought to his management the questioning approach that is a vital ingredient for success. He has applied proven methods to achieve the perfection of the great wines—control of yields, modernized facilities, new oak barrels, and all the crucial details involved in attaining this noble aim. The 54-acre (22-hectare) vineyard, located at the foot of a slope on favorable soil planted with mostly merlot vines, produces a complex wine of opulent finesse. To add to the intellectual delight of tasting this outstanding *grand cru*, remains were discovered in 1969 in the neighborhood of the château of a Gallo-Roman villa, decorated with mosaics depicting the fertile vine, which may well have been one of Ausonius's residences in around the fourth century.

production area	54 acres (22 hectares)		10,000 cases	
grape varieties	65% M, 30% CF, 5% CS			
soil	Clay-calcareous			
maturation	50% new barrels			
comments	Often uneven up till 1985, recent vintages superb			
2nd wine	Clos de la Gaffelière			
Vintage	**Rating**	**Peak**		
1990	10	2000	Elegant	
1991	5	1997	Poor ripening	
1992	5	1997	Light	
1993	5.5	starting	Fruity	
1994	7	2002	Well constructed, elegant	
1995	7.5	2005	Round	
1996	7.5	2004	Meaty and fine	
1997	7.5	2006	Stylish, pure	

Saint-Emilion premier grand cru classé B
Château Magdelaine

The Chatonnet family reigned over Magdelaine for two and
a half centuries. Then Georges Jullien married one of the
daughters, and while keeping on his notary's practice in Saint-
Emilion, he contrived to maintain the domaine's reputation at
a very high level. His son, on the other hand, showed little
interest in the vines, and sold them in 1953 to the Libourne
firm of Moueix. As at Pétrus, the jewel of their possessions,
Moueix applied unstoppable methods designed to upgrade a
growth that started out with an excellent *terroir*. The 26-acre
(10.5-hectare) vineyard is V-shaped, with different soil types
on either branch—one forms a limestone plateau, the other clay
slopes. Merlot vines dominate by nine to one, with 10 percent
cabernet franc. The grapes are harvested by the same team of
pickers as at Pétrus: about a hundred pickers operating at the
best time of day, to avoid morning rain and dew that could affect
the concentration of the musts. The wine of Château Magdelaine
offers all the seductiveness of the merlot grape when it has
been developed with great skill: finely balanced, and made
velvety, fruity, and delightful to the point of inviting the
abandonment of all moderation.

production area	26 acres (10.5 hectares)		3,000 cases	
grape varieties	90% M, 10% CF			
soil	Clay-calcareous on limestone			
maturation	33% new barrels			
comments	Merlot wine; balance achieved, but takes a little getting used to			
Vintage	**Rating**	**Peak**		
1990	10	**2005**	Full-bodied, rich	
1992	5	**1997**	No ripeness	
1993	6	**2000**	Gentle harmony	
1994	6	**starting**	Fruity	
1995	7	**2001**	Dense	
1996	7	**2002**	Spicy and firm	
1997	7	**2003**	Harmonious, well made	

Saint-Emilion premier grand cru classé B
Château Pavie

Adolphe Pigasse, a doctor of medicine, invested his entire income in vines, establishing a fine estate that was sold at his death to the Fayard-Talleman family. It was then bought up by the wine merchant Bouffard, followed by Albert Porte, in the aftermath of World War I. In 1943 Château Pavie became the property of the Valette family, which is still running the business today and also possesses other Saint-Emilion growths. Gérard Perse, who owns the Château Monbousquet and the Château Pavie-Decesse, purchased the Château Pavie in 1997. The major part of the 91-acre (37-hectare) vineyard, facing due south, mounts an assault on the hill, which reaches its highest point at 295 feet (90 meters). Here the soil is calcareous, whereas at the foot of the hill it is deep clay or sandy clay. The underground winery has been fitted out at the top of the hill, in some old stone quarries, and the château is on the hillside, with the fermenting house and offices just below. The diversity of the soils and the three grape varieties—55 percent merlot, 25 percent cabernet franc, and 20 percent cabernet sauvignon—together with the great age of the vines and their low yield, make the wine a harmonious one, full of delicate shades, a wine more about finesse than about power.

production area	91 acres (37 hectares)	13,000 cases	
grape varieties	55% M, 25% CF, 20% CS		
soil	Clay, limestone, sand		
maturation	40% new barrels		
comments	The fruitiness and finesse are there; recent vintages have been "long." When a property is sold, the quality of the wine suffers.		

Vintage	Rating	Peak	
1990	10	2000	Balance and finesse
1991	5	1997	Problem with ripeness
1992	5	1997	Ultra light
1993	6	1997	Elegant, fruity
1994	6.5	1999	Well structured
1995	7	2001	Round, but body?
1996	7	2002	Fruity, direct, characteristic Pavie
1997	6	2002	Doesn't have the finesse of great Pavie

Saint-Emilion grand cru
Château Le Tertre Rotebœuf

One might think that the hummock on which the estate's vineyard lies borrowed its picturesque name from the belching sounds of bullocks as they toiled at drawing the plow. Here we have 14 acres (5.7 hectares) of vines arranged in an amphitheater bought by François Mitjaville and his wife about twenty years ago at Saint-Laurent-des-Combes. They tend their little vineyard with loving care. The charming eighteenth-century-style country seat has been renovated, as has the winery. The new oak barrels are renewed a third at a time each year. Eighty percent merlot grapes and 20 percent cabernet franc is the blend used in Château Le Tertre Rotebœuf, which in the space of a few years has proven itself worthy of a place alongside the great Saint-Emilions. The media, always looking out for something new, have helped it on its way down the path to glory, but all the credit should go to this talented and painstaking couple, who have contrived to draw all this richness out of the *terroir* and the microclimate while making their wine carefully and intelligently. Their wine is like them: warm, frank, and rich with profound, healthy qualities. Those taken with this full, attractive growth are fighting over the insufficient production, as its price goes up and up.

production area	14 acres (5.7 hectares)		2,500 cases	
grape varieties	80% M, 20% CF			
soil	Clay-calcareous			
maturation	New barrels			
comments	Powerful and smooth, unfortunately bought by speculators			
Vintage	**Rating**	**Peak**		
1990	10	2000	Unbelievably concentrated	
1991	6	starting	An astonishing success	
1992	6	2000	Fruity, velvety	
1993	7	2000	Strong personality	
1994	7.5	2004	Round, well-built	
1995	8	2005	Body, complexity	
1996	8	2006	Concentrated, complex	
1997	8	2007	Charm and power; incredible success	

Saint-Emilion grand cru
Château de Valandraud

Jean-Luc Thunevin is familiar with wine and wine lovers, having been a Saint-Emilion wine merchant. Maybe this experience explains the unbelievable success of his creation, the wine of Château de Valandraud, so called by juxtaposing the word *Val* (the valley of Fongaban) and *Andraud*, the maiden name of his wife, whose family has lived in Saint-Emilion since the fifteenth century. The thirty-year-old vineyards are in two sections, one over by Pavie-Macquin, the other at Saint-Sulpice-de-Faleyrens. Vinification is taken very seriously at Valandraud. The harvest is over in two days and is sorted on the spot. It is then sorted again in the fermenting house. After manual destemming, the berries pass through a hand-turned wine press. The must ferments in oak vats, then the wine is stored in new barrels, contrary to common practice, before it has been through its malolactic fermentation. Thunevin considers his wine to be the better for it, an opinion backed up by buyers of Château de Valandraud, who are willing to pay stratospheric prices for a bottle of this deep garnet-red wine, not to be forgotten in a hurry.

production area	6 acres (2.5 hectares)		700 cases
grape varieties	75% M, 20% CF, 5% Malbec		
soil	Gravel, clay, sand on limestone		
maturation	New barrels		
comments	The latest fad among wine lovers; horribly expensive		
2nd wine	Virginie de Valandraud		
Vintage	**Rating**	**Peak**	
1994	6.5	2002	Great, round
1995	7	2002	Rich, harmonious
1996	7.5	2005	Jansenistic for its appellation
1997	7	2005	Beautiful fullness

Pomerol
Château Certan de May

In the sixteenth century the fiefdom of Certan was granted to the de Mays, a Scots family who had settled in France back in the Middle Ages, and who a royal decree authorized to plant vines on its lands. The Revolution led to the dismantling of Certan, however, and the part still held by the de May family was sold in 1925 to Madame Barreau-Badar, who has operated it to this day with her son Jean-Luc. This tiny 12-acre (5-hectare) domaine lies in the uppermost section of the Pomerol plateau, not far from Pétrus and Vieux-Certan. The venerable old vines, with their small yield, are planted on a gravel-clay soil, with two-thirds merlot alongside one-third cabernet. The whole winemaking process is long and drawn out. The grapes are harvested late and very ripe; maceration lasts for a month, with numerous pumping-over operations; the wine is refined for many long months in oak casks; and fining with fresh egg whites is followed by no filtering. A rare and expensive wine, Certan de May is a noble star of the appellation, and the 25,000-odd bottles sell like hotcakes. Dark purple in color, with a deep aroma of truffles, full-bodied and sappy, it is concentrated, the better to dazzle.

production area	12 acres (5 hectares)		2,000 cases	
grape varieties	70% M, 25% CF, 5% CS			
soil	Gravelly clay			
maturation	50% new barrels			
comments	Superior quality, due to the Certan plateau, proper harvesting, exemplary vinification			
2nd wine	La Petite Eglise			
Vintage	Rating	Peak		
1990	10	2000	Round	
1993	6	2000	Well-structured	
1994	6.5	2002	Concentrated	
1995	7.5	2003	Supple and mature	
1996	7	2003	Concentration?	
1997	6.5	2004	Tannic, to be kept	

Pomerol
Château Certan-Giraud

This 18-acre (7.5-hectare) domaine is the smallest section of the fiefdom of Certan, which was divided up during the Revolution. It was initially called Certan-Marzelle, and one-third of the harvest is still sold under that name by Cruse of Bordeaux. Later, in 1956, it was bought by the Giraud family, who gave it their own name. Located in the center of the Pomerol plateau, just next to Pétrus, the vineyard comprises 80 percent merlot and 20 percent cabernet franc grapes. The wine is made not on the spot but at Château Corbin, which is also owned by the Girauds, in the neighboring appellation of Saint-Emilion. Château Certan-Giraud has a reputation for being a high-quality Pomerol at an affordable price. It has the truffle flavors that are so characteristic of the wines of the Pomerol plateau, a meaty, fruity generosity, and a delightfully enjoyable softness.

production area	18 acres (7.5 hectares)		4,000 cases	
grape varieties	80% M, 20% CF			
soil	Gravelly, clayey sand			
maturation	New barrels and vats			
Vintage	Rating	Peak		
1990	9	1997	Round	
1991	5	past its best	Light	
1993	6	1999	Fruity, round	
1994	6.5	2000	Well constructed	
1995	7	2002	Full-bodied	
1996	7	2002	Light, fruity	
1997	6.5	2003	Supple and fruity	

Pomerol
Château La Conseillante

La Conseillante is just across the road from Château Cheval Blanc; the château itself is no more than a charming little house, but with a big reputation. It all began in the eighteenth century with Catherine Conseillan, nicknamed "The Iron Lady" because she was a metal merchant at Libourne, but also well known for her hardened character. It was she who set up the 30-acre (12-hectare) vineyard and named it La Conseillante. After a spell in the Fourcaud family, the estate was bought in 1871 by Louis Nicolas, a wine merchant at Libourne, who went as far afield as Russia to make his wine known. From then on, La Conseillante was to remain in the Nicolas family. The vineyard is on various soil types—*graves,* sand, clay—and includes iron slag in its composition. The merlot grape dominates the cabernet franc and a spot of malbec.

So as to control yields and concentrate the musts, the vine is pruned hard and severely thinned, and the grapes are sorted on harvesting. Old-fashioned methods and cutting-edge equipment are combined in making this growth, which is highly regarded by those seeking elegance, finesse, truffle flavors, and a velvety body.

production area	30 acres (12 hectares)		5,000 cases
grape varieties	65% M, 30% CF, 5% M		
soil	Clay-gravel on iron pan		
maturation	New barrels		

Vintage	Rating	Peak	
1990	10	starting	Silky velvet, concentrated
1991	5	past its best	
1992	5.5	1997	The suppleness of the merlot grape
1993	6.5	1999	Lingering, spicy
1994	7	2000	Elegant
1995	7.5	2001	Voluptuous
1996	7	2001	Polished, delicate
1997	6.5	2002	Floral suppleness

Pomerol
Château L'Eglise-Clinet

The château, which is in fact no more than a rural construction, was built in 1850 up against a small Romanesque church erected by the Hospitallers of Saint John of Jerusalem, the ruins of which were demolished during the nineteenth century. Denis Duranton bought it from Pierre Lasserre together with the 14-acre (5.5-hectare) vineyard right in the center of the high plateau, behind the church, opposite the cemetery at Pomerol. The vines, many of which escaped the frost in 1956, are old stock. Carefully preserved and cultivated, they produce a low yield, which however concentrates the juice. The merlot grape accounts for 80 percent of the blend, and cabernet franc for 20 percent. Denis Duranton makes the wine with attention to the tiniest details, laying it down for a long period of maturation in new wood. The quality of the *terroir* and the extreme attention paid both to the grapes and to the winemaking process are apparent in the wines of Château L'Eglise-Clinet. The small output is the target of impulse buying by tasters, who admire this growth the color of night, with its dark, velvety aromas of chocolate, furs, and leather, and its vaulted structure reminiscent of a Romanesque church.

production area	14 acres (5.5 hectares)		1,700 cases	
grape varieties	80% M, 20% CF			
soil	Gravelly-clay			
maturation	40% new barrels			
2nd wine	La Petite Eglise			
Vintage	Rating	Peak		
1990	10	2000	Quality doubled 1989–1990	
1991	7	1999	Unbelievable for the vintage	
1992	5	1997	Fluid	
1993	6	2001	Toned-down tannins	
1994	7	2002	Concentrated and supple	
1995	8	2005	Harmonious, lingering	
1996	8	2005	Lingering, fruity	
1997	7.5	2005	Meaty and gay	

Pomerol
Château L'Evangile

There is probably an interesting story behind this biblical name, but it is a mystery, for the archives of the Léglise family, which owned the château during the seventeenth century, went up in flames during the devastating period of the French Revolution. Bought in 1862, Château L'Evangile fell to the Ducasse family. Upon the death of Louis Ducasse in 1982, his widow took over the running of the domaine with invaluable support from Michel Rolland, who saw to the vinification and maturation. In 1989 Baron Eric de Rothschild, part owner of Château Lafite, purchased Château L'Evangile. A great figure of the Médoc at Pomerol—this would have been unthinkable back in 1855! The vineyard is huge for the appellation, and was replanted following the 1956 frosts. It covers 37 acres (15 hectares) of varied soil types—pure clay, gravels, and sand. Such diversity in the *terroirs* gives the wine its harmonious proportions, combining power, build, and finesse. Sixty-five percent merlot and 35 percent cabernet franc is vinified following traditional methods and matured in one-third-new barrels, blending to give the L'Evangile growth an aroma of violets, silky tannins, and a tender body on a powerfully built frame.

production area	37 acres (15 hectares)		4,500 cases	
grape varieties	65% M, 35% CF			
soil	Clay, gravel, sand			
maturation	40% new barrels			
2nd wine	Blason de l'Evangile			
Vintage	Rating	Peak		
1990	10	starting	Perhaps the best Pomerol of the vintage	
1993	7	starting	Complex, sublime	
1994	7.5	2000	Straightforward, elegant	
1995	8	2003	Rich, round	
1996	7.5	2003	Elegant; the tannins need rounding off	
1997	7	2004	Floral and full	

Pomerol
Château Gazin

With its single 60-acre (24-hectare) vineyard, this is Pomerol's largest viticultural estate. It has been in the de Bailliencourt family for several generations. Before the entrance to the winery there is a boundary stone bearing the Maltese cross, to recall the former proprietors. The château, a fine charterhouse topped with a pinnacle turret, overlooks the vineyard. When the owner died during the 1960s, Château Gazin had to sell off a 12-acre (5-hectare) section to its renowned neighbor, Pétrus, to settle its problems of joint possession. Etienne de Bailliencourt remained as sole master of the domaine with his sons. At Gazin they combine progress and tradition. Tradition is represented by the use of concrete vats, and fining with egg whites (possibly with some slight filtration); progress, with malolactic fermentation in new casks. Needless to say, the wine is matured for a long period—18 months—in oak casks, half of which are new. The merlot grape accounts for 90 percent of the blend, and the two Cabernet varieties for the other 10 percent. Given the size of the vineyard, a considerable amount of wine is produced (around 100,000 bottles a year), and Château Gazin is a remarkable ambassador for Pomerol growths around the world. Its *terroir* gives it strength and vigor, with a characteristic aroma of truffles, on the flattering round grain of a good strain of merlot grape.

production area	60 acres (24 hectares)		8,000 cases
grape varieties	90% M, 3% CF, 7% CS		
soil	Clay-limestone on iron pan		
maturation	50% new barrels		
comments	uneven from 1970 to 1985		
2nd wine	L'Hospitalet de Gazin (since 1986)		
Vintage	**Rating**	**Peak**	
1990	10	2000	Full-bodied, round, profound
1991	5	starting	Astringent
1992	5	1997	Easy
1993	6	1999	Fruity, unctuous
1994	7	2000	Complex, distinctive
1995	7.5	2002	Powerful, fruity
1996	7	2003	Full, good extract
1997	6.5	2004	Ripe tannins and roundness

Pomerol
Château Lafleur

In its humble buildings, Château Lafleur houses a rare growth that sells for a small fortune. The vines, on 10 acres (4 hectares) of clay and red gravels, have remained unchanged for forty years, in neat rows divided into four sections by two paths in a cross shape, like a formal garden. The estate was created by Henry Greloud in the late nineteenth century, then taken over by André Robin. Upon the latter's death, his daughters Thérèse and Marie took over the inheritance, continuing to observe their father's motto, *Qualité passe quantité* (Quality before quantity). In 1981 the property reverted to the descendants of Henry Greloud, Sylvie and Jacques Guinaudeau. This young couple, who also own Château Grand-Village, set about renovating Lafleur in keeping with the personality of the place. The old facilities were renewed, and the winemaking process was placed in the capable hands of Jean-Claude Berrouet, the enologist at Pétrus. From then on, with rigorousness the watchword, from being just good, the wine became consistently good. The growth, obtained from equal amounts of merlot and cabernet franc, is the color of ink, its deeply penetrating bouquet announces a powerful, full-bodied wine with a domineering virility that does not fade with passing years, but over time will mellow into generous roundness.

production area	10 acres (4.5 hectares)		2,400 cases	
grape varieties	50% M, 50% CF			
soil	Clay and gravel			
maturation	New barrels			
comments	For many, the best of the Pomerols			
2nd wine	Pensée de Lafleur			
Vintage	**Rating**	**Peak**		
1990	10	1997	Harmony and power	
1992	6	1997	Harmonious	
1993	7.5	2000	Full-bodied, plenty of almost astringent tannins	
1994	7.5	2002	Rich, full-bodied	
1995	8	2005	Velvety, round tannins	
1996	7.5	2005	Supple, tight-knit	
1997	7	2006	A very classic flower	

Pomerol
Château Lafleur-Pétrus

Lafleur-Pétrus's name is no mystery, since the 32-acre (13-hectare) vineyard is sandwiched between Lafleur and Pétrus and has been in the hands of the Jean-Pierre-Moueix firm of Libourne since 1952. The 1956 frost caused extensive damage, and a substantial section of the vineyard had to be replanted. The merlot grape is preponderant, with a 90 percent share, the other variety being cabernet franc. The vines have now reached their prime, producing their maximum yields. Christian Moueix, enologist Jean-Claude Berrouet, and the entire Pétrus staff watch over these grapes, whose distinctive flavors are formed by the gravelly soil and ideal winemaking conditions. They are honored with oak casks that are entirely renewed over a three-year period, and in which they mature for almost two years. The wine reaches a pleasant maturity after five or six years. It is concentrated, with a fine, deep ruby color, elegant and smooth, with tender, delicate aromas. Small output, a famous name, and a price tag to match.

production area	32 acres (13 hectares)		6,500 cases	
grape varieties	90% M, 10% CF			
soil	Gravelly clay			
maturation	33% new barrels			
comments	Vineyard extension, fine *terroirs* added on			
Vintage	**Rating**	**Peak**		
1990	10	1997	Polished, harmonious	
1993	6	starting	Supple	
1994	6.5	2000	Better built, full-bodied	
1995	7.5	2002	Dense, elegant	
1996	7	2003	Vigorous, lingering	
1997	6.5	2004	Ripe raisins, beautiful vinification	

Pomerol
Pétrus

Pétrus is not a classified growth. It is also different for having a name and label that do not use the word *château*, because the domaine has none.

Ever since 1961, Pétrus has been distributed by the dynamic Moueix firm, which in addition to being a *négociant* also owns several estates. The wine went on to achieve fabulous success, resulting in an irresistible price inflation from a baseline aligned on the price of the best wines. After Buckingham Palace, Pétrus found its way into President Kennedy's White House, when it became that rare, inaccessible bottle, the hallmark of luxury. Joint proprietor Christian Moueix and enologist Jean-Claude Berrouet vie with each other in carefully cultivating this jewel of a vineyard covering 28 acres (11.5 hectares), where the merlot grape likes the blue clay soil. The vines are pruned hard, then thinned and harvested by a hundred and fifty pickers working only in the afternoon.

Much research goes into making this wine, which is matured in new barrels. Pétrus is a dense wine that gives full expression to the merlot grapes, with an added touch of cabernet franc. The unspeakable delight of its aromas, its sensuous opulence, combine with its renown and reputation to give the fortunate drinker the feeling of being placed before one of the century's masterpieces.

production area	28 acres (11.5 hectares)		3,500 cases	
grape varieties	95% M, 5% CF			
soil	Clay			
maturation	New barrels			
comments	The first wine to attract the speculators; much imitated			
Vintage	Rating	Peak		
1990	10	2000	Powerful	
1992	5.5	1997	Strong selections	
1993	6.5	2000	Good tannins	
1994	7	2002	Fruity	
1995	8.5	2005	Concentrated, complex, long	
1996	7.5	2005	Fruity, woody	
1997	7.5	2006	Complete, balanced, long	

Pomerol
Château Petit Village

The estate's names would appear to come from the set of buildings of various styles and heights, which from a distance do indeed resemble a little village. The vineyard as a whole forms a triangle over an area of 27 acres (11 hectares) at a place named Catusseau. It was devastated by the 1956 frost and had to be almost entirely replanted. Today the vinestocks have reached their prime. The two cabernet varieties have equal shares in the 20 percent left to them by the merlot grape. Bruno Prats has managed Petit Village with all the skill, talent, and perfectionism that he brings in the Médoc to his second classified growth of Saint-Estèphe, Château Cos d'Estournel. Under his leadership, the wine has become more characterful, serious, and dependable. Its growing success did not go unnoticed among shrewd investors, and the Axa Millésimes firm bought up Petit Village in 1989. An influx of capital is always welcome in a high-level business venture, where investment is crucial in achieving technical enhancements and overcoming the constraints involved in producing noble wines. The Petit Village growth has a spicy aroma, a hint of a woody flavor, and a full-blown fruitiness.

production area	27 acres (11 hectares)		4,000 cases
grape varieties	80% M, 10% CF, 10% CS		
soil	Gravel on clay-limestone		
maturation	50% new barrels		
comments	Owned by Axa Millésimes since 1989; J.-M. Cazes (Lynch-Bages) is in charge.		

Vintage	Rating	Peak	
1990	10	starting	Round, tender
1992	6	starting	The great success of this difficult vintage
1993	6.5	1999	Round, dense
1994	7	2002	Fruity, good extraction
1995	7.5	2004	Tannic, complex
1996	7	2004	Very fruity, average complexity
1997	7.5	2004	Supple, velvety, elegant

Pomerol
Château Le Pin

This tiny, 5-acre (2-hectare) property, which carries on where Vieux Château Certan leaves off, had belonged to Madame Laubrié since 1924. When she died, the Thienpont family, which already owned Vieux Château Certan, bought this plot in 1979. Since then, Jacques Thienpont has teamed up with Michel Rolland to turn this into an exceptional growth, avowedly taking as their model the greatest of the greats: Pétrus. To achieve this aim, the same luxurious methods are followed: using almost exclusively the merlot grape; holding yields at about 1.43 tons per acre (25 hectoliters/hectare); grapes handpicked, sorted, and 60 percent destemmed; fermentation in stainless steel, then oak vats; maturing in new barrels; and fining but no filtration. The *terroir* sees to the rest, with its gravel and clay soil on iron slag. Château Le Pin has been a great commercial success. It represents a small output, about 6,000 bottles of a growth that is rich—both in concentration and in price—and opulent, and which but for a roundness of very ripe fruit and an oakwood and caramel flavor would be rather overpowering.

production area	5 acres (2 hectares)		900 cases	
grape varieties	100% M			
soil	Gravel, sandy clay			
maturation	New barrels			
comments	Limited production, numerous buyers, high prices			
Vintage	**Rating**	**Peak**		
1990	10	2000	Vey balanced, concentrated	
1992	5	starting	Lighter	
1993	6	2000	Supple, charming, delicious	
1994	7	2003	Smooth, melting, delicate	
1995	8	2005	Round	
1996	7.5	2005	Elegant	
1997	7	2006	Ripe raisins, smoothness	

Pomerol
Château Trotanoy

The Trotanoy vineyard has held on to the old vines that escaped the phylloxera epidemic thanks to the nursing of E. Giraud. In 1949 the domaine was bought by the Pécresse family. Jean-Pierre Moueix of Pétrus then purchased it in 1953, and Jean-Jacques Moueix set up in the bourgeois house built in 1890. Then Jean-Claude Berrouet took charge of the wine's destiny.

The growth had already made a name for itself, but one can always strive for greater excellence; after all, is not Pétrus a model to stimulate emulation? The 17-acre (7-hectare) vineyard is located on a hillock on soil made up of *graves* and clay. This soil, slippery when it rains and rock-hard in dry weather, gave the château its name, a deformation of *trop ennoyé,* meaning too difficult to till. The merlot grape, however, is in its element here, and with its 90 percent, dominates the cabernet franc. It also thrives on the microclimate, as the old vines emerged unscathed after the 1956 frost. The grapes are harvested in the afternoon to avoid the morning damp. They are carefully sorted and pressed in the old-fashioned way and matured for twenty months in wood, fined but not racked. Despite partial replanting of the vines, which has resulted in some not-so-glorious vintages, the wine has a deep purple color, aromas of violets and blackcurrant, and savors of truffles and coffee, which linger on its velvety tannins.

production area	17 acres (7 hectares)		3,500 cases
grape varieties	90% M, 10% CF		
soil	Gravel and clay		
maturation	33% new barrels		
Vintage	Rating	Peak	
1990	10	starting	Silky texture
1993	6	2000	Body with suppleness
1994	7	2002	Silky, lingering
1995	7.5	2002	Well structured, floral
1996	7	2004	Even, full
1997	6.5	2005	Charming, with finesse

Pomerol
Vieux Château Certan

When the Certan estate of the de May family was split up during the Revolution, 33 acres (13.5 hectares) were bought in 1858 by Charles de Bousquet, who had the old château rebuilt among the vines. In 1924 Georges Thienpont, a wine merchant from Belgium, bought the domaine. The Belgian graft took well, and the Thienpont family is still firmly ensconced three generations later, with the same passion for this outstanding *terroir*.

The vineyard, on the edge of the plateau, enjoys a micro-climate that removes any risk of spring frosts. The thirty-year-old vines on clay and gravel offer an unusual mix for Pomerol, with 60 percent merlot blending with 30 percent cabernet sauvignon, 10 percent cabernet franc, and a little malbec. For long a leader of the great Pomerols, during the 1950s Vieux Château Certan was overtaken by Pétrus. This growth is still much sought after, however, and it is exported in large quantities. Owing to the complexity of the blend, it is often compared with the great Médocs. A well-built, complex wine, it is harsh in the first few years and then reveals a balanced richness, fine tannins, and a velvety, spicy fruitiness.

production area	33 acres (13.5 hectares)		5,000 cases	
grape varieties	60% M, 30% CF, 10% CS			
soil	Gravel, sandy clay			
maturation	50% new barrels			
comments	Still on the Certan plateau, a Pomerol for laying down. The second wine has been made since 1985			
2nd wine	La Gravette de Certan			
Vintage	Rating	Peak		
1990	10	starting	Fruity, smooth, long	
1992	5.5	1997	Fruity, supple	
1993	6.5	1999	Fruity, empyreumatic	
1994	7.5	2000	Velvety tannins	
1995	8	2003	Round	
1996	7.5	2004	Meaty, concentrated	
1997	7	2005	More merlot than cabernet, yet structured	

Pomerol
Château La Violette

Its floral name would appear to have come from the subtle
aromas of violets that some discriminating tasters found in the
wine when the Servant family was choosing this scented name
for its domaine. Just as the violet is a mere slip of a flower, so the
vineyard covers only 11 acres (4.5 hectares) in several small plots,
on the famed Pomerol plateau with its characteristic subsoil
containing a good dose of iron slag. The château itself and the
winery are right in the middle of the village of Catusseau.

Madame Servant, a keen viticulturist, cultivates her vines like
a garden and uses traditional methods to make wine from their
grapes—80 percent merlot, 20 percent cabernet franc. A long
maturation in wood completes this careful process. Her daughter
and son-in-law are also involved in effectively running the estate.

The La Violette growth has been in great demand since
1982 for its aromas of truffles and of course violets, its generous,
elegant body, and the excellent aging quality of its vintages, at
highly competitive prices.

production area	11 acres (4.5 hectares)	2,000 cases
grape varieties	80% M, 20% CF	
soil	Gravel on iron pan	
maturation	60% new barrels	
comments	Sensual, floral wine with a round fruitiness, to be drunk at 5 to 10 years old	
2nd wine	Pavillon la Violette	

VINTAGES, 1982-1997

YEARS		HARVEST		PEAK	MARK
1982	Perfect spring, fine flowering, hot, dry weather; end of summer very hot. Sunny harvest.	13 September	High alcoholic strength, very ripe tannins, low acidity; generous, well-developed wines, powerful rather than subtle. Sauternes: raisined, nonbotrytized grapes; uninteresting wine.	1992–2000	17
1983	Poor spring; hot and then very wet summer; September dry and hot. Sunny harvest.	24 September	In the Médoc, the south more noteworthy than the north. Wines concentrated rather than flabby. Sauternes: grapes ripe and botrytized.	ready for drinking	16
1984	Poor spring, flowering difficult; fine but very short summer, rainy and cool. Wet harvest.	6 October	Not much merlot, grapes not ripe. Sauternes: a few interesting wines, harvested very late.	for finishing (the best ones)	11
1985	Poor spring, but successful flowering. Hot, dry summer; hot, dry autumn. Sunny harvest.	1–30 October	The merlots early, the cabernets late. Balanced, classic, likable wines. Sauternes: weather too dry; raisined, nonbotrytized grapes; uninteresting wines.	1995–2005	18
1986	Fine end of spring. Hot, dry summer; autumn uneven; fine Indian summer. Harvest generally sunny.	10–15 October	Generally speaking, the cabernets are better than the merlots. Full-blooded, tannic wines. Sauternes: grapes ripe and botrytized.	1998–2010	17
1987	Poor spring, average summer, dreadful autumn. Wet harvest.	7 October	Dilute harvests; mellow, light, uninteresting wines. Sauternes: more gray rot than noble rot.	ought to be drunk	12
1988	Spring normal; summer normal; in autumn, fine Indian summer that "made" the vintage. Perfect harvest.	7 October	Good, balanced, sinewy wines. Excellent Sauternes when harvested late.	1998–2010	17
1989	Early, hot spring; summer perfect; fine autumn. Perfect harvest.	1–25 September	Rich, full wines, ripe tannins. Sauternes: botrytized. Excellent.	2000–2005	18
1990	Early, hot spring; very hot summer; fine autumn, just right. Perfect harvest.	1–end of September	Rich, fruity wines; supple, round tannins. Sauternes exemplary, very rich, botrytized to perfection.	2000–2005	19
1991	Early, then very cold spring, flowering hardly disturbed at all. Dry summer but too short; rainy autumn. Wet harvest.	end of September	Lack of ripeness, and dilution. Sauternes: gray rot.	ready for drinking	13
1992	End of spring cold and rainy. Rainy summer, likewise autumn. Wet harvest.	15 September– 15 October	Lack of ripeness, grapes swollen, dilute. Merlots relatively superior to the cabernets. Sauternes: neither ripeness nor botrytis.	ready for starting	12
1993	Rainy spring; hot, thundery summer; rainy autumn. Wet harvest.	10–30 September	Merlots relatively superior to the cabernets. Average ripeness. Sauternes: gray rot.	2000	13
1994	Hot spring and summer. Autumn: torrential rain. Wet harvest.	15 September– 10 October	Merlots relatively superior to the cabernets. Average ripeness. Sauternes: small harvest of botrytized grapes.	2003–2005	14
1995	Early spring; hot, dry summer; rains in September. Harvest between showers.	20 September– 10 October	Fine merlots and cabernet sauvignons, not always ripe. Sauternes: good harvest of botrytized grapes.	2005	15
1996	Early spring, summer hot then cool, nights unusually so. Autumn rains and sunshine. Harvest between showers.	20 September– 10 October	Fine concentration (similar to 1986), with acidity present (similar to 1988). Sauternes: fine, sinewy, botrytized wines.	2010–2015	16
1997	Spring hot and dry. Early bloom, but stretched over a long period. Tropical summer. Exceptionally fine autumn.	(15 August) 8 September– 6 October	White grapes harvested August 15 to save from rotting. Red wines silky, agreeable, suitable for keeping a while. The harvest was very spread out, and of mixed quality. Sauternes: a great year, similar to 1990.	2004	14

GLOSSARY

appellation d'origine contrôlée (AOC) France's strict system of regulating the identification of French wines (and spirits in general). The system is based on geography—rather than, for example, grape variety—and essentially seeks to protect and distinguish the finest French product from generic wines. There are fifty-seven appellations in Bordeaux, ranging from the general (Bordeaux) to the very specific (Barsac, Moulis).

ascence The development of volatile acidity. Affected wine will smell of vinegar (acetic pungency).

alcoholic fermentation The transformation of the sugar in the must into alcohol while giving off carbon dioxide.

ampelography The science of the vine and grape varieties.

bacterium Microorganism present in the must and wine. Often undesirable, the cause of disease affecting wine (acetic bacteria), bacteria can be extremely useful (lactic bacteria).

barrel or cask Wooden recipient. The Bordeaux barrel contains 225 liters (just under 60 U.S. gallons).

black rot Fungal disease of the vine affecting the leaves and grape bunches.

blend A mixture of wines from the same origin, usually from the same estate but made with different grapes or from different plots. This is how the *grand vin* (first wine) and the second wine are obtained.

botrytis *Botrytis cinerea,* a fungus (mold) that attacks the grapes and causes rot that can either be gray, which is disastrous, or brown (noble rot), which is sought after by sweet wine producers.

bung Wooden, glass, cork, or Teflon stopper for the mouth of a cask, or bunghole.

cap Solid matter that floats atop the must—or the wine—contained in the fermenting vat. The cap is regularly washed out, as it contains the "soul" of the wine (see **pumping over**).

chaptalization Increasing the alcoholic content of the wine by adding sugar before or during fermentation. A technique recommended by Antoine Chaptal, a minister of Napoleon I. Also known as sugaring. Chaptalization is regulated, and in the south of France it is illegal.

château French term for winemaking estate, including vineyard. "Domaine" has roughly the same meaning.

commercial wine Any wine whose drinking qualities have been recognized following analysis and wine tasting.

coulure An accident occurring during flowering that prevents fruit from forming. The main culprits are cold weather and rain.

cross-breed Result of crossing two varieties of grape vine. There are no crossbreeds in the Bordeaux vineyard, although there are plenty of examples in Germany.

cru French term most often translated as growth, though cru can also mean vineyard. "Cru bourgeois" indicates wine from the Médoc region that meets certain standards, apart from the 1855 classification. A "cru classé" is a classified growth, and when speaking of Bordeaux refers to those châteaus included in the 1855 classification.

crusher Appliance for crushing the grapes, i.e., breaking the grape skins.

cryo-extraction Concentration process applied to white grapes by freezing them. The ice in the berry stays in the winepress, while the unfrozen juice runs off. Cryo-extraction is an artificial version of what occurs naturally to grapes used for making

eiswein (ice wine). Used in the Sauternes.

débourbage Separation of the *bourbes* (solid matter) from the must prior to fermenting.

decant To pour off the wine contained in a bottle into a decanter so as to leave the sediment in the bottle. Decanting serves two purposes: it removes the sediment and airs the wine.

destemming Separating the stalk on which the grapes grow from the actual grapes themselves. The stems are discarded, while the grapes go off to the vat after crushing.

direct producer A nongrafted grape vine of American origin. There are none such in Bordeaux (nor in any of the other wine-producing vineyards).

domaine *See* **château**.

downy mildew A fungus that attacks vine leaves.

eiswein German for ice wine, a highly sweet, acidic wine that takes its name from the process of extracting juice from frozen grapes for a higher concentration of sugar. Comparable to the sweet whites that come out of the Sauternes region.

enology The science of winemaking. An enologist has a degree in enology.

enzymatic fermentation A special fermentation process occurring in an oxygen-free (anaerobic) environment through the action of enzymes. This intracellular fermentation in the full grape, or Beaujolais-type fermentation, is not used in the Bordeaux region.

fifth growth (cinquième cru) Refers to the fifth tier of the 1855 classification. The wines in this group are Château d'Armailhac, Château Batailley, Château Belgrave, Château Camensac, Château Cantemerle, Château Clerc-Milon, Château Cos-Labory, Château Croizet-Bages, Château Dauzac,

Château Grand-Puy-Ducasse, Château Grand-Puy-Lacoste, Château Haut-Bages-Libéral, Château Haut-Batailley, Château Lynch-Bages, Château Lynch-Moussas, Château Pédesclaux, Château Pontet-Canet, and Château le Tertre-Rotebœuf.

filtration The passing of the wine through a porous partition or filter, to remove impurities. "Earth filtration," or *kieselguhr,* is done with an alluvial deposit. Sterile filtration is sufficiently thorough to remove all biological impurities.

fining Process to clarify wines by adding a product, such as egg whites, that will cause impurities to clump together and fall to the bottom of the vat. This makes the wine clearer and mellower.

first growth (premier cru) Refers to the first tier of the 1855 classification. The wines in this celebrated group, including one upgrade, are Château Haut-Brion, Château Lafite-Rothschild, Château Latour, Château Margaux, and Château Mouton-Rothschild (promoted in 1973).

fortifying Adding alcohol to a wine. This is illegal unless you are making natural fortified wine, which is not the case for Bordeaux.

foxed Having a peculiar, unpleasant taste, specific to *direct producers* (American vinestocks). The French anglicism *foxé* sometimes translates into *renarder.*

fourth growth (quatrième cru) Refers to the fourth tier of the 1855 classification. The wines in this group are Château Beychevelle, Château Branaire-Ducru, Château Duhart-Milon, Château Lafon-Rochet, Château Marquis de Terme, Château Pouget, Château Prieuré-Lichine, Château Saint-Pierre, Château Talbot, and Château La Tour Carnet.

graft The upper section of the vine, which is grafted onto a rootstock (the *Vinis vinifera* graft is sensitive to phylloxera, while the roots are immune).

graves Generically, areas of stony, gravelly terrain. Graves is also the proper name of a large wine-growing region southeast of the town of Bordeaux.

growth *See* **first growth, second growth**, etc.

hybrid Produced by crossing two species of vine, one of which may be *Vinis vinifera*. Not to be confused with crossbreed. The understocks are hybrids.

inert gas Gas (usually nitrogen) that replaces oxygen so the wine is not in contact with air (oxygen being an oxydizing agent).

layering Method of propagating vinestocks prior to the appearance of phylloxera.

lees More or less solid deposits at the bottom of a vat (or cask) that appear after racking, composed of exhausted yeasts, protein, etc. The lees feed and protect the wine.

malolactic fermentation (MLF) Lactic bacteria cause malic acid to turn into lactic acid, giving off carbon dioxide. MLF is sometimes described as biological deacidification, since it mellows the wine. All the red wines undergo MLF; white Bordeaux wines do not, although white Burgundy wines do.

marc The solid matter removed from the fermenting vat and pressed to yield *vin de press,* or press wine. Also the solid matter removed from the winepress, and the name of a spirit obtained by distilling the marc.

must Cloudy, unfermented grape juice.

mutage The process by which fermentation is stopped in the **must** (see above).

noble rot *See* **botrytis.**

overripening Stage grapes reach when they are past the ripe stage. In Bordeaux, grapes are only overripened to produce sweet wines.

oxidation Any substance that fixes oxygen. This includes wine, or rather most of its components. It results in aging.

palus French term for rich, heavy, alluvial soil. The palus is not suitable for producing the highest quality wine but offered an ideal training ground for early Bordeaux vintners, and played a role in defeating the various "American blights."

pasteurization Elimination of microorganisms by heat (60°C). This method is not used in Bordeaux, except for some minor sweet wines.

photosynthesis The process whereby the leaf uses light to produce the sugar that will be taken to the berry.

phylloxera A disease caused by a plant louse *(Phylloxera vastatrix)* imported from the USA in around 1860, which infests the vine roots. To combat this parasite, all *Vitis vinifera* vines had to be grafted onto American rootstocks.

powdery mildew (oidium) Serious disease caused by fungus attacking vine leaves and fruit.

pressing Compression of the grape or the marc in a winepress, so as to extract the juice. Pressing grapes produces must (white); pressing marc produces press wine (red).

primeur French for young wine.

pruning A process of clipping the vine aimed at restricting its growth so that it will bear more fruit.

pumping over The process of pumping up wine from the bottom of the vat over the cap at the top of the vat so as to extract its aromatic and phenolic substances. Performed several times a day for several days, it also helps to expose the must to the air. (*See* **cap.**)

racking Transferring wine from one container to another, leaving behind the lees.

raising Partial drying of the grapes, on the vine or on grids, evaporation of the water contained in the grapes. Overripening such as is practiced in Sauternes combines raising and botrytization.

reverse osmosis Method of concentrating the must by passing it through a semipermeable membrane, a technique that is not unknown among the great Bordeaux growths.

rootstock The root onto which the upper section of the vine is grafted. This rootstock imported from America is phylloxera-resistant.

second growth *(deuxième cru)* Refers to the second tier of the 1855 classification. The wines in this group are Château Brane-Cantenac, Château Cos d'Estournel, Château Ducru-Beaucaillou, Château Dufort-Vivens, Château Gruaud-Larose, Château Lascombes, Château Léoville-Barton, Château Léoville Las Cases, Château Léoville-Poyferré, Château Montrose, Château Pichon-Longueville, Château Pichon-Longueville-Comtesse de Lalande, Château Rausan-Ségla, and Château Rauzan-Gassies.

stalk Woody structure bearing the grape.

sugaring *See* **chaptalization.**

sulfating In vine growing, the spraying of a sulfate solution onto the vine to eliminate fungus, such as powdery mildew. In wine making, the addition of sulfur dioxide to the must or wine to ward off oxidation and microbial diseases.

tannins Astringent and bitter phenolic substances that are vital to the quality of red wines, particularly red Bordeaux.

terroir Refers to both the actual soil grapevines are grown in and the entire natural environment of a relatively small area, such as a vineyard. See footnote on page 9 for a complete description of *terroir*.

thermovinification A winemaking process that relies on heating the must or grape harvest to 60°C. No great Bordeaux wine is produced by this brutal method.

third growth *(troisième cru)* Refers to the third tier of the 1855 classification. The wines in this group are Château Boyd-Cantenac, Château Calon-Ségur, Château Cantenac-Brown, Château Desmirail, Château Ferrière, Château Giscours, Château d'Issan, Château

Kirwan, Château Lagrange, Château la Lagune, Château Langoa-Barton, Château Malescot-Saint-Exupéry, Château Marquis d'Alesme-Becker, and Château Palmer.

topping up Filling up a barrel "on ullage." i.e., having lost some liquid due to evaporation.

ullage Typically, the amount of space left at the top of a filled bottle, barrel, or cask after evaporation. This space should be minimized by **topping up** (see above).

vatting time The period during which the must is turned into wine in a vat, and which includes fermentation and maceration. It may last anything from a few days to a month, for red wine.

veraison A French word also used in English to describe the stage when the grapes soften and begin to change color.

vion de goutte Red wine that runs off from the vat.

vin de presse (press wine) Red wine that runs off from the winepress.

vin de saignée Juice "bled" from a vat, either to make rosé wine or to concentrate what is left in the vat.

vinestock Variety of grapevine. There are several hundred of them. In the Bordeaux region, only three white and three red varieties are used to any great extent.

Vitis vinifera The only species of vine (out of a total forty) suitable for producing quality wines.

volatile acidity The sign of the presence of acetic acid in wine, which gives it a vinegary quality perceptible with as little as 0.7 gr./liter. There is a legal limit to volatile acidity, and a wine is no longer "commercial" when it oversteps this standard.

wine Beverage produced by fermenting the juice of fresh grapes.

yeast Single-cell microorganism *(Saccharomyces cerevisae)* responsible for alcoholic fermentation.

CHÂTEAU INDEX, WITH ADDRESSES

Italic page numbers indicate an illustration; a "c" refers to a caption. See also alphabetical château listing on page 137.

Margaux

CHÂTEAU BEL AIR MARQUIS D'ALIGRE, 153
M. Pierre Boyer
33460 Soussans

CHÂTEAU BRANE-CANTENAC, 22, 139
M. Lucien Lurton
33460 Cantenac
Tel. 05 57 88 83 33

CHÂTEAU CANTENAC-BROWN, 22, 144
Axa Millésimes
M. Jean-Michel Cazes
33460 Margaux
Tel. 05 57 88 81 81

CHÂTEAU DAUZAC, 22, 27, 152
M. André Lurton
Labarde
33460 Margaux
Tel. 05 57 88 32 10

CHÂTEAU DESMIRAIL, 22, 145
M. Denis Lurton
33460 Cantenac
Tel. 05 57 88 83 33

CHÂTEAU D'ISSAN, 22, 147
Société fermière viticole de Cantenac
33460 Cantenac
Tel. 05 57 88 35 91

CHÂTEAU DURFORT-VIVENS, 20, 22, 140
M. Gonzague Lurton
33460 Margaux
Tel. 05 57 88 83 33

CHÂTEAU GISCOURS, 22, 146
M. Eric Albada Jelgersma
Labarde
33460 Margaux
Tel. 05 57 97 09 09

CHÂTEAU KIRWAN, 20, 22, 148
Schröder & Schÿler & Cie
M. Jean-Henri Schÿler
33460 Cantenac-par-Margaux
Tel. 05 57 88 71 00

CHÂTEAU LASCOMBES, 20, 22, 141
Société Viticole
BP 4
33460 Margaux
Tel. 05 57 88 70 66

CHÂTEAU MALESCOT-SAINT-EXUPÉRY, 22, 149
M. Roger Zuger
33460 Margaux
Tel. 05 57 88 70 68

CHÂTEAU MARGAUX, 10, 18, 19, 20, 22, 26, 30c, *31*, 33, 35c, *38–39*, 74, 125c, *130–31*, 138
Société Civile Agricole
Château Margaux
Mme Mentzelopoulos
33460 Margaux
Tel. 05 57 88 83 83
19, avenue Montaigne
75008 Paris
Tel. 01 44 43 43 20

CHÂTEAU PALMER, 20, 22, 25, 133, 150
M. Bertrand Bouteiller
33460 Margaux
Tel. 05 57 88 72 72

CHÂTEAU PRIEURÉ-LICHINE, 22, 151
M. Sacha Lichine
33460 Cantenac-par-Margaux
Tel. 05 57 88 36 28

CHÂTEAU RAUSAN-SÉGLA, 20, 22, 25, 143
33460 Margaux
Tel. 05 57 88 82 10

CHÂTEAU RAUZAN-GASSIES, 20, 22, 25, 142
M. Jean-Michel Quié, manager
33460 Margaux
Tel. 05 57 88 71 88

CHÂTEAU SIRAN, 154
Mme Miailhe
33460 Labarde
Tel. 05 57 88 34 04

Saint-Julien

CHÂTEAU BEYCHEVELLE, 22, 161
M. Blanc
33250 Saint-Julien-Beychevelle
Tel. 05 56 73 20 70

CHÂTEAU BRANAIRE, 22, 162
M. Patrick Maroteaux
Saint-Julien-Bêychevelle
33250 Pauillac
Tel. 05 56 59 25 86

CHÂTEAU DUCRU-BEAUCAILLOU, 22, 155
M. Jean-Eugène Borie
33250 Saint-Julien-Beychevelle
Tel. 05 56 59 05 20

CHÂTEAU GRUAUD LAROSE, 22, 125, 156
33250 Saint-Julien-Beychevelle
Tel. 05 56 73 15 20

CHÂTEAU LAGRANGE, 22, 160
M. Marcel Ducasse
33250 Saint-Julien-Beychevelle
Tel. 05 56 73 38 38

CHÂTEAU LÉOVILLE BARTON, 20, 22, 157
M. Antony Barton
33250 Saint-Julien-Beychevelle
Tel. 05 56 59 06 05

CHÂTEAU LÉOVILLE LAS CASES, 20, 22, 25, 158
SC du Château Léoville Las Cases
33250 Saint-Julien-Beychevelle
Tel. 05 56 73 25 26

CHÂTEAU LÉOVILLE POYFERRÉ, 20, 22, 25, 159
M. Didier Cuvelier
33250 Saint-Julien-Beychevelle
Tel. 05 56 59 08 30

CHÂTEAU SAINT-PIERRE, 22, 163
Domaines Martin
33250 Saint-Julien-Beychevelle
Tel. 05 56 59 08 18

CHÂTEAU TALBOT, 22, 164
M. Rustmann
Mme Bignon
33250 Saint-Julien-Beychevelle
Tel. 05 56 73 21 50

Pauillac

CHÂTEAU BATAILLEY, 22, 172
33250 Pauillac
Tel. 05 56 59 01 13

CHÂTEAU CLERC-MILON, 22, 173
Baron Philippe de Rothschild SA
33250 Pauillac
Tel. 05 56 73 20 20

CHÂTEAU D'ARMAILHAC, 22, 171
Baron Philippe de Rothschild SA
33250 Pauillac
Tel. 05 56 73 20 20

CHÂTEAU DUHART-MILON-ROTHSCHILD, 22, 170
Head office:
33, rue de la Baume
75008 Paris
Tel. 01 53 89 78 00

CHÂTEAU GRAND-PUY DUCASSE, 22, 174
Mestrezat & Domaines
17, cours de la Martinique
BP 90
33027 Bordeaux Cedex
Tel. 05 56 01 30 10

CHÂTEAU GRAND-PUY LACOSTE, 22, 175
M. François-Xavier Borie
33250 Pauillac
Tel. 05 56 59 05 20

CHÂTEAU HAUT-BATAILLEY, 22, 177
Mme François des Brest-Borie
33250 Pauillac
Tel. 05 56 59 05 20

CHÂTEAU HAUT-BATES LIBÉRAL, 22, 176
Mme Villars
33250 Pauillac
Tel. 05 56 58 02 37

CHÂTEAU LAFITE-ROTHSCHILD, 10, 18, 20, 22, *32*, 33c, 44, *115*, 119c, 125, 165
M. Éric de Rothschild
33250 Pauillac
Tel. 05 56 73 18 18
Head office:
33, rue de la Baume
75008 Paris
Tel. 01 53 89 78 00

CHÂTEAU LATOUR, 10, 11c, *12–13*, 18, 20, 22, 33, 166
SCV de Château Latour
33250 Pauillac
Tel. 05 56 73 19 80

CHÂTEAU LYNCH-BAGES, 22, 178
Axa Millésimes
M. Jean-Michel Cazes
33250 Pauillac
Tel. 05 56 73 24 00

CHÂTEAU MOUTON ROTHSCHILD, 10, 20, 22, 25, 28, 167
Baron Philippe de Rothschild SA
33250 Pauillac
Tel. 05 56 73 20 20

CHÂTEAU PICHON-LONGUEVILLE, 20, 22, 25, 168
Axa Millésimes
M. Jean-Michel Cazes
33250 Pauillac
Tel. 05 56 73 17 17

CHÂTEAU PICHON-LONGUEVILLE-COMTESSE DE LALANDE, 20, 22, 25, *72–73*, 74c, 169
Mme de Lencquesaing
33250 Pauillac
Tel. 05 56 59 19 40

CHÂTEAU PONTET-CANET, 22, 179
Famille Guy Tesseron
33250 Pauillac
Tel. 05 56 59 04 04

Saint-Estèphe

CALON-SÉGUR, 22, 25, 182
Mme Philippe Capbern-Gasqueton
33180 Saint-Estèphe
Tel. 05 56 59 30 08

CHÂTEAU MONTROSE, 22, 181
SCEA du Château Montrose
M. Jean-Louis Charmolüe
33180 Saint-Estèphe
Tel. 05 56 59 30 12

COS D'ESTOURNEL, 22, 26, 35c, *36–37*, *82–83*, 84c, 180
33180 Saint-Estèphe
Tel. 05 56 73 15 50

HAUT-MARBUZET, 183
M. Henri Duboscq
33180 Saint-Estèphe
Tel. 05 56 59 30 54

PEZ, 184
M. Jean-Claude Rouzaud
Rue de la Mairie
BP 14
33180 Saint-Estèphe
Tel. 05 56 59 30 26

Moulis

CHÂTEAU CHASSE-SPLEEN, 51, 185
Mme Villars
33480 Moulis-en-Médoc
Tel. 05 56 58 02 37

CHÂTEAU POUJEAUX, 51, 186
M. Jean Theil SA
33480 Moulis-en-Médoc
Tel. 05 56 58 02 96

Haut-Mèdoc

CHÂTEAU BELGRAVE, 22, 188
Groupe CVBG (Dourthe-Kressman)
Mme Inquimbert
33112 Saint-Laurent-Médoc
Tel. 05 56 35 53 00

CHÂTEAU CAMENSAC, 22, 189
M. Henri Forner
Route de Saint-Julien
33112 Saint-Laurent-Médoc
Tel. 05 56 59 41 69

CHÂTEAU CANTEMERLE, 22, 190
33460 Macau
Tel. 05 57 97 02 82

CHÂTEAU LA LAGUNE, 22, 187
Messrs Jean-Michel
and Alain Ducellier
33290 Ludon-Médoc
Tel. 05 57 88 82 77

CHÂTEAU SOCIANDO-MALLET, 191
M. Jean Gautreau
33180 Saint-Seurin-de-Cadourne
Tel. 05 56 59 36 57

Médoc

CHÂTEAU LA TOUR-DE-BY, 192
Pagès, Cailloux, Lapalu
33340 Bégadan
Tel. 05 56 41 50 03

CHÂTEAU LES ORMES SORBET, 193
M. Jean Boivert
33340 Couquèques
Tel. 05 56 73 30 30

CHÂTEAU ROLLAN DE BY, 194
M. Jean Guyon
33340 Bégadan
Tel. 05 56 41 58 59
Paris :
Tel. 01 40 67 19 17

CHÂTEAU TOUR-HAUT-CAUSSAN, 195
M. Philippe Courrian
33340 Blaignan-Médoc
Tel. 05 56 09 00 77

Pessac-Léognan

CHÂTEAU BOUSCAUT, 22, 56, 197
Mme Lurton-Cogombles
33140 Cadaujac
Tel. 05 57 83 10 16

CHÂTEAU CARBONNIEUX, 20, 22, 25, 56, 125, 198
M. Anthony Perrin
33850 Léognan
Tel. 05 57 96 56 20

CHÂTEAU COUHINS-LURTON, 22, 56, 74, 200
M. André Lurton
Head office: 33420 Grézillac
Tel. 05 57 25 58 58

CHÂTEAU DE FIEUZAL, 22, 201
M. Gérard Gribelin
124, avenue de Mont-de-Marsan
33850 Léognan
Tel. 05 56 64 77 86

CHÂTEAU HAUT-BAILLY, 22, 56, 202
M. Jean Sanders
33850 Léognan
Tel. 05 56 64 75 11

CHÂTEAU HAUT-BRION, 10, 14c, 17, 20, 22, 25, 33, 35, 56, 196
Domaine Clarence Dillon
33608 Pessac Cedex
Tel. 05 56 00 29 30

CHÂTEAU LA LOUVIÈRE, 210
M. André Lurton
33850 Léognan
Tel. 05 56 64 75 87

CHÂTEAU LA MISSION HAUT-BRION, 20, 22, 25, 56, 203
Domaine Clarence Dillon
33608 Pessac Cedex
Tel. 05 56 00 29 30

CHÂTEAU LATOUR-MARTILLAC, 22, 56, 204
Famille Kressman
33650 Martillac
Tel. 05 56 72 71 21

CHÂTEAU LAVILLE HAUT-BRION, 22, 205
Domaine Clarence Dillon
33608 Pessac Cedex
Tel. 05 56 00 29 30

CHÂTEAU MALARTIC-LAGRAVIÈRE, 22, 74, 206
M. Alfred-Alexandre Bonnie
33850 Léognan
Tel. 05 56 64 75 08

CHÂTEAU OLIVIER, 22, 56, 207
M. Jean-Jacques de Bethmann
33850 Léognan
Tel. 05 56 64 73 31

CHÂTEAU PAPE CLÉMENT, 22, 25, 56, 208
M. Léo Montagne
BP 164
33600 Pessac
Tel. 05 56 07 04 11

CHÂTEAU SMITH HAUT-LAFITE, 22, 56, 209
M. & Mme Cathiard
33650 Martillac
Tel. 05 57 83 11 22

DOMAINE DE CHEVALIER, 22, 35, 56, 74, 199
M. Olivier Bernard
33850 Léognan
Tel. 05 56 64 16 16

Graves

CLOS FLORIDÈNE, 35, 211
M. & Mme Denis Dubourdieu
Château Reynon
Beguey
33410 Cadillac
Tel. 05 56 62 96 51

Sauternes and Barsac

CHÂTEAU CAILLOU, 22, 228
Mme Bravo
33720 Barsac
Tel. 05 56 27 16 38

CHÂTEAU CLIMENS, 22, 56, 227
Mademoiselle Bérénice Lurton
Mme Lurton-Belondrade
33720 Barsac
Tel. 05 56 27 15 33

CHÂTEAU CLOS HAUT-PEYRAGUEY, 22, 133, 213
M. & Mme Jacques Pauly
33210 Bommes-Sauternes
Tel. 05 56 76 61 53

CHÂTEAU COUTET, 22, 56, 227
M. Baly
M. Constantin, winery master
33720 Barsac
Tel. 05 56 27 15 46

CHÂTEAU DE FARGUES, 56, 224
Comte Alexandre de Lur-Saluces
33210 Fargues-de-Langon
Tel. 05 57 98 04 20

CHÂTEAU DE MALLE, 20, *40–41*,
43c, 223
Comtesse de Bournazel
33210 Preignac
Tel. 05 56 62 36 86

CHÂTEAU DE MYRAT, 22, 232
Comte Xavier de Pontac
33720 Barsac
Tel. 05 56 27 15 06

CHÂTEAU DE RAYNE-VIGNEAU, 22,
56, 218
Mestrezat & Domaines
17, cours de la Martinique
BP 90
33027 Bordeaux Cedex
Tel. 05 56 01 30 10

CHÂTEAU DOISY-DAËNE, 22, 229
EARL Pierre & Denis Dubourdieu
33720 Barsac
Tel. 05 56 27 15 84

CHÂTEAU DOISY-DUBROCA, 22, 230
M. Louis Lurton
33720 Barsac
Tel. 05 56 72 69 74

CHÂTEAU DOISY-VÉDRINES, 22, 231
M. Pierre Castéja
33720 Barsac
Tel. 05 56 27 15 13

CHÂTEAU D'YQUEM, 20, 22, 25c, 35,
56, 75, 212
Comte Alexandre de Lur-Saluces
33210 Sauternes
Tel. 05 57 98 07 07

CHÂTEAU FILHOT, 20, 22, 222
SCEA du Château Filhot
M. de Vaucelles
33210 Sauternes
Tel. 05 56 76 61 09

CHÂTEAU GILETTE, 225
M. Christian Médeville
33210 Preignac
Tel. 05 56 76 28 44

CHÂTEAU GUIRAUD, 22, 56, 214
M. Xavier Planty
33210 Sauternes
Tel. 05 56 76 61 01

CHÂTEAU LAFAURIE-PEYRAGUEY, 22,
56, 215
33210 Bommes-Sauternes
Tel. 05 56 76 60 54

CHÂTEAU LA TOUR BLANCHE, 22,
56, 216
M. Jausserand, manager
Bommes
33210 Langon
Tel. 05 57 98 02 73

CHÂTEAU NAIRAC, 22, 233
Mme Tari-Heeter
33720 Barsac
Tel. 05 56 27 16 16

CHÂTEAU RABAUD-PROMIS, 22, 56, 217
M. Dejean
33210 Bommes
Tel. 05 56 76 67 38

CHÂTEAU RIEUSSEC, 22, 56, 219
Head office:
33, rue de la Baume
75008 Paris
Tel. 01 53 89 78 00

CHÂTEAU SIGALAS RABAUD, 22, 220
Famille Lambert des Granges
33210 Bommes-Sauternes
Tel. 05 56 95 53 00

CHÂTEAU SUDUIRAUT, 20, 22, 56, 221
Axa Millésimes
M. Jean-Michel Cazes
33210 Preignac
Tel. 05 56 63 27 29

Saint-Emilion

CHÂTEAU ANGÉLUS, 22, 236
Bouärd de la Forest Family
33330 Saint-Émilion
Tel. 05 57 24 71 39

CHÂTEAU AUSONE, 22, 56, 234
Vauthier Family
33330 Saint-Émilion
Tel. 05 57 24 70 26

CHÂTEAU BEAUSÉJOUR, 22, 237
Duffau-Lagarosse Heirs
33330 Saint-Émilion
Tel. 05 57 24 71 61

CHÂTEAU BEAU-SÉJOUR BÉCOT,
22, 238
M. & Mme Gérard Bécot
33330 Saint-Émilion
Tel. 05 57 74 46 87

CHÂTEAU BELAIR, 22, 239
Mme Dubois-Challon
33330 Saint-Émilion
Tel. 05 57 24 70 94

CHÂTEAU CANON, 22, 240
SC Château Canon
33330 Saint-Émilion
Tel. 05 57 55 23 45

CHÂTEAU CHEVAL BLANC, 22, 57,
68, 235
Fourcaud-Laussac Heirs
33330 Saint-Émilion
Tel. 05 57 55 55 55

CHÂTEAU DE VALANDRAUD, 247
M. Jean-Luc Thunevin
33330 Saint-Émilion
Tel. 05 57 55 09 13

CHÂTEAU FIGEAC, 22, 57, 242
M. Thierry Manoncourt
33330 Saint-Émilion
Tel. 05 57 24 72 26

CHÂTEAU LA GAFFELIÈRE, 22, 243
Comte Malet de Roquefort
33330 Saint-Émilion
Tel. 05 57 24 72 15

CHÂTEAU MAGDELAINE, 22, 244
Éts Jean-Pierre-Moueix
54, quai du Priourat
BP 129
33502 Libourne
Cedex

CHÂTEAU PAVIE, 22, 56, 245
Consorts Valette SCA
33330 Saint-Émilion
Tel. 05 57 55 43 43

CHÂTEAU TERTRE ROTEBŒUF, 22, 246
François & Émilie Mitjavile
33330 Saint-Émilion
Tel. 05 57 24 70 57

CLOS FOUTET, 22, 56, 241
Lurton Brothers
33330 Saint-Émilion
Tel. 05 57 24 70 90

Pomerol

CHÂTEAU CERTAN DE MAY, 248
Mme Bareau
33500 Pomerol
Tel. 05 57 51 41 53

CHÂTEAU CERTAN-GIRAUD, 249
SC des Domaines Giraud
1, Grand Corbin
33330 Saint-Émilion
Tel. 05 57 74 48 94

CHÂTEAU GAZIN, 253
Messrs Nicolas
& Christophe de Bailliencourt
33500 Pomerol
Tel. 05 57 51 07 05

CHÂTEAU LA CONSEILLANTE, 250
Nicolas Heirs
33500 Pomerol
Tel. 05 57 51 15 32

CHÂTEAU LAFLEUR, 254
M. & Mme Jacques Guinaudeau
Château Grand-Village
33240 Mouillac
Tel. 05 57 84 44 03

CHÂTEAU LAFLEUR-PÉTRUS, 255
Éts Jean-Pierre-Moueix
54, quai du Priourat
BP 129
33502 Libourne Cedex

CHÂTEAU LA VIOLETTE, 261
Head office:
Servant-Dumas
Avenue de la Libération
BP 248
33506 Libourne Cedex
Tel. 05 57 51 70 27

CHÂTEAU L'EGLISE-CLINET, 251
M. Durantou
33500 Pomerol
Tel. 05 57 25 99 00

CHÂTEAU LE PIN, 258
M. Jacques Thienpont
Pomerol
33500 Libourne
05 57 51 33 99

CHÂTEAU L'ÉVANGILE, 252
SC du Château L'Évangile
Pomerol
33500 Libourne
Tel. 05 57 51 15 30

CHÂTEAU PETIT VILLAGE, 257
Axa Millésimes
M. Jean-Michel Cazes
33500 Pomerol
Tel. 05 57 51 21 08

CHÂTEAU TROTANOY, 259
Éts Jean-Pierre-Moueix
54, quai du Priourat
BP 129
33502 Libourne Cedex

PÉTRUS, 57, 67,68, 256
Mme Lacoste

VIEUX CHÂTEAU CERTAN, 260
M. Alexandre Thienpont
33500 Pomerol
Tel. 05 57 51 17 33

PRODUCTION CONDITIONS

(appellations mentioned in this book)

RED GRAPE VARIETIES

cabernet sauvignon

cabernet franc

merlot

malbec

carmenère

WHITE GRAPE VARIETIES

semillon

sauvignon

muscadelle

Officially, the basic yield may be increased by 20 percent (the PLC or classification ceiling). A maximum yield has been introduced on an experimental basis (for five years).

AOC (APPELLATION D'ORIGINE CONTRÔLÉE)

MÉDOC (4,700 HECTARES)
Alcoholic content: 10 to 12.5°
Yield: 50 to 66 hl/ha (2.86 to 3.77 tons/acre)

AOC

HAUT-MÉDOC (4,200 HA)
Alcoholic content: 10 to 12.5°
Yield: 48 to 66 hl/ha (2.74 to 3.77 tons/acre)

MARGAUX (1,300 HA)
MOULIS (600 HA)
SAINT-JULIEN (900 HA)
PAUILLAC (1,100 HA)
SAINT-ESTÈPHE (1,400 HA)
Alcoholic content: 10 to 13°
Yield: 47 to 66 hl/ha (2.69 to 3.77 tons/acre)

PESSAC-LÉOGNAN RED (1,000 HA)
Alcoholic content: 10 to 13°
Yield: 45 to 66 hl/ha (2.57 to 3.77 tons/acre)

PESSAC-LÉOGNAN WHITE (300 HA)
Alcoholic content: 10 to 13°
Yield: 48 to 66 hl/ha (2.74 to 3.77 tons/acre)

GRAVES WHITE
Alcoholic content: 9.5 to 12.5°
Yield: 50 hl/ha (2.86 tons/acre)

SAUTERNES AND BARSCA (2,000 AND 700 HA)
Alcoholic content: 12.5° established, 13° (minimum) potential
Yield: 25 to 28 hl/ha (1.43 to 1.6 tons/acre)

SAINT-EMILION GRAND CRU (3,500 HA)
Alcoholic content: 11 to 13°
Yield: 40 to 60 hl/ha (2.29 to 3.43 tons/acre)

POMEROL (750 HA)
Alcoholic content: 10.5 to 13.5°
Yield: 42 to 60 hl/ha (2.44 to 3.43 tons/acre)

PHOTOGRAPHIC ACKNOWLEDGMENTS

Photography: Michel Guillard (Scope), except: Jean-Luc Barde, page 21; Christie's, page 24; Bibliothèque Nationale, page 29; Château Margaux archives, page 31; Archives Départementales de la Gironde, pages 12–13, 18, 26, 28, 34; "Photographies Burdin," pages 196, 203, 205; Editions Féret, page 251.
Cover photograph: Laziz Hamani.